# ENDORSE

A riveting account of a normal man doing extraordinary things through the power of God. Wonderfully written, this is one of those books that is hard to put down once you start. If you want to know what "in the trenches" chaplain ministry is all about, read this book.

—Chaplain (COL) Paul Vicalvi (RET)
Former Commandant
United States Army Chaplain Center and School

I have read many books of memoirs of soldiers who experienced combat up close and personal from the Civil War through World War II and Nam, right up to Iraq and Afghanistan. This book by Chaplain (CPT) Jeff Bryan may be the best of them because this is the memoir of a caring Christian chaplain who dealt with the trauma, sacrifice, and death on a daily basis in Iraq. Putting his own fears and apprehension aside, he was able to influence the lives of brave young soldiers who protected freedom. These are stories of war and personal sacrifice and also stories of FAITH and perseverance through Jesus Christ and HIS vessel Jeff Bryan. You must read this book and learn... and pray! Thank you, Chaplain Bryan, for your service to America...and to the Gospel!

—Joseph S. Bonsall
Member of The Oak Ridge Boys and
author of *G.I. Joe & Lillie* and *From My Perspective*

*Memoirs from Babylon* is a poignant story of a world most Americans only see in TV sound-bites offered by media news celebrities. Unlike those slices of human experience, Chaplain Jeff Bryan offers the longer, more thorough, version of the prickly juxtaposition between faith and the realities of war. Regardless of your views of the global war on terror, I think we could agree that the brave men and women of our armed forces deserve the finest of spiritual support, while they carry out their critical roles on behalf of our nation. Chaplain Jeff Bryan is one of those "real life" heroes who have walked with American sons and daughters through the "valley of the shadow of death." My proudest moments as a seminary president are when I realize that our alums (which include Chaplain Bryan) are providing powerful spiritual ministry to the neediest sectors of our society. Chaplain Bryan's *Memoirs from Babylon* will give every reader a clear picture of human experience faced with the most gut-wrenching realities. Here is a story of the power of faith and hope that sustains our troops under fire.

—Byron D. Klaus, President
Assemblies of God Theological Seminary
Springfield, Missouri

Chaplain Bryan has written an engaging and inspirational account of his service as a combat chaplain in Iraq during a critical phase of Operation Iraqi Freedom. His motivation in writing his memoirs has been consistent—to pay tribute to the heroic American soldiers he was privileged to serve. Chaplain Bryan's story of his battalion's entry into The Triangle of Death deserves critical acclaim as an eye witness account of spiritual strength and mission success in the midst of suffering and loss. I am pleased to recommend this remarkable book to anyone who wishes to understand the value that chaplains bring to the United States Army and to the soldiers they accompany into armed conflict for God and Country.

—John W. Brinsfield, Ph.D., D.Min.
Army Chaplain Corps Historian

An informative, moving and deeply authoritative book! Chaplain Jeff Bryan gives us a powerful insight into the nature of war, and the power of God to bring men through the tragic crucible of war, to bring them closer to Him, renewed in their Faith, and empowered by God to go on to greater achievements. I believe that a new "Greatest Generation" is coming home, and this book affirms and enlightens that belief. An untold story of this war is an army of Christian Soldiers coming home, ministered by our chaplains in their hour of greatest need, empowered with the love of Christ and a deep sense of patriotism, prepared to go on to accomplish mighty deeds in the years to come. This book renews our faith...our faith in God, and our faith in our nation and our future. Well done, Chaplain!

—Lt. Col. Dave Grossman (RET)
Author of *On Killing and On Combat*

*Memoirs from Babylon* is a book that I intended to skim but found I could not put down. It is a stirring story of a troubled youth who nearly destroyed himself as he searched for meaning and purpose. Although the first two decades of Jeffery Bryan's life were punctuated by one blind alley after another, he eventually found some companions on life's journey who pointed him to Jesus Christ who became his savior, healer, counselor and guide. Jeff Bryan battled enormous odds to become a combat chaplain in the U.S. Army. From that vantage point he became the kind of strong and honest companion he had searched for during the early years of his pain-filled life and during his time as an enlisted man in the Army. Chaplain Bryan has found purpose and fulfillment in being an encourager to the men he walked with into the darkness and chaos of combat. Here we find a chaplain who has ministered to men in the midst of some of the fiercest fighting of the Iraq War—not from the relative safety of chapels and desks, but behind the lines. This is a cameo portrait of a man's man who is at once strong, tender, confident and humble. This book will change the lives of many who read it.

—Lyle W. Dorsett, Billy Graham Professor of Evangelism
Beeson Divinity School, Birmingham, Alabama

As a young infantry company commander deployed to Iraq, it was my privilege to know Chaplain Jeff Bryan. In one of the most dangerous areas of Iraq, the men of Task Force Polar Bear fought an entrenched insurgency to provide a safe and secure environment for the civilian populace. With complete disregard for his personal safety, Jeff was everywhere on the battlefield ministering to his flock. Whether it was on foot, by Bradley Fighting Vehicle, Abrams tank, or Blackhawk helicopter, Chaplain Bryan went where he was needed. Compassionate, brave, and fearless, Jeff was a true combat multiplier in every sense of the word.

—MAJ Rich Ince, Former Commander
Alpha Company, 2-5 Cavalry (Operation Iraqi Freedom, 2007-2008)

From enlisted infantry soldier on the DMZ, chaplain candidate, to combat chaplain for the Lord in Iraq, that's Chaplain (CPT) Jeff Bryan. You have to read this great book on Jeff's experiences with the God Squad in Iraq and continue to pray for all our troops in harm's way, family members, and wounded warriors!

—Chaplain (COL) Gary "Sam" Sanford (RET)

Ch (CPT) Jeff Bryan has captured what it means to serve infantry troops in combat. A former rifleman himself, Jeff knows only one way to do ministry in combat: be with troops and share their danger and hardships. Chaplain Bryan is a true soldier's chaplain—faithful, courageous, and always present to provide the hope and encouragement his soldiers need. I highly recommend his book.

—Chaplain (COL) Scott McChrystal (RET)
Senior Chaplain Endorser
Assemblies of God

Recently, I had the privilege and honor of reading *Memoirs From Babylon* by Chaplain Jeff Bryan. It was an informative book about his experiences with the 31st Infantry in Iraq. For over 15 months, he ministered and gave spiritual strength to nearly 1,200 members of a task force in an area known as the Triangle of Death. Chaplain Bryan worked closely with the men and women on the field of battle, and his devotion to God and to those whom he served is commendable. For a true assessment of the fears and faith in God by Jeff on the field of battle, and from my review of Memoirs From Babylon, I highly recommend its reading and endorse it fully.

—Morris Barker, National Commander
Former Prisoners of War Association
Waco, Texas

Jeff Bryan's memoir is a transparent and sobering account of his experience in one of the deadliest regions in the world. With candor and humility, he details his passion to provide spiritual support to troops on the front line. Facing the deaths of countless comrades and horrific encounters with bloodshed, Chaplain Bryan is to be commended for his service to our country and his tried and tested faith that shines like gold.

—Dr. Ravi Zacharias
Author and Speaker

# MEMOIRS FROM

# BABYLON

## A COMBAT CHAPLAIN'S LIFE IN IRAQ'S TRIANGLE OF DEATH

### CHAPLAIN JEFF BRYAN

FOREWORD BY MATT EVERSMANN

FROM BLACK HAWK DOWN

**Memoirs from Babylon:** *A Combat Chaplain's Life in Iraq's Triangle of Death*

By Jeffery A. Bryan

www.combatchaplain.com

Published by Combat Chaplain Ministries and Lightning Source (a subsidiary of Ingram Content Group), 1246 Heil Quaker Boulevard, La Vergne, TN USA 37086

All Scripture quotations, unless otherwise indicated, are taken from The Holy Bible, New International Version, copyright 1973, 1978, and 1984 by International Bible Society.

Interior design and typeset by Katherine Lloyd, The DESK

Bryan, Jeffery A.
Memoirs from Babylon: A Combat Chaplain's Life in Iraq's Triangle of Death

ISBN: 978-0578-07449-8

1. Iraq War 2. Bryan, Jeffery 3. Chaplains, Military

Printed in the United States of America

# DEDICATION

*Sergeant Christopher P. Messer; Corporal Joseph J. Anzack, Jr.;*
*Private First Class Byron W. Fouty; Sergeant Alex Jimenez;*
*and every other American who participated in Operation Iraqi Freedom.*

★

*Tanisha, who was in my heart with each step of my journey.*
*She was with me as I walked in the shadows of real heroes, and who,*
*more than anyone else, remains the strength behind my ministry.*

# TABLE OF CONTENTS

# ACKNOWLEDGEMENTS

*Thanks to Chaplain (COL) John Brinsfield, Jr. (RET);
Lela Gilbert; Paul Smith; Greg Johnson; James and Laurel Pence;
Katherine Lloyd; Kirk DouPonce; Arthur Brong; my brother Gary;
and everyone else who supported the story.*

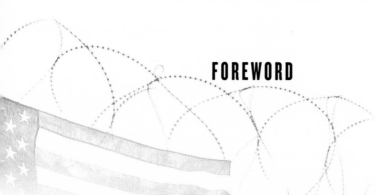

# FOREWORD

Remember the scene from *The Longest Day* where the British chaplain was chest deep in the river searching for his communion set? Not only was he deep in the river, he was under direct fire from the Germans on the far side! Yet, despite the constant enemy fire and the dire predicament, the chaplain continued the search to find the mission kit. While it made a light-hearted moment during the combat scenes in the movie, it really is a great representation of the chaplaincy and the military.

From August 2006 to October 2007, I was deployed to Yusufiyah, Iraq, as a member of the 4th Battalion, 31st Infantry, along with our Chaplain, Captain Jeff Bryan. We entered the aptly named "Triangle of Death" to find our new battlefield rife with Al Qaeda terrorists as well as the abominable sectarian violence that ravaged that country. There was no doubt that we were in for a fight during this deployment. For almost six months straight, we dodged IEDs, daily mortar fire, as well as direct assaults from an unyielding enemy. The constant exposure to danger was enough to challenge even the most battle-hardened infantry soldier. Trust me when I say, the most difficult thing one can ever ask a soldier to do is not to fight, but to go back into the fight. Yet, that is exactly what we did. We, the Polar Bears, armed with our unit motto "Pro Patria (for country)," moved directly into the enemy stronghold and defeated them on the field of battle. The surge worked and we made a difference. But combat comes with a cost-physically, emotionally and psychologically. What this all boils down to is that someone needs to be there, right there, right at the point of impact to keep the soldier on an even keel. Someone needs to hear our troubles, our fears, and our deepest thoughts. For the soldiers of Task Force Polar Bear, that man was Chaplain Jeff Bryan.

The Chaplain Corps covers the entire spectrum of soldiering. There are chaplains who serve the needs of the Army (as well as the Marines, Air Force, and Navy) and there are chaplains that serve the Lord and His children. Jeff Bryan most certainly is the latter. He was perhaps the most unsung hero of the deployment. His actions will never be quantified. But, if you ask any soldier who served with Jeff, they will assuredly tell you that he was ALWAYS THERE! He was on the IED-laden roads traveling to minister to the soldiers at the most distant patrol bases. He was flying in Black Hawks on air assault missions; he was riding in boats on the Euphrates River along with his flock. Like the chaplain in the movie, Jeff made the battlefield his home and fulfilled his duties in the harshest environment imaginable. Make no mistake: Jeff Bryan is a warrior chaplain who brought our Lord's message to the soldiers every single one of the 447 days we lived in Iraq.

The lay person will debate just war and the writings of St. Thomas Aquinas as long as there are wars. But, regardless of one's position on the necessity or application of warfare, the needs of those whom we send to do this business must be met. Their eternal safety and protection lies in the hands of their chaplain. We were blessed to have a spiritual leader like Jeff on the battlefield and we are all certainly blessed to call him our friend.

—Matt Eversmann

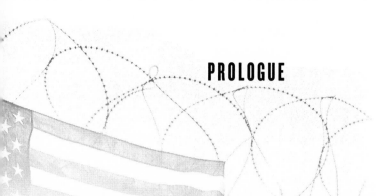

# PROLOGUE

O ne dark evening as I lay on a small bunk inside a comfortable little trailer at Camp Striker, Iraq, I thought about the sacred memorial ceremony I would be conducting the next day for three soldiers from the Army's 1st Battalion, 89th Cavalry Regiment. Private First Class (PFC) Adare W. Cleveland, PFC Matthew C. Bowe, and Sergeant (SGT) Sean M. Dunkin, three of America's bravest young men, had volunteered to hunt and kill the enemies of the United States so that terrorism would not be allowed to encroach on their homeland. Earlier in the week, they were killed by an Improvised Explosive Device (IED). Their unit, to which I was not officially assigned, asked if I would conduct the memorial service in absence of their chaplain.

While the late hours of the evening ticked by, constant recollections of my deployment began unraveling my already shattered nerves. My thoughts ricocheted back and forth from casualties, to family, to the future. As I tried unsuccessfully to sleep, thoughts of sharing my experiences, possibly through a book, began to stir. Many accounts of war have been written, but few by chaplains. But rare as they are, history has at times been kind to us and provided some accounts from battle-hardened chaplains. These included Chaplain (MG) Francis L. Sampson, a chaplain with the paratroopers who parachuted into France on D-Day; and Chaplain (CPT) John H. Craven, a naval chaplain who maneuvered the hellish jungles of the Marshall Islands, Saipan, and the Tinian Islands while in the Pacific.

Their stories embody honor and sacrifice—exactly what the Chaplain Corps symbolizes—but were written many years ago. Thus, I was led to ask, who is going to tell the story of modern combat chaplains? Will their efforts from this era be overlooked or forgotten? My own efforts were not ignored by my unit, but I always knew that any credit I received belonged to the warriors whom I served and the many chaplains who went to war before me. They're the ones who truly deserve it.

Were it not for those recurring questions that evening, I might never have written about my own experiences on the battlefield. My desire is to illustrate how life's most terrifying and difficult circumstances can produce a multi-dimensional environment for learning. Sometimes we mature the most while desperately trying to overcome the pain found only in the dark nights and long days of our souls.

On that forlorn night at Camp Striker, the desire to write this book intensified into something that I needed, rather than just wanted, to do. But the point at which I truly decided to fulfill the vision and put pen to paper occurred in May, 2007. Several months after the 1-89 Cavalry's memorial ceremony, came the overwhelming summer heat and an abominable peak in violence. Fighting and death became the general day-to-day occurrence. I realized from first-hand experience just how important a recorded account of America's new war from a chaplain's perspective would be.

With an intense desire to tell the story of the 10th Mountain Division soldiers whom I served, I preserved my experiences in detail. First, my goal is to help you, the reader, better understand authentic faith. Although my exploits center on front-line battle, a person does not have to travel to a war zone to understand that life itself can be a brutal brawl. You can face the most terrifying fight of your life without ever leaving home. Cancer, the loss of a child, financial turmoil, and similar trials can easily put one's faith in significant check. We all struggle with our faith at times. Yet, my experiences in Iraq have reinforced my conclusion that hope is something always worth fighting for.

Second, I hope to provide a historical account of the war in Iraq. Operation Iraqi Freedom will go down in history as one of the most politically polarizing conflicts in which America has been involved. Hopefully my first-hand account from the front lines will shed some important light on it.

Last, I hope this book will provide a positive portrayal of military chaplains. Sadly, there are weak-hearted, egocentric, selfish chaplains who avoid danger, choosing to guard their own safety rather than seek the welfare of the soldiers to whom they should be ministering. However, the authentic ministry of dedicated chaplains is found wherever you find suffering, danger, and fear.

Many believe that there are no front lines in the War on Terror, but that is simply false. Find out the truth for yourself. Join me on my journey as I share experiences found only in the deadliest place in Iraq, the infamous Triangle of Death.

"When the great day of battle comes, remember your training…you must succeed, for to retreat is as cowardly as it is fatal. Americans do not surrender. During the first days and nights ashore you must work unceasingly, regardless of sleep, regardless of food. A pint of sweat will save a gallon of blood. The eyes of the world are watching us. The heart of America beats for us. God is with us. On our victory depends the freedom or slavery of the human race. We shall surely win."[1]

—General George S. Patton, Jr.

Sincerely,
Chaplain Jeffery A. Bryan
"For God and Country!"

---

1   Carlo D'Este, *Patton: A Genius for War* (New York: Harper Collins Publishers, 1995), 434.

# THE MAKING
# OF A SPIRITUAL
# WARRIOR

As streams of sweat trickled down my face, I used my dirty uniform sleeve to push up my ballistic protection sunglasses. Perspiration soaked nearly every inch of my body in the 120-degree heat. An afternoon filled with adrenaline rushes, fear, and excitement—in other words, a normal day—began to disappear with the fading sun.

It was the thirteenth of December, 2006. The firefight hadn't lasted very long, but it became an important event in my life and ministry. My role might not have been to rain gunfire back upon the enemy, but it was equally important. As the chaplain of the 4th Battalion, 31st Infantry, living with troops at remote outposts was typical ministry, and being involved in combat was a part of everyday life.

That day, PFC Isbell, one of my outstanding young soldiers in Delta Company, stood guard on the rooftop of a remote building named Battlefield Position 151. Isbell, like most of the men in the unit, was an adventurous American teenager who joined the military in hopes of experiencing war firsthand.

The small house, practically covered with piles of sandbags, was captured in an earlier battle when we initially sought to establish control of the area. It was located inside Qarghuli Village, one of the worst areas in the Triangle of Death. Like many Iraqi houses, it was a two-story building consisting of dirt floors, hand-built steps, and a primitive brick foundation. The only major difference between this house and its neighboring ones was the presence of American soldiers. Coils of rusty razor wire, half-buried metal pickets, and chest-high stacks of sand bags protected the windows, the walls, and even the doors. They were not completely effective against rocket and mortar attacks, but they were the best defense we had.

Now, instead of serving as someone's home, the little house was an observation point for troops. It was also an important checkpoint for missions involving the deadly Route Malibu, a treacherous span of highway running north and south, directly through the center of Qarghuli Village.

The Polar Bear soldiers worked long, tiring hours fortifying their outposts. I helped them erect barriers and fill sandbags, learning important lessons about safety in the combat zone. One lesson was that there is no such thing as an absolutely safe location on a battlefield. Sometimes soldiers place too much hope in their protective fortifications and live under a false sense of security. Situational awareness of one's surroundings, no matter how protected one is, serves as the most time-tested method of safety.

For the most part, the soldiers determined their level of security. If it took them three weeks to fortify a position, rest and relaxation became rare commodities. However, regardless of how much work went into the outposts, the spooky neighborhoods only became more ominous as time passed. No shovel, axe, or hammer could change a community of darkness into a colony of good. Only a substantial psychological transformation could do that. On this day, I could smell death in the village. A deep sense of hidden evil wafted through the air.

The unseen dangers of the area seemed only inches away from me. The hair on my arms stood on end. Qarghuli Village had traditionally served as one of Saddam Hussein's safest havens. Among all Iraqis, the people who lived there were the most loyal to him, most ideologically similar to him, and most armed by him. A protective swath of Baath Party members—Hussein's elite—permeated the landscape.

They were the kind of people who did not allow outsiders to enter their sanctum. From the outside it seemed to be the picture-perfect village. It was isolated, self-sustaining (through farming), and beautiful enough to be considered a paradise. Lush tropical vegetation gave the farming community magnificent and serene landscapes. However, in the midst of this beauty there were the apocalyptic realities. Improvised explosive devices (IEDs) and gunshots erupted frequently each day. One usually did not have an idea of what was going on nor who was exchanging gunfire. The only sure thing was that somebody, somewhere, was being attacked.

And that is exactly what happened while I crouched on the roof with Isbell. SGT Steve Tennant, my chaplain assistant, and I had spent the afternoon with 2nd Platoon, Delta Company. Because the building had only recently been secured, no heavy machine guns were emplaced upon the roof yet. I hunched my body behind a small wall of concrete blocks and plump sandbags, creating a smaller target. PFC Isbell paced the roof and said, "You know, Sir, I grew up in church and hope that I can learn more about God while I'm here."

He walked back and forth across the roof, telling me about his perspectives of God, his faith, and his personal life that seemed so far away. It was the kind of discussion I loved having with my troops. It always made the visits to their outposts worthwhile. But as we talked, I grew steadily more nervous. PFC Isbell began watching the small yard surrounding the house instead of the thick, vegetated banks of the nearby Euphrates River, a much more likely hiding place for snipers. The danger of being shot by snipers while on a rooftop worried me, which was why I hunkered down. I knew that the enemy always watched us. Earlier in the week, I had been sitting with other soldiers in a vehicle at a nearby outpost when, moments after I exited the vehicle, a shot struck the bulletproof window next to my seat.

Fear was a part of life here.

I always tried to avoid imposing on the duties of the soldiers because that was not why I visited. But my fears led me to remind PFC Isbell that he needed to keep low and watch the side of the building facing the Euphrates. Our enemies were grateful for the river because its shores served as significant military and political boundaries. They could covertly cross over from the Anbar Province, attack us at night, and retreat across the water back into the province, knowing that we would not be allowed to pursue.

I respectfully placed my hand on Isbell's side to encourage him to turn around. That very second, sporadic shots—often called "spray and pray" by the men—came raining on us. About twenty-five armed attackers began firing at Isbell and me with AK-47s. The remaining men of 2nd Platoon dashed up the broken concrete stairs and positioned themselves for the fight.

Isbell returned fire as the rest of the platoon got in place. Soon most of the group was shooting back at the assailants. Some soldiers were covering the areas to our left and right so that enemy personnel could not flank us. PFC Isbell yelled out, "Hey, Sir! This would be a great time for a prayer." Already on one knee, I yelled my prayer while the men fired their weapons. "God, please destroy our enemies and make our bullets very accurate. Please give us victory. In Christ's name I ask this Father, Amen!"

First Lieutenant Dudish, the team leader, yelled, "This is the most awesome thing I have even seen! We have the chaplain with us in a firefight!" As usual, it was apparent that the enemy's effort was futile. Our superior marksmanship training, advanced equipment, and prayers quickly brought control to the situation.

One enemy team approached the opposing riverbank in a small truck. Our bullets struck it and the enemy troops riding in the back of it. The Americans lined their green rifle lasers upon them and filled the cab with bullets. The driver hastily sped off, spilling his wounded comrades out the back of the truck and onto the ground.

PFC Isbell remained at the far left corner of the small roof and the other members of the element fanned out to his right. I immediately sat on one knee behind the center man, who was hunched down behind the wall firing his M-4. I told the platoon leader, "I'm giving you permission to take control of my chaplain assistant for whatever defense purposes you need." He then placed SGT Tennant, my bodyguard, on the far right flank.

Darkness fell while the men shot at the enemy. Soon the enemy's bravado began to wane. A few minutes later a deathly silence fell across the land.

Then, when everything appeared to be over, crack! A sniper's bullet cut a deadly trajectory through the sky, missing our heads by inches.

As my adrenaline-laced nerves fought to cool down, the men of the platoon told me that it was awesome for them to have had a chaplain with them during a firefight. I told them that it was more awesome to be the chaplain in their firefight. Being present among my men in such incidents was never about going back to the rear with exciting stories; it was always about bringing and demonstrating real faith to them on the front lines.

While with the troops in the Triangle of Death, I always kept in mind something that another chaplain told me at the beginning of our tour. Because of the massive number of casualties we had taken, I was considering getting out of the Army upon my eventual return home. He told me, "That would be a real shame if you left the Army. You were born for this." At the time, I didn't believe him. Being in this war and seeing men die hurt too much. But, as time passed, I realized that he was right.

Serving as the 31st Infantry Regiment's chaplain that day at Battlefield Position 151 was not a success in itself. The sacred honor and success was in the attitude my men had towards me. The firefight was not the first attack I had been involved in and it was not even close to being my last, but that day I ventured beyond verbal ministry and into the dangerous realm of missionary ministry. It was all about demonstrating authentic faith in the foxhole.

## LEARNING ABOUT BEING A SPIRITUAL WARRIOR

It has been my good fortune to experience many cultures throughout the world during my time in the military. One thing that I am always reminded of when I return to the United States is that many good people of faith—people who could be spiritual warriors—often wait too long in their own lives to discover God's purpose. As they anxiously anticipate the day when destiny will arrive at their doorstep, life passes them by.

Eventually, they realize that their lives are nearly over, and that any opportunities they might have had are now gone. Sadly, they also fail to experience the great joys which God intended for them. During their senior years, they realize that they foolishly wasted precious energy and resources hopelessly comparing their own experiences with those of others, believing that their destinies would one day discover them.

In truth, being a spiritual warrior is more a state of toughness and character than words. The passion which lies inside a person's heart and willingness to go wherever the Lord leads is an important factor in living a fulfilled life.

How we pursue our dreams and aspirations tells more about us than anything else. As Pastor Alvin Blackard, a pastor of a church I once attended said, "The proof of passion is found in one's pursuit." I have learned from faith that absolutely nothing can stop me from achieving a God-given objective, except for me. I have also learned many times over that successful people generally do practical things each day so that they edge closer to their divine purpose. Many leaders understand that even though possible, most people's God-given destinies won't unfold in a single day.

General George S. Patton, Jr., the famous military strategist, once said, "*A man must know his destiny. If he does not recognize it, then he is lost. By this I mean, once, twice, or at the very most, three times, fate will reach out and tap a man on the shoulder. If he has the imagination, he will turn around and fate will point out to him what fork in the road he should take. If he has the guts, he will take it.*" I have always told people that "right now" is the fundamental foundation of their future. At this very moment, our clocks of purpose are steadily ticking. The fact is, with each breath we have the opportunity to be doing something to enhance ourselves and fulfill the divine purpose of our life.

My personal destiny led up to the blazing firefight at BP 151. I heeded the wisdom of General Patton and reached out for my fate. When I found it, I grabbed it with all of my might. A person's willingness to be stable during turbulent circumstances is a matter of character. Each trial I faced throughout life served as a stepping stone along the path to my greater destiny. Whether growing up as a small boy in the rural farmlands of southwest Kansas or struggling for my faith as a chaplain in battle, I learned that life can be a war in its own right. You see, life and combat are not diametrically different in their natures as is often perceived. One is simply the worst-case scenario of humanity's cruel nature; the other is war.

# EARLY INFLUENCES

In the humid air of Pascagoula, Mississippi, Dr. Jerry Bryan and his wife, Thelma, anticipated the birth of their second son. Their first child, Gary, was already exploring his brave new world during December, 1972. After working a second job in the Ingalls Naval Shipyard to pay off college bills, Jerry decided that his family needed to move to the Midwest and fulfill the American dream. He planned to open a chiropractic office and enjoy a prosperous life with his family. With that in mind, my parents packed the family's belongings and moved to Kansas.

Growing up as a small child in the farmlands of the Wheat State, I enjoyed opportunities many kids only dream about. We lived in the bantam town of Ness City, a community of about 2,500 people. Life seemed marvelously passive and serene. Everyone knew everybody else and life was simple, slow, and safe.

When I was not playing with other local kids, my parents would take me to a nearby farm owned by friends of the family, where we enjoyed picnics and games. My family frequently took me on fishing trips and nature treks. I believe these outdoor expeditions encouraged a strong sense of adventure in me.

I developed a great sense of respect for nature and freedom. However, I began to realize that another challenging world existed, one where I would not find the same goodness as that found in the country. Instead, I found ravaging meanness. Back in town, specifically at school, bigger kids teased and bullied me about my size. As they did, the question of "why" evolved, along with my anger.

Many of the youths refused to let me play sports with them because of my stature, often taunting me with the name "Little Jeff." The times I was allowed to play were rare, as the best positions were reserved for the larger boys. Disheartened, I watched from the lonely sidelines as the fun passed by. Boredom quickly settled in and my adventurous spirit led me to the local library. In the absence of sports I found something else. I began to read about people who had faced similar adolescent dilemmas and overcame them. As I read, I sensed a deep hunger to better understand who I was and where my life was supposed to go.

I fell in love with the library and retreated into an imaginary world found between the pages of anything I could read. The countless rows of shelves, stuffed with books, became an escape where I could become anything I wanted. I spent hours reverently poring through collections of military history. Sometimes I even made it past the pictures and read the books. This bizarre thing called war, along with the brave combatants who took part in it, began replacing my uncertainties with inspiration.

With a heightened sense of awareness for anything relating to soldiers, my admiration for movie stars and sports figures diminished. Nothing stimulated my curiosity more than the war stories I read at the library. At the same time, I learned war through first-hand accounts from veterans, men whom I knew as family friends, neighbors, and relatives. One veteran who profoundly influenced me was our neighbor, Ben Tittle. He had served as a sailor in the United States Navy during the famous D-Day landing of WWII. He told me about the day of the invasion, when he drifted off of Omaha Beach and watched helplessly as countless boats capsized because of harsh seas and enemy gunfire. He told me how a massive landing ship transport (LST), loaded with hundreds of young men, was struck by rockets and sunk, right next to his ship. He showed me photos of the overturned hulk. My eyes watered and my throat tightened as I listened to the heart-wrenching story of how his friends perished under that boat. Even though I didn't fully comprehend it, I sensed a beautiful mixture of humanity and experience within him as he recounted the terrible pain that battle produced.

Ben never lacked for dramatic stories. Almost as though it were a sacred ritual, I would visit him and he would mesmerize me with accounts blazing with vibrant details, always leaving me in awe. I often walked across the street several times a day to sit next to him and listen to breathtaking tales of heroism about his comrades who had given their lives.

As I look back, I believe that Ben's stories touched a special place in my heart and attracted me to values such as courage, sacrifice, loyalty, determination, and selflessness. Hearing them from someone who had been to the ghastly front lines of combat personified real heroism in ways a book or movie never could. His soul-riveting legacy was genuine heroism, not the superficial sacrifice so often portrayed by actors in movies or wealthy athletes in sports.

Whenever possible, my parents enlisted veterans as influential models for me. Many of their friends had served in either Korea or Vietnam. When we visited their homes, my mother routinely urged them to entertain me with their stories and memorabilia. She knew they enjoyed having an interested ear for their stories; she also knew those stories inspired me. Nothing fascinated me more than hearing the dramatic accounts of those who served in battle for their freedom, for their comrades, as well as their loved ones. It was a done deal. I wanted to be like them. I decided to become a soldier.

## EVOLVING INTO A SOLDIER

My mother had certainly gone above and beyond in her endeavors at finding me positive leaders to observe, but she was not able to overcome every challenge I faced. Nothing changed the fact that I was a small boy, a liability that attracted bullies. Although role models helped move me forward, fear of others and low self-esteem pushed me back even more.

When I was seven years old, my parents drove me to a local United States Marine Corps recruiting station. In those days, they were called recruiting stations, not career centers. The military wasn't interested in employing career-minded recruits; they wanted tough, hardened fighters. They were not places for the faint-hearted, but I wasn't worried. As far as I was concerned, the military needed misfits like me, guys who needed nothing more than some training and a chance to become heroes. Given that opportunity, I was their man, or at least their kid.

As soon as we walked in, I saw a flawlessly-dressed Marine non-commissioned officer (NCO). He looked as though he had just walked off the cover of the recruiting poster on the nearby wall. His black dress shoes were shined to a mirror finish and his creased pants reminded me of a set of boards. Behind him, a set of colorful military flags was displayed. He stood next to a green steel government desk; one look at his face and I understood why the Marine Corps chose a bulldog as their mascot.

The room smelled of stale coffee; the cheap, generic kind that is found in government coffee pots around the world. From the coffee pot to the papers on the desks, everything was in its proper place: coat hangers, file cabinets, books, even the waste baskets seemed intentionally positioned.

The only thing that was out of place was me.

My parents humored me by going along with my attempt to enlist. They stood by as I asked the sharply dressed man if I could sign up for duty. Of course, my parents were not serious about me joining the military at seven, but they were excited to see me inside a real Marine Corps workplace, talking to a real Marine, and hopefully finding confidence.

But as our visit progressed, the mood turned sour and the game fell apart. The NCO refused to humor me for more than a couple minutes. Instead of encouraging me to return in the future, he sternly lectured me on why I was going to have to wait until I turned eighteen years old to become a warrior. His lack of empathy crushed me. My hope of entering his exalted world of war, or at least of a military that would consider me as a future enrollee, was dashed. I was back to being a misfit that nobody wanted.

My parents were not pleased that the visit had become counterproductive. I never knew exactly what they said to the NCO after they had me step outside, but I doubt it was pleasant.

As we left, I hung my head low and retreated back into my shell. All I could think about for days were painful questions. What kind of weakling was I to be so solidly rejected by the military? What was I going to do with the rest of my life? I felt like a colossal failure and was running out of time at the age of seven years old. I needed an identity and I needed it soon before my final few sparks of hope petered out.

## A JUVENILE WARRIOR

I remained angry for years over the incident at the Marine recruiting station, but I also remembered that it was the no-quit attitude of service members that inspired me in the first place. With that, my imagination wasted no time in running wild with curiosity about other ways I could be a warrior. I decided I would prove my capabilities as a clandestine commando.

Late one evening, when I was nine, I decided that it was time to prove my worth to myself. I knew that as soon as my neighborhood became quiet I would have the opportunity to experience covert operations up close and personal, just like an elite warrior. The clock on my bedside blinked away the seconds and minutes, almost as if it were enticing me to stay. But that wasn't going to happen. Not this night.

I quietly grabbed the gear I had selected for the mission: my tiger-striped camouflage pants and shirt and a woodland camouflage bandana I carefully wrapped around my face. The bandana made me look more like an outlaw than a commando. I pocketed my survival knife that I'd ordered from *Soldier of Fortune* magazine. The knife came with a cheap compass and an even lower quality fishing hook tucked deep inside the handle.

I regarded my expedition as an all-too-serious maneuver. I planned to sneak around the town in the darkness of the Midwestern night, proving to myself how capable I was at stalking, concealment, and the high-risk art of escape and evasion. Then, when I had lived beyond the edge and experienced the things that only the most proficient combatants were allowed to take part in, I would return home with no one the wiser. I was convinced the mission had to be reasonably easy because of the countless stories I had read of how daring men, such as Spetsnaz troops (Russian Special Forces; literally meaning "special purpose") infiltrated enemy territory, conducted highly secretive reconnaissance or assassination operations, and safely returned home-all within a few pages.

At a predetermined time, the perfect time, I slipped out through a small basement window and made my way through our yard and became one with the darkness. My tiny shadow followed close behind through the night's moonlit stillness and I could hear my heart pounding at double, triple, and even quadruple speed out of pure fear—mainly because I was afraid my parents would catch me.

Crickets chirped in the cool Midwestern air while large puffy clouds passed quietly overhead. I could hear an occasional sound from traffic on the interstate at the edge of our town. What was I doing out here? Despite the second guessing, my juvenile reasoning processes successfully persuaded me that, if I were to be considered among the best, I had to continue my mission.

Unfortunately, all I proved that night was that adrenaline and pre-adolescent imagination don't mix well. Recollections of the brave Army Rangers who scaled the high cliffs at Point-du-Hoc at Normandy and the famed Green Berets who heroically patrolled in the mosquito-ridden jungles of Vietnam flooded my imagination. Thoughts of these events drove me to not fail my self-appointed mission.

I maneuvered through a jungle of shadows, buildings, and vegetation in ways—I imagined—that would have made the shock troops of the French Foreign Legion proud. Eventually, I approached two tall grain silos at the local farmers' co-op. They pierced the heavens like skyscrapers through the darkness. While taking in the magnificent structures, I caught something out of the corner of my eye. Terror suddenly gripped me in a way that I had never felt before.

A police squad car was heading my way.

What could have happened? How could my operation have gone wrong? I tried to run but it was too late. As a brilliant spotlight swept across the small field of grass, I immediately dropped to the ground. With nowhere to run, the only tactic I had at my disposal was concealment. I felt an adrenaline rush that filled me with a sense of exhilaration like I never had before. What could quickly become the worst day of my life I now saw as an opportunity to prove myself. Would I crumble under the stress or embrace the challenge and refuse to quit?

The desperate reality of being a soldier was now more than just some three-page story from an issue of *Soldier of Fortune* magazine. Now, with the sudden pressure of evading people who wanted to capture me, I wanted to wake up safely in my bed back at home. Should I surrender? But being caught by the police meant certain confinement in jail for running away from home, trespassing, curfew breaking, and even evading the police. I envisioned prison, years of hard labor, and the scorn of my parents. None of those options was worth surrendering for. Yet, as I lay on my chest in the waist-high grass, I realized that I was, in fact, still evading. They hadn't caught me yet.

Gradually, the passion I had always felt about being a soldier overcame my fears. Whatever was going to happen was going to happen. I had gotten myself into this mess as a soldier, and I was going to get myself out as one.

With that thought, I crawled on my belly toward a deeper ravine just a few feet from a small bridge. I lay quietly on the ground and waited. I was determined not to be a helpless victim. If my pursuers wanted to catch me they would have to throw all they had into the effort. The black-and-white squad car rolled to a halt on the dark road, only ten feet from me. Its bright spotlight projected an intense beam right over my head, missing my grass-covered body by inches.

I remained stiff as a corpse—not even breathing—as the beam swept back and forth overhead. After a few minutes, the police drove away. Once they were completely out of sight, I crawled out of the grassy ditch and into another row of shadows along the old road. After a second of considering my coolness under fire, I took a deep gulp of fresh air and then ran home as fast as my nine-year old legs would carry me. I darted through dark yards, jumped over rickety fences, and moved so fast that at one point I wondered if I was actually touching the ground. As I neared my neighborhood, my heart rejoiced. Ahead of me was the final pathway to freedom and security: my basement window.

If my parents knew about my adventure, they never brought it up. However, after that night, it really did not matter. I had already learned many important lessons that would steer my life. One involved the importance of considering decisions before executing them. I did not fully grasp all the implications, but I knew that if the police had caught me, I would have been severely punished. I asked myself, "Was the stunt worth the risk?"

Also, I thought about how I had taken part in a strange sense of freedom that evening. My successful evasion of the local authorities made me feel powerful. I felt that, because I was able to avoid everyone, I honestly could have done anything I wanted to. But I also understood the difference between right and wrong when it came to opportunity. Just because I had the ability to do wrong didn't mean I should. I gained a new appreciation for powerful people who use their strength to protect those weaker than themselves, and a disdain for those who exploit their power.

## ANOTHER TIME, ANOTHER PLACE

Several years later, my parents went through a bitter divorce. My mother packed the old Ford Thunderbird and moved my brother and me to Atchison, Kansas, on the opposite side of the state. With plenty of anger issues from the dissolution of my family, I grew obnoxious, ill-willed, and spiteful. I became known by relatives in the area as, "The kid who's angry with everyone and everything."

Life in Atchison brought an immediate need for a kid like me to fit in. It was a vastly different community, both in size and culture, than my hometown of Ness City. While my mom worked long hours at a nursing home, I got into fights at school, hung out with my cousin Ferol, and looked for trouble with a rebellious crew of quarrelsome, foul-mouthed, weed-smoking teenagers.

The uniform that clothed my anger consisted of a light blue denim jacket with heavy-metal rock band patches sewn all over it, a faded concert t-shirt, and a pair of tattered jeans with gaping holes at the knees. I also sported long, brown hair that rolled lazily past my shoulders and onto my back. I did everything possible to be like the toughest kids I could find.

At that unsettled time, another inspirational figure arrived in my life: Uncle Carl. Uncle Carl served as a positive light as I increasingly turned toward a darker path. He had served in the Army in WWII as a supply soldier, seeing action in the grueling heat of the Philippine jungles.

He told me that when the Army was cut off by Japanese forces and rations were completely exhausted, his unit killed horses and ate them in order to survive. It was that toughness that stood out to me and I wanted it badly in my own life. Little did he know that his strength was increasingly becoming one of my only reliable anchors.

I felt as though his willingness to put up with my rebellious ways came from his military-honed toughness. How he must have had to restrain his frustrations at some of my foolish teenage antics. Although I spent most of my free time with troublemaking youths, Uncle Carl remained consistent both as a friend and advisor. He was always there for me, even when I knew deep down that I did not deserve it. We went fishing together and often just sat around, shooting the breeze. I often felt that he was the only person in the world who accepted me for who I was.

Like most small towns in America, Atchison had its share of local youth hangouts. A handful of fast-food restaurants along the main street served as perfect parking spots during the weekends. I learned one weekend just how badly teenagers, poor attitudes, and excessive boredom mix.

While driving through the McDonald's parking lot, I decided to stop and get something cold to drink with two friends, Jimmie and Brian. I failed to observe that Mike, a local troublemaker, and his entourage of weed-laced friends, stood near the front entrance. We frequently clashed at school. Apparently Mike had heard that I would soon be leaving for the Army after graduation. As I approached, he yelled, "I think the Army is weak. It sucks just like you!"

Two of his buddies joined in, "You got a problem?"

I looked around, hoping to find support in Jimmie and Brian, but they were still in the car. I kept walking, hoping they would be content with just taunting me. Instead, the situation exploded. As I neared the door of the restaurant, they moved in like hungry lions. As they slammed their fists at me, I swung back wildly. I landed some haymakers, jabs, and painful body blows, but they outnumbered me and eventually I was knocked to the ground. They began kicking me, but I took hold of someone's foot and pulled him to the ground. I grabbed his head and gouged my fingers deep into his eye sockets.

"He's ripping my eyes out!" he yelled.

Suddenly a police car roared into the parking lot. The onlookers scattered like roaches. Mike and his buddies ran away as well. I stumbled back to my car.

"What the heck happened to you guys?" I said to Jimmie and Bryan.

"We didn't want any part of that, man. Sorry!"

The police threw their hands up in frustration as cars poured by them out of the parking lot.

For the next few days I lay in bed and again thought about my life. A concussion, bruised ribs, and multiple cuts moved me to consider my need for direction. This was a typical week in my life. The only thing that changed from week to week was when, where, and whom I fought.

## HEARTBREAK AND GRACE

My downward spiral into juvenile delinquency troubled my mom. Trying to support me and deal with my fights and frequent suspensions from school forced her into a vicious cycle of work and heartbreak; which eventually led her to a nervous breakdown. She simply wanted to save me from myself. If anything was clear to her, it was that my path into fighting and drugs would lead to prison or death. Because she was a devout Christian, she prayed for me every day, believing that God would intervene at some point and redirect my life for some greater purpose.

She knew something had to change, and soon. My high school graduation was at hand. Although it signaled a new stage in my life, this new freedom would only mean I had more time to think about the lack of purpose I had. I told my friends and family, "If I graduate, it will only be because the teachers hate me and want to get rid of me."

In 1990, a crisis for the world became a blessing for me. President George H.W. Bush announced to the American people that political efforts to rid an invasive force of Iraqis from the nation of Kuwait had failed and military operations were being directed toward a removal of Saddam Hussein's military forces. The conflict steadily escalated and officially became known as Operations Desert Shield (initial phase) and Desert Storm (later phase).

As I watched the news and saw the awesome array of American military power staging for a colossal fight, I remembered the hope of purpose and character I looked for in the military when I was a child. The military was a place where young men and women could find meaning in their lives. The armed forces had perfected the art of transforming nominal people into phenomenal leaders. On January 3, 1991, I decided to join the military.

Uncle Carl drove me to a nearby recruiting station. Once there, the most difficult part of the process was deciding which branch of the service I was going to join. The Army's commercials and advertisements stated that they could make leaders out of ordinary folks. The Marines promised to make the most proficient and professional warriors in the world. The Navy said they would show me the world and give me training far greater than any normal job. The Air Force posited that I could own the sky if I joined them. For only a handful of choices, the opportunities were amazing.

The Navy, with its magnificent warships, striking uniforms, and sacred traditions, was clearly remarkable. Many of my heroes, like Ben Tittle, had proudly served and any opportunity for me to do the same would be marvelous. But I wanted to serve as a "dog-faced grunt" (a term often given to infantry soldiers during WWII), a role the Navy did not offer.

The Air Force would have been an excellent choice because it held professionalism in the highest tier of priorities. Their "esprit de corps" was indisputable and their powerful aircraft, impressive. I considered trying out for pilot school for large bombers, but my lack of civilian college eliminated such a possibility. They offered many other fascinating jobs, but a "light fighter" rifleman was not one of them.

While continuing to weigh my options, I thought back to how I had always dreamed of being a front-line foot soldier. That left only the Army and the Marine Corps. I considered the pros and cons of both, but the memory of my embarrassing experience at the Marine Corps recruiting station tipped the scales in favor of the United States Army.

Because the "Corps" failed to believe in me then, I chose not to seek them now. The Air Force and Navy had no options for infantrymen. The clear choice was to follow in the footsteps of my great grandparents, uncles, and cousins. The Army became the one organization to look past my weaknesses and offer me what I wanted. They had a purpose for me if I was willing to "be all that I could be," and that was exactly what I was determined to do.

I signed the paperwork, rushed home, and began packing my belongings for my future at a place called Fort Benning, Georgia.

# 2

# FORT BENNING: BASIC TRAINING

**M**y first week at Fort Benning was spent entirely at the 30th Adjutant General Battalion (Reception). It was isolated from much of the base so that the moans and groans of America's youth could not be heard by the rest of the world. Angry and power-thirsty corporals herded us around like a terrified flock of sheep. Inside the WWII-style barracks bay, we prepared for basic training. That day arrived much too quickly.

A semi-trailer "cattle truck" pulled up in front of the large reception building. Within an hour, the trailer would shuttle a frightened flock of lambs to the basic training barracks. This was a sacred passage taken by countless generations of soon-to-be infantrymen, one where the weak and strong are separated, the killing machines of war are assembled, and the iron-like guardians of freedom become forged.

We boarded the truck and were thrown about in the back of the trailer as it rumbled toward its destination. I felt like I was cooking in the burning Georgia heat. I peeked through a couple of the small breathing holes and tried to suck in some fresh air.

It felt as though we had been traveling for an eternity across "the home of America's shock troops" before we felt the enormous vehicle's metallic brakes screech to a halt. I knew my life was about to change forever.

I knew at that moment that I had made the single biggest mistake of my life by enlisting. The choices leading up to the ride in the cattle truck were all self-inflicted shots to my morale. I had nobody to blame but myself and there was nothing I could do now to change the situation. I had gotten myself into this mess and now rationalized that it had to have been for a good reason. Nevertheless, as I succumbed to a new depth of fear, I couldn't remember what in the world it was.

Boom! The back doors blasted open and, out of nowhere, hordes of sadistic drill sergeants wearing campaign hats hustled around the rear corners and screamed, "Pick up your *!##!!* gear and get off of my *##*!! truck!"

They began grabbing the troops and throwing them out of the trailer onto the ground. They reached for several men in front of me and tossed them out as if they were dolls. Anyone who did not move fast enough became prey.

I will never forget the terror that shot through me as I jumped out and ran for my life, narrowly missing the instructors' clutching hands. I tried to hide myself inside a small group of soldiers. The drill sergeants chased us in every direction, screaming at the top of their lungs, "Get over here you **%#! No, move over there you $$!!&**"

I was so terrified that I saw events almost as if they were unfolding in slow motion. As the monsters raced around me, I could hear my heartbeat and see soldiers being shoved back and forth. In my efforts to not get caught, I kept moving. The group was then ordered to form up and run up a set of dark stairs leading into the barracks. The drill sergeants began throwing our bags, emptying their contents all over the floor, as we stood side by side, waiting for the nightmare to end. Eventually it did and the "worst first" came to a close.

Weeks passed and we endured the madness. In the process, we became warriors. The young lad who had wanted so badly to quit now became a potent, highly articulate soldier, one bent on finishing anything with a confident, no-quit attitude. Over the nearly two months I spent at basic training, I decided that I would leave only by graduating.

Although I was not a Christian at that point in my life, on Sundays I ventured out of the barracks, away from the drill sergeants, to go to the

Infantry Chapel. I regularly attended religious services with a small group of fellow trainees. Although it provided me a serene place to hang out for awhile, I could not understand the strange peace other soldiers left with. I began to wonder if I was missing something. No matter how hard I tried to figure it out, I just couldn't get a handle on it. Maybe I was not cut out to be one of the religious guys.

Finally, graduation day arrived. My mother and her friend Loretta traveled from Kansas to see the ceremony. Unfortunately, Uncle Carl was ill and could not make the trip. The traditional pomp and parade kept us standing on the ceremony field until it seemed that everyone within a hundred miles had spoken. This display for the civilians came at a cost to us in the form of sweat and exhaustion. The visitors rested in the shade while we stood under the scorching sun. Not exactly my idea of fun. I had waited for months for a breath of freedom and I was ready to experience it.

Immediately after the service I told my mom, "We have to get our belongings and get as far away from here as possible. I don't care what direction we go: north, south, east, or west. We just need to leave!" I had had enough of Fort Benning, the place affectionately referred to in military cadences as "the place where the mud is eighteen inches deep and the sun is blazing hot."

The drill sergeants had drilled us mercilessly in an effort to make us into effective soldiers, to teach us how to survive the realities of war which soldiers might face. But I had overcome their torture and wanted to get away to reflect on my accomplishment. I had never encountered this level of positive feeling before. For the first time in my life, I was convinced that I truly was a winner. But soon my merit-based self-worth would be tested.

## KOREA

After basic training and advanced individual training (AIT) school, I served two years with the Kansas National Guard, becoming proficient in both infantry and artillery tactics. My assignment eventually became frustrating because it involved driving great distances for monthly duties. I turned to fellow soldiers for advice about seeking an active-duty assignment. After hearing their personal experiences, I decided to make the change. An Army recruiter provided me with a list of available options. After reviewing them, I was convinced that both my current duties and future prospects were limited if I remained with the National Guard. So I volunteered for active-duty service with the 1st Battalion, 506th Infantry Regiment. It was a highly decorated unit recognized several years later in the award-winning film, *Band of Brothers*. One of the reasons I chose them was because some of my friends described their exploits along the volatile swath of land in South Korea known as the Demilitarized Zone (DMZ).

One said, "It's real risky, man! One time while on a patrol, we ran into a Bengal tiger. Another time we met some North Koreans while on a foot patrol and got into a firefight."

Another soldier recounted his clandestine reconnaissance missions along the border.

Hoping to experience conflict on the DMZ, I finished a pile of paperwork, shipped to Fort Leonard Wood, Missouri, for medical processing, and eventually traveled to Camp Greaves, Korea. Once I arrived on the controversial Korean peninsula, I realized that my only daring encounters were to be with the bitter cold, searing summer heat, rigorous training routines, and bar fights. It did not take long for my eagerness to turn into frustration.

I talked with the chaplain. He appeared to be a good, religious man, something I was not, or could not hope to be. This left me again feeling separated from anything religious because I knew that I could never be like him. I left his office feeling more distraught than before, and sadly concluded that my lonely unease from the isolation was something that church could not fix.

Full of despair, I decided that my life was wasting away in a country that couldn't care less what happened to me. In the depths of my soul I felt that my destiny as a combat soldier had been stripped away from me like it had been during Desert Storm (it was over before I finished basic training).

I missed out on other important conflicts during my time spent in Korea, including Operations Restore Hope and Continue Hope in Somalia. These missions were intended to be humanitarian efforts aimed at feeding the tiny African nation. Instead, they quickly turned out to be defensive battles amidst a militant community. I desperately wanted to help, but was reduced to watching CNN journalists describe what would become known as the legendary Battle of the Black Sea.

Remorse, emptiness, and regret over the fact that I could not help the brave men in Somalia overwhelmed me. I began drinking heavily, indulging in all-night binges that shocked my comrades. One time as I lay on the floor in a puddle of booze, a squad leader named SGT Frank West said, "That's a crying shame, Bryan. You're going to drink yourself to death."

In my mind it was official. I was a loser. I couldn't even convince my fellow soldiers that I was tough. I desperately wanted to be somebody, but the more I tried, the more I fell on my face. Everyone around me had a purpose. I was drinking my life away without one.

When my deployment to Korea was up, and after twelve months of wrecking my life, I left the remote base. Late one evening, without saying goodbye to anybody, I signed out of the unit and traveled back to the United States, broke, disappointed, and disgruntled because of my overwhelming sense of failure. I had set out to encounter my destiny—combat—but came away feeling as though God, whoever or whatever that was, had, for some mysterious reason, kept me from it.

## A FAILED RELATIONSHIP WITH THE ARMY

Upon returning to the United States, I received orders assigning me to the prestigious 2nd Battalion, 502nd Infantry Regiment of the 101st Airborne Division (Air-Assault) at Fort Campbell, Kentucky. Unlike the 506th back in Korea, the 502nd was a unit that would certainly be mobilized in a conflict. I looked forward to being an important part of it when that happened.

After taking leave, Uncle Carl, my mom, and I traveled from Kansas to Kentucky. My mom rode up front with Carl while I sat in the back of his truck. After I arrived at the installation's reception center (also known as the Fort Campbell Repo-Depot), I unloaded my gear, said goodbye to my family, and claimed a small living space in the old WWII barracks.

The next few months were packed with duties as I transitioned into the 502nd Infantry. My life seemed to be going reasonably well, at least in a professional sense, because I was able to perform my duties as a rifleman. My co-workers appreciated the fact that they could depend on me as a reliable team member. I was given ample opportunities to earn merits and awards, but it didn't take long to realize that the large-scale Air-Assault Division was not going to face major combat operations anytime soon.

Major conflicts were fading, and smaller humanitarian missions became the political challenges of the day. And I wasn't even likely to experience those. This disheartening realization caused me to sink into the same kind of depressive slump I had succumbed to in Korea.

After two years at Fort Campbell, the only themes in my life were girl-friends, late-night parties, and cyclic bouts with alcohol. I had nowhere to run from myself and needed to psychologically numb my anguish. Although I had become proficient at my job as a rifleman, that wasn't enough to sus-tain me during my time off. It seemed as though my perpetual cycle of shattered hope was going to follow me for a long time, including through a possible future away from the Army.

A sense of hopelessness, which revolved around unanswered questions about faith, gradually eroded my already fragile morale. The enormous bur-den of an uncertain eternity caused me to crumble emotionally. Eventually, the stress overcame me and I retreated to my barracks room. Each lonely night, I numbed my pain by huffing the fumes of markers, gas, and paint as I listened to the ballads of Jim Morrison and The Doors.

Surprisingly, I consistently passed the Army's random drug tests. But even though I had somehow managed to not get caught, I couldn't out-run time and reality. Juanita, my girlfriend from a nearby town, witnessed my gradual demise. One evening I pulled my car over to the side of a dark country road, got out, and drew my pistol. I began screaming out my frus-trations with life and firing my pistol randomly into the dark woods. Not surprisingly, Juanita decided to reconsider our relationship. I had nothing to counter her belief that drugs were changing me. She left me soon after.

One evening I drove my car to the old downtown district of Clarksville, Tennessee, and parked by a river. As I watched the current, I felt as though I was drowning in despair. I sat alone in the dark Chrysler LeBaron with a loaded .380 pointed directly in my mouth. Sweat poured down my face and

my hand trembled. Only the fear of a greater unknown kept me from squeez-
ing the trigger.

The question, "What's going to happen to me if I do this?" pounded in
my head. Were hell and judgment real? If I followed through with a bullet in
my head, I would find out the hard way. If I didn't go through with it, then
I was going to have to live with myself. I also considered that I might be cutting my life short when purpose lay just ahead. If I pulled the trigger, I would
never know. Finally, I reasoned that the only way to discover the mystery of
life was to face it headlong, not run from it. I slowly laid the gun down on
the passenger seat next to me and drove home.

Throughout the next two years with the 101st, I hoped for some abstract,
life-changing religious experience, like a lightning bolt from heaven. I had
rejected the idea of killing myself but remained unsatisfied with my life's
direction. But for me, change did not come as a bolt of lightning; it came in
the form of another soldier.

A Christian soldier from another unit began visiting my barracks each
week. He invited my cohorts and I to his church located on the outskirts
of Oak Grove, Kentucky, a small town outside one of the Fort Campbell's
gates.

After I watched others repeatedly reject him, I felt bad, so I offered to go.
We visited his small, spirited church one Sunday and the guilt of not being
a better man sank into me. After the service, we sat in his car and he offered
to help me answer the question of eternal hope.

I sat with a blank stare on my face, looking at his dashboard. Trying not
to sound disrespectful, I told him that it was not possible for a guy like me
to resemble a good one like him. He told me I could never be good in and of
myself, but only with God's help. However, everything he said went in one
ear and out the other. My mind was filled with excuses because I was not
ready to turn my back on the alcohol and girls.

I stepped out of his car, walked away, and never saw him again.

My last few months at Fort Campbell involved a couple of strategic alerts,
but each one only teased me with the possibility of combat. Each alert eventually turned out to be nothing more than a disappointment. The mission
preparations consistently ended with a few loaded aircraft and a bunch of

disgruntled troops. At that point, it was clear that my longing to experience combat would never be fulfilled. The vision of war which I had dreamed of facing for so many years had amounted to nothing.

There comes a point when all soldiers have to decide whether or not they will continue to serve or leave the service. When my day to answer this important question arrived, I met it with a cynical laugh. I felt the Army had duped me into believing that I would "be all I could be" when I initially signed up in 1991. Now they expected me to reenlist? As far as I was concerned, reenlistment was not even a consideration.

I had expected to experience combat, but was left out in the cold. Not a single doubt was in my mind: I would leave the military, let my hair grow long (as it had been in high school), and live however I wanted to. My only questions were, "How fast can I pack my belongings, sign my final leave forms, get in my car, and drive through the installation's main gate?"

In preparation for leaving the barracks one last time, I dumped the belongings out of my green Army duffel bag and onto the small bed. I stepped outside on the balcony of the building and nodded my head in remembrance of the many soldiers who had shared the room with me and had already moved on. Now I was saying farewell to it all: the good times and the bad. And those memories were the only things I had left.

I learned years earlier in Korea that discontented soldiers have unique ways of paying homage to the units upon which they frowned. The most common means of disrespect that I witnessed took place when a soldier painted his combat boots silver and threw them high over a telephone wire on his final day of duty. The only response to the hanging footwear was a few laughs the next morning when troops gathered for their first formation.

Sometime around midnight, I prepared to abandon the Army and its false hopes, but not before I left a token of my anti-appreciation—a scarecrow soldier. Constructed from one of my old uniforms and stuffed with the rest of my army paraphernalia, the scarecrow was held together with boot strings. From there, I threw my mini-me into a tall tree, easily visible for the unit to see the next morning.

I sent another pair of boots sailing over a nearby electrical wire. I looked back at the scarecrow of a man I had constructed and watched as he blew back and forth in the wind. As I stared at it for a few seconds, I thought about the unfulfilled promise I had made to myself so long before about becoming a bona-fide combat veteran. I turned, walked to my car, started it and drove away, completely oblivious as to how my life was about to change.

## SALVATION: BECOMING A SOLDIER OF THE SPIRIT

After leaving the Army, I moved into a small apartment in Clarksville, the town just outside of Fort Campbell. I began working odd jobs at stores around town; however, none offered me a sense of importance. Whether the work was at a pawnshop, a furniture store, a car dealership, or a high-end clothing store in the local Governor's Square Mall, jobs with minimal pay and limited opportunity for advancement meant little to me.

Sometime in December of 1996, I was walking across a strip-mall parking lot. I had almost made it to my car when a huge, muscular man approached me. He had blond, flat-top hair, arms like telephone poles, and legs like oak trees.

"Hey, how's it going?" he said. "My name's Dino. I work at a ministry called Club Beyond and was wondering if you'd like to lift weights or play some basketball?"

My curiosity overcame me. Why was he talking to me? I wondered why such a monster-sized guy was acting so nice.

"I'm sorry," he continued. "If this is a bad time to talk, maybe we can later."

Saying goodbye, the man left. "What was that all about?" I wondered. "It couldn't be good."

Throughout the day, my mind returned to the man in the parking lot. What was his motive? Had I done something that drew the wrong kind of attention from him? Was he an undercover cop tailing me for something I had done years before and forgotten about? Was he a serial killer or a psychopathic madman seeking an unsuspecting victim? My mind formulated dozens of possibilities.

Later that month, I was walking through another parking lot in another area of the city when the same man approached me again.

"How's it been going? I still hope that we're able to play basketball some-time."

I said, "I have to go," and walked away.

Near the end of the month I had taken a job as a salesman in Belk, a clothing store at the local mall. While folding clothes one day, I noticed a large man wearing a muscle shirt and athletic shorts walking up the store's main aisle.

"You see that man over there?" I said to another clerk.

"Yes," she answered.

"I think he's stalking me. If I disappear over the next few days, tell the police about him."

The man wasted little time in finding me. As he approached, I asked the first question.

"Why are you following me?"

A certain part of me thought that I had mentally flipped, thinking just how crazy it was to confront a guy that I knew nothing about. But I had had enough. He tried to say something, but before he could finish his first word I beat him to it.

"Why are you following me? That's all I want to know."

"I'm not following you," he said. "But since we keep running into each other, maybe we could sit down and talk sometime. I would like to have a chance to get to know you."

I shook my head and said, "Give me your phone number." After he wrote it down on a piece of scrap paper, I snatched it out of his hand and then walked away, thinking, "I will get to the bottom of this tomorrow, once and for all."

The next day, while sitting at home, I looked at the man's phone num-ber. I thought about not calling him. After all, what if he was a psychotic killer? Finally, I decided to make the call. I had once been a soldier and could fight well if I needed to. Besides, the mystery surrounding this man could only be solved by speaking with him more in-depth.

I called him, and asked, "Are you interested in meeting me here at my apartment?"

He replied, "Yes. That would be cool."

Perhaps not my wisest decision, I was determined to face the fear and deal with this potential threat. To ensure my safety, I carefully hid an aluminum baseball bat behind a door, a sharp hunting knife on a counter top, and my .380, freshly loaded with deadly hollow point shells, in a nearby drawer. Even the chair I offered him was a part of my survival plan. If he went psycho, I would have him pre-positioned in a corner where I could easily reach my pistol and blow three holes in his chest before he had any chance of killing me.

He arrived later in the evening and I cautiously invited him in.

We started talking; he introduced himself as Dino and said that purpose in life was sharing the love of Jesus Christ with others. I listened as he discussed intriguing thoughts on mortality and every man's need for a relationship with God.

He asked, "Where are you going to spend eternity and how can you be sure of it?"

"I have no idea," I said. "I know I haven't lied, killed, or stole anything lately."

I cringed at my half-hearted attempt at humor because I knew I had never felt those things would keep me in any good graces with a God I didn't know or understand. As far as I was concerned, I was headed for hell and had no realistic hope of a heaven, wherever and whatever that was.

Dino opened a Bible and told me about how God had come into the world. That he died and rose again, not for churchgoers, but for sinful people.

It was that simple; God loved me and created me to spend eternity with him. He had a plan for me that I could not know unless I came to know Him. As tears flowed down my face, I accepted Christ as my personal Lord and Savior and asked Him to forgive me of my sins.

That evening, I became a soldier of the spirit—a warrior staring his destiny directly in the face—and this time I would be prepared by the grace of God to find it.

# SEEKING
# GOD'S WILL

President John F. Kennedy said, "The cost of freedom is always high, but Americans have always paid it. And one path which we shall never choose is the path of surrender or submission." My neoteric spirituality provided me with an entirely new perspective on life. It emboldened me with a "never surrender" attitude that I believe would have made President Kennedy proud.

My past had been contaminated with selfishness and drugs, but my newfound hope in God enveloped everything I thought, said, or did. I had been transformed from a wavering warrior of self to a shining shield bearer of hope and prayer. Even the weapons I possessed changed. Before, they were limited to the destruction of physical enemies, but had since been exchanged for Scriptures. God's Word is a formidable weapon against anything, including the psychological and spiritual obstacles of pride and anger that I once faced.

Now, the incomparable power of the Most High God enabled me to lay down my narcissistic life in exchange for one of service to Him. Instead of despair and frustration, my days were filled with inspiration and the yearning to learn as much as possible about the Christian faith. So great was my spiritual hunger that I began reading my Bible daily and learning about the time-tested truth of a never-surrender attitude. Years earlier I had learned creeds in the military about never surrendering, but now I realized that in my own strength I would always end up a casualty. However, my stubbornness and type-A personality were volatile fumes resting within my faith. God was about to ignite them into a raging inferno in my soul that would eventually cause a shockwave leading me back to the Army.

Dino was busy teaching me about the importance of spiritual maturity. We were becoming as close as brothers. But now we faced a challenge. Our homes were quite some distance away from each other, and that forced us to attend separate churches. Although we still met often, the distance between us grew more problematic.

A few months later, I began working at a small health food store. There, I met the Marr family, who were members of a small church in the Kentucky backwoods. They invited me to attend services with them, so every Sunday we all packed into their large Lincoln Town Car. As we drove through the countryside, we sang hymns and talked about God.

The Apostolic Full Gospel House of Prayer, located in the quiet woods of the beautiful Kentucky countryside, became the place I would always recognize as my first church. Charismatic songs echoed in the small building as we danced and lifted our hands in worship. The congregation demonstrated to me what loving one's neighbor was about. Unfortunately, after several months of fellowship with the Marrs and the church, a job change forced me to move into another apartment across town. The trip to the small Pentecostal church became increasingly difficult. To make matters worse, the monsoon-type thunderstorms that pounded the Bluegrass State made the back roads hazardous, leaving me with no choice but to search for another church.

The search didn't take long because my new job was within a block of a large, thriving church. First Assembly of God of Clarksville consisted of two massive brick buildings, one of which had a beautiful steeple and cross. My first evening there, I sat in the back of the sanctuary and carefully watched the pastor. His name was Louie Montoya or "Pastor Louie" as I would soon learn to call him. His dynamic mixture of charisma, knowledge, and personality made him an incredible preacher. He rarely veered from his sermon's tight course, yet his personal stories made his messages relevant.

I introduced myself after the service and we instantly hit it off. Within days he became an important mentor. Pastor Louie's wisdom as a spiritual leader helped me understand practical Christian living. His counsel was a sweet blend of humorous common sense and strong personal confidence, qualities which I sought to emulate. Later, these traits would help me become a leader who could both accomplish my goals and laugh at myself when necessary.

As I worked more and more with the church, Pastor Louie and his wife Linda became like family members. I joined them in children's ministries, nursing home, and prison ministries. The church eventually hired me as custodian, van driver, errand runner, and fix-it guy. As far as I was concerned, working in God's house was the greatest job in the world. After work, I would punch out and often spend time in the sanctuary praying.

One time, Pastor Louie paid me extra to rid the building's roof of a plague of pigeons. The birds had been nesting in the air conditioning units, filling them with excrement and hideous odors. The problem had been ongoing for some time and the staff was in gridlock over humane, yet effective solutions. In the end, my name was brought up and I found myself saddled with the job of saving God's house from "the flying rats."

After several unsuccessful attempts at clearing the roost, I found the one sure means of accomplishing the mission: a trusty old Daisy pellet gun. With my rifle, bags for the dead birds, and some sunscreen, I climbed an old ladder and found two good hiding places. One by one I shot at the birds, lowering the population by a handful. When the sun's heat grew unbearable, I climbed back down to find a shadier vantage point.

About that time, Pastor Louie drove up in his large, grey Buick. Seeing me with the rifle, he expressed concern about me shooting in an open area because onlookers might misinterpret it and call the police. Nevertheless, he began joking around and soon wanted to join in on my mission.

Hoping into the passenger seat, we drove around the buildings and parked where I could get a good shot at a large flock. When we stopped, we both got out of the car. I aimed the small rifle at the line of birds on the roof, and slowly took aim. Just as I squeezed off the shot, we heard sirens. Within seconds, six police cars came barreling in from all directions. They surrounded us with weapons drawn.

"Drop the weapon now! Put your hands on your head! Step towards the trunk of your vehicle!"

I carefully dropped the pellet gun and we crept backwards. The police pushed us into spread-eagle positions, frisked, and questioned incessantly. We related our story and the officers thankfully let us off with a warning.

"You can't be firing weapons within city limits," we were told. "Someone called and reported you guys. Just don't do it again."

After they left, Pastor Louie nearly fell over from laughter. My face turned beet red because I had almost caused my pastor to fall into the annals of criminal lore: Baby Face Nelson, John Dillinger, Al Capone, and Pastor Louie.

Every day was not only an opportunity to learn spiritual wisdom from Pastor Louie and the church, but also to consider God's plan for my life. Over time I became aware of the Lord's desire for me to enter the ministry and serve His people. Pastor Louie taught me how to maintain a practical balance in ministry: to have fun and enjoy work, yet keep a heartfelt compassion for those I serve. The desire to become an ordained, full-time minister became an uncontrollable fire in my bones. After more time, and prayer, and leading from the Holy Spirit, I packed my belongings and said goodbye to the Montoyas and the church.

Shortly before I left Clarksville, the thought of attending a local Bible college came to mind. I picked up the Nashville phonebook and asked God to guide me. I found the North American Baptist Bible College, and within the week I took a trip to visit the beautiful school that was situated on the outskirts of the city. Across its carefully manicured courtyards stood colonial style buildings, silently reflecting the school's long history of theological training.

Walking into the school, I was directed by a secretary to the office of the university's dean, Dr. Don B. McCoy. An overwhelming feeling of peace and assurance swept over me. Dr. McCoy looked directly at me and we both knew in some strange way that our paths were providentially meant to cross.

Although Dr. McCoy and I initially discussed ministerial training at the collegiate level, he took a personal interest in me and we began meeting. He often traveled nearly forty-five miles from his office in Nashville to my apartment in Clarksville to visit. We spent many afternoons playing tennis, having lunch, and studying the Bible together. Each meeting with this intelligent, godly man deepened my hunger for intellectual maturity as a leader.

Even though Dr. McCoy and I developed a strong bond, I wasn't comfortable enrolling in the American Baptist Bible College. My theological views leaned toward Pentecostal rather than Baptist. It had nothing to do with one faith being better than another, just differing theological perspectives. Nevertheless, I sensed a need to look for a college that reflected my understanding of how God works in people's lives

It was terribly difficult to tell him that I was going in a different direction, but I had to because he was my friend. I had no idea how he would take it and I was prepared for the worst. My hands became clammy and my heart thumped like a drum as I told him. When I finished, I waited quietly for whatever was going to come. Would it be a harsh, crushing response? Would it be the end of our friendship?

Dr. McCoy said, "I love you like a son. No matter where you go or which path you take, you have my full support, including whichever school you enroll in. Whatever denomination you choose, the important thing is that you stay faithful to the Lord."

As a spiritual mentor and a friend, Dr. McCoy proved to me that God sends wise leaders into our lives. Very few people, with the exception of my mother, Dino, Pastor Louie, and Dr. McCoy, showed me the unconditional love of Christ with their lives. But these four selflessly shared of themselves, trying to bring me closer to God. Their efforts ultimately enabled me to become a soldier of the faith.

## LEAVING FOR BIBLE COLLEGE

During the fall of 1997, I finalized my plans to attend Central Bible College in Springfield, Missouri. It was a huge change, because never in my life had I aspired to study in school and certainly not college. But now, after a spiritual transformation of my values, my world view, and my hope, I was excited about the opportunity to learn.

The apostle Paul said, "God takes the foolish things of the world to shame the wise," (I Corinthians 1:27). This was certainly true of me: a young man who had ridiculed education and was now working on a degree for pastoral ministry. I knew that it was a goal that God wanted me to embrace, and anything less than total commitment would be shameful to Him. Bible college was also an important stepping stone on the providential path toward my future. It was clear to me that pleasing Him involved my willingness to act, not Him forcing me to do anything.

So my dad and I loaded my belongings into an old, beat-up, U-Haul truck, and I left Clarksville. A quick glance over my shoulder left me with one last mental snapshot: my friend Michael, sitting on the cement porch with his chin in his hands and his elbows on his knees as I drove out of town. Seeing the old neighborhood shrink in the mirror was tough, but I was determined to act on God's leading. Thus I forced myself to travel the new highways that pointed to my future.

## CENTRAL BIBLE COLLEGE

After I arrived at Central Bible College, I faced a new set of challenges. Countless meetings with school officials, centering on my old records and poor grades, made me wonder whether they would let me enroll. Regardless of my misspent youth, I knew God had a plan for me and it involved college. I was a fighter and was not going to let anything distract me from my destiny. Finally, they admitted me and I began following my new path toward ministry.

It wasn't long, however, before fear and doubt crept into my heart. I hadn't been anywhere near a school for years, let alone enrolled in one. Six long years had passed since high school and now I was facing the daunting task of relearning practically every study skill I had known. Hectic class schedules, annoying tuition bills, and years of separation from academics pushed at me from every side.

I knew God's plan for me was to be a minister, but I was uncertain about the specific direction. The school emphasized three options: "The training of preachers, missionaries, and evangelists." This creed was engraved on a small, brick memorial at the center of the campus.

I liked to travel, so the missionary option was plausible, but my duty on the Demilitarized Zone in 1993 had tainted me. I felt that I would not do well as a missionary. Other students and staff disagreed.

"You would make a great missionary," they said.

"You have no idea how much I hated being sent to another country by the Army," I would reply.

The idea of being a pastor failed to stoke my fire because I felt that it involved too many administrative duties. Besides that, it sounded too difficult for a stubborn guy like me. Pastors had to smile and shake hands during spats with people. I was the type of guy who quickly let others know when they frustrated me.

The last option was becoming an evangelist. I liked to travel, but I could leave the country whenever I wanted to. Also, I was already sharing my faith, like an evangelist, with others. Evangelism was a simple and straightforward lifestyle, the perfect fit for a guy like me who fell into no clique and fit no mold.

Others who knew me believed that none of these choices were the best fit. They argued that I should become a military chaplain. One group of students from the school organized an outreach to soldiers at a nearby Army post and repeatedly asked me to join them in their ministry.

"Why me?" I asked.

I was usually told, "Your prior service in the military can help you to serve those in the military. Your soldier attitude would be useful in relating to troops and leading them spiritually. Besides, you would not have to waste time learning everything from scratch because you already know how to be a warrior."

The outreach group drove nearly two hours each weekend to conduct religious services at the base. Even though their weekly expedition involved many things that I enjoyed, my answer remained the same. When the team leaders asked if I would be interested in ministering with them I said, "No. I'm done with the military."

Not only was the idea of a return to the military unpleasant, but so was any thought of becoming a chaplain. Being a clergyman in the armed forces was dead last on my list of potential ministries. I was certain that I would never be involved in any ministry to the military.

Thoughts of my former experiences as a rifleman misguided me into believing that grunts were the only hard-core people in the military. Would God expect me to forget all of that and blindly become a chaplain? I had once proudly served among the infantry, the "Shock Troops" of America's Army, but that was then and this was now. I felt that no civilian could ever understand how I had come to love the spearhead soldiers of war but loathed any rear-echelon attitude.

My rejection of the chaplaincy was never an implication that all chaplains were bad, although most of the ones I had seen were. Nevertheless, there were chaplains who could be considered legendary, often referred to by soldiers as "water walkers." They were the ones who lived what they preached, went anywhere for the mission, and put soldiers before themselves. I only heard others talk about those chaplains. All but one of the chaplains I served with were nominal at best and almost always absent from where the troops were.

Certain that chaplaincy was not for me, I concluded that ministry with the military ministry team was likewise not for me. The idea of visiting a basic training post in order to watch a bunch of new recruits bored me. They would be learning how to wear uniforms, march, and speak military words. I thought about how pathetic it seemed. There were not going to be any heroic feats of military courage, missions of glory; only the primitive education of troops who were learning to simply exist within a military system.

After hearing enough of my arrogant arguments—I was practically laughing at the group—the "military missionaries" eventually stopped inviting me.

After the invitations stopped, the pressure to become involved in military ministry ceased—until my mother visited me one weekend. During her sojourn, we talked about life and faith. Gradually, she steered the conversation toward military chaplaincy. As I sat in disbelief, she told me, "I've been thinking about all of the soldiers you used to serve with. Imagine if you could have shared the love of the Lord with them. Imagine what a difference it would have made for them if SPC Bryan would have been a chaplain."

In the weeks that followed, I often recalled that conversation and wondered about it. What if I would have been a chaplain for those soldiers? The chaplaincy was something completely different than the combat arms occupations I had worked in, but it would be considered a ministry. Unless my mother or someone else could guarantee that I would be able to serve as a hardcore chaplain—on the front lines with the troops—I would continue to have no part of it.

The following months continued stirring up the question in my mind. What if my mother and the students at school were right? Maybe God could use me as an effective chaplain. My mom worked with a retired Army chaplain. He had told her, that the Army needed chaplains badly because of low numbers in service with the organization.

Mom wanted me to meet the guy and putting it off I replied, "I will sometime."

I knew my arguments against the chaplaincy were gradually weakening. I finally asked myself, "When was the last time I actually met a chaplain?" My resistance was proving to be little more than shallow arrogance and pride. But I was not at a turning point yet. I still needed a sense of clarification from God.

So for now, I intended to stick to what I had learned while in the Army: standing orders. Standing orders are directives last given by any senior leader in the absence of further commands. If a soldier has been sent to guard a building, he isn't supposed to leave that position until further orders are given to do so. In my case, God had burdened my heart for inner-city evangelism, and that was what I was going to do unless He guided me elsewhere. Determined to serve in the darkness of America's inner cities, I packed my belongings into my recently purchased 1989 Cadillac Fleetwood Brougham, attended my college graduation, and left for Los Angeles.

## LEAVING BIBLE COLLEGE FOR THE INNER CITY

The day I graduated from Central Bible College, I drove west along the old, mostly abandoned Route 66 towards Los Angeles, California. Throughout the trip, which lasted about four days, I thought about how exciting it would be to help homeless people, drug addicts, prostitutes, and runaways. Eventually I pulled into the parking lot of the Teen Challenge ministry center in Hawthorne, California, a drug rehabilitation ministry ran by a pastor I had met years before. The center lay tucked away in a crowded community shadowed by more than 200 other cities that comprised the greater Los Angeles area.

Pastor Phil Cookes, the director of the ministry, introduced me to his staff and showed me where I would live. He also gave me a tour of the neighboring cities where I would minister. These cities included Lynwood, Compton, and South Gate. One evening, I sat in the comfort of my new room in Hawthorne, on the second story of a renovated motel that the ministry owned. I would only be there a month before moving to Lynwood, an even more dangerous place.

A large man by the name of Randy Sillicato was my roommate. An incredibly nice fellow, Randy had once been a methamphetamine addict in Tajunga, California prior to completing the ministry program in Hawthorne. Unfortunately, the recovery unmasked a depressive disorder, which led to a massive weight gain.

Randy and I became great friends and he would often ask, "Hey Jeff, What was it like being a soldier?"

"I always appreciated the camaraderie of troops and the no-nonsense attitude of the military leaders. I am proud to have served, but that's a part of my past."

"Have you ever thought of going back in as a chaplain?"

I sighed and told him, "I have not planned on it, but I sometimes wonder if God might be trying to lead me that way."

One day, after visiting Long Beach on a break from work, I came home to bad news. As I walked to my room, another staff member stopped me and asked, "Did you hear what happened to Randy?"

"No, what happened?"

"Randy died a little while ago. He had a heart attack as he was climbing the stairs in the old motel building. He actually fell down the stairs and the medics tried to resuscitate him three times."

I was crushed. Randy was the one good buddy I had in this place, a thousand miles from my home. His family asked me to speak at his funeral a week later. During the event, I said, "The last time I saw Randy was in our room. Before I walked out, I turned, looked at him, and said I love you man." He said to me, "I love you too, bro."

There are two things about Randy I'll never forget. One was what a great guy he was. The second was that he had pointed out that God will follow us to the farthest places if that is what it takes for us to hear Him.

After Randy's death, I continued weighing the pros and cons of civilian versus military ministry. I enjoyed conducting Bible studies for the students in our program who had only recently come off drugs. Praying and counseling, helping cook meals for them, all gave me deep gratitude for the opportunity to serve. I was content—almost.

After serving nearly eight months with the Hawthorne Ministry Center, I began to feel that my life was not heading in the right direction. Early on, my ministry had gone well, but then I became frustrated with the complete lack of income, heavy work load, and the constant sense of being treated as an outsider by some of the staff members. Except for my car, I had given nearly everything I had to join the group. I spent all my savings moving to California, and lived in a lonely room the size of a walk-in closet in one of the worst neighborhoods in the country.

I loved Teen Challenge, but knew that I could not sustain myself without an income and would eventually need to seek out another ministry. At one point, one of the assistant leaders of the rehab ministry suggested I join in a food stamp enrollment program.

"I would never do that," I said. "My mom and dad always taught me to work hard and earn my own way. I don't think that I'm better than someone on welfare, but I do believe my reputation as a minister would be destroyed because I am more than capable of earning a living."

My desire to leave the Teen Challenge center was confirmed by a peace from God. Nevertheless, I felt that I needed to leave in a respectful manner. So, I waited for the right time when neither I nor God would look foolish. I was careful to still perform my duties, but I gradually withdrew from day-to-day interaction with others. I struggled with my decision because I genuinely cared for those whom I served. Once I departed, there would be no returning because of the rift it would cause. Teen Challenge needed people to come to the inner city, not to leave it.

The months passed and finally, the day came when I sensed an answer from the Lord. It was a typical afternoon in the inner city: the "Ghetto-Bird" (a police helicopter) flew its occasional path over our neighborhood, gunshots rang out somewhere down the street, and a layer of cool, moist air floated in from the Pacific Ocean.

Alan, a former student who had once asked me to pray with him concerning his faith, walked by the main building of the center. He approached me and said, "God wants me to tell you something, Jeff. I have no idea why I am saying this, but I feel as though I am supposed to. He has great plans for you. He doesn't want you to be held back from those opportunities."

I knew that he had no idea I was thinking about leaving, because I had told no one. I choked for a second and then said, "Thanks, man. I appreciate you telling me that." After much prayer that evening, I was convinced that Alan's comment was a divine sign for me. I knew it was time to leave.

I skipped breakfast the next morning, packed my belongings in my car, went to the director's office, and told him I would be leaving the ministry center within the hour.

An hour or so later, I headed toward East Los Angeles. I was ready to get on with my life, find time to recover from the loss of Randy, and discover what the Lord had in store me. As I drove away I reflected on my tenure in the inner city and how it had changed me in both positive and negative ways. Helping the needy was invigorating. The sheer thrill of being in the "city of drama" was enlightening. But the daily struggles of surviving were exhausting.

I had managed to live in some of the toughest neighborhoods in America and suddenly I realized it was the military that had imparted that survivor attitude in me. The Army had ultimately done it for God; they just weren't aware of it at the time.

I was not yet ready to concede the idea of returning to the Army, but a pivotal event would soon change both the world—and me—forever.

## MY NOMAD EXPERIENCE

As I drove east, the uncertainty of my future worried me. Where was I going to restart my life? I prayed throughout the drive and hoped to have an answer soon.

The first idea that came to mind involved a Christian university that I had read about. Obtaining the directions, I drove to the Talbot School of Theology, located in La Mirada, California, and began a lengthy foot march across its sprawling campus. Knowing I would need a job, I searched out and found a student bulletin board with dozens of help-wanted flyers tacked all over it. One in particular stood out. It read: "Looking for a young, hard-working Christian male for construction work. Lodging provided."

Without hesitation, I called the phone number of Mr. Hal. L. After discussing a few basic terms, we met and worked out an employment agreement. My new home was going to be his recreational Golden Falcon camping trailer which was parked in his backyard. The yard resembled a construction zone because of all the unfinished projects and tools that were scattered across it. He was going to pay me ten dollars an hour for completing those unfinished projects.

I started within the week. My work included mowing, painting, digging holes for sprinkler systems, moving cement blocks, and chopping wood. It only took two days for me to realize that Mr. L. was one tough taskmaster. One of his requirements was that I clock in every morning, on the minute, using an obsolete time card machine that hung on a wall next to his back porch. He told me, "You will punch in exactly on the minute, morning and sundown. I will be very upset if you go over even a minute or two."

I was miserable. There had to be more to life than back-breaking labor, nominal pay, and isolation from the world. As time passed, I became increasingly frustrated that my life extended no further than Mr. L's backyard. Angry at God, I prayed, "How could you have gotten me into this, Lord? Why did you lead me here only to forget about me?" Unbearable feelings of failure swept over me every day. I had come to California as a willing servant and now found myself repeating the question Jesus offered on the cross, "Father, why have You forsaken me?"

I had asked God to make me a warrior of faith. Instead, I was a washout, a loser, a slave in a foreign land. Instead of blessing people, I lived to work and survive. One day I reached my limit of patience. I retreated to my bed in the rickety old camper, sat down, and cried.

While hunched over on the edge of my bunk, I went to the source of strength that had gotten me through my spiritual battles: God. I blindly flipped open my Bible and saw the book of Job staring directly back at me. I read Job and realized that there was a significant parallel between Job's trials and mine. I understood that God had not abandoned me, but was guiding me into substantial character-building situations in order to be a more developed spiritual warrior.

In the Bible, God directed his people, Moses, Jonah, Job, and Jesus, into situations of extreme isolation, confusion, and need. He wanted them to face seclusion so that they could understand His "all-sufficient comfort and power." After thinking about this one day, I considered how God had brought those men through nomadic experiences of extreme loneliness so that they could become legendary men of faith. At that point, my trials began to make sense. God had brought me to Mr. L's backyard so that I could become a more resilient, mentally hardened, and highly effective spiritual combatant.

## SAYING GOODBYE TO THE BACKYARD

Shortly after the lesson about Job, I respectfully gave Mr. L a two-week notice. He was gracious and allowed me to stay for a few extra days while I searched for a new job. I found a position as a fitness instructor at a YMCA in nearby Fullerton, California. However, while I was juggling the transition between my final day at the backyard and the interview for the new job, the world changed forever.

On September 11, 2001, I woke up in the trailer and turned on the little television next to my bed. Shepherd Smith from Fox News was describing the terrible carnage caused by an airplane accident in New York City. Apparently, a Boeing 747 had flown directly into one of the World Trade Centers. As clouds of black and gray smoke poured from the tower behind him, a second plane flew directly into the second tower of the World Trade Center. I trembled as I watched.

I listened intently to radio news commentators discussing the unfolding tragedy as I worked in the backyard that morning. Nonstop coverage permeated every radio station. Eventually, I finished my work and drove to the YMCA for a new employee orientation meeting. As I spoke with my future boss, I couldn't help glancing at a television behind her and watching the horror that was escalating throughout the eastern U.S.

Not only had the World Trade Center been attacked, but also the Pentagon. And one aircraft crashed into a field in Shanksville, Pennsylvania.

The following week, I moved from Mr. L's to the home of Robert and Tina Zurrica, friends I met at a local church. Staying with them was a great blessing because it provided me a comfortable place to lay my head and reasonable rent. As for the YMCA, it proved to be an unexpected dream job. Lifting weights and teaching aerobics classes inside a gym with glass walls, waterfalls, and a heated pool inspired me to develop myself physically.

As good as it was, though, it was not enough to quench a strange yearning in my soul. A dark cloud settled over our nation following the attacks in New York. Suddenly and unexpectedly the nation was involved in a war on terror. That war struck a deep chord of patriotism in my soul. Reason dictated that the United States would not stand idly by after her innocent citizens were burned, crushed, and forced to jump from buildings to their deaths. As I worked in the beautiful gym, surrounded with palm trees, I struggled as an ever-increasing desire to serve my country warred with equally powerful memories of my enlisted years.

On one of my days off, I visited a nearby Army recruiter and asked, "What kind of jobs do you have available right now? Are there any benefits to being prior service?"

He told me, "Not many positions are available right now due to the turnout of people wanting to join because of the attacks in New York. The few jobs left, at least for prior service, are helicopter pilots, infantry, and military chaplains. Any experience you have can always help." He also said, "There are a couple of drawbacks for you: one is that you would lose your last rank. The other is that you will have to complete basic training again because you have been out so long."

Those things were not enticing, but one thing was certain. If I went through the effort required, I would find myself going to battle. The recruiter and I traveled to the San Diego MEPS (Military Entrance and Processing Station) so that I could retake the ASVAB (Armed Services Vocational Aptitude Battery) test, which I had originally taken ten years earlier. The results of that test would affect my decision.

My test results came back strong. I carefully considered the available options for occupations. Finally, I told the recruiter that I wanted to pray about the decision and leave it in God's hands for a week. A few days later as I was weightlifting, I sensed God speaking to my heart. It was a clear to me that God's answer was, "No."

I returned and told the recruiter that I was certain that rejoining was not the right thing to do at the time because it was not God's plan for me. As far as I was concerned, my time as a soldier was finished and combat was something that I was never going to experience.

I went on with life, thinking that I might return to the Midwest and figure out what I should do with the rest of my life. One weekend, while visiting a buddy's house, I received a startling revelation. My friend's mother, supposedly a devout churchwoman, prophesied a revelation of God's will for my life. She said, "God is going to reveal the great purpose of your life to you within the next three to four months."

As the family and I talked, my mind alternated between faith and doubt. How could she know what was troubling me in the deepest part of my heart? Sensing this, she stated, "You don't have to believe me, but I believe that God wanted me to tell you that." With caution, I shelved the message in the back of my mind. If it was truly from God, at least according to the Bible, it would have to eventually come to pass. Although the prophecy seemed too risky to fully buy into at the moment, about four months later, events happened that corroborated it.

In the meantime, my days of waiting in California for God to guide me back to the Midwest were ending. I increasingly sensed a peace within my soul about leaving. A week arrived when I felt the time was right, so I gave the Zurricas a final rent check and packed my car.

The last week of December, 2001, I said goodbye to a year of the most challenging personal battles I had ever faced. Now I was headed to Kansas. During the drive, I thought about how God had brought me through the forfeiture of almost everything I owned for the ministry, the tiring trip to the Golden State, Randy's death, and Mr. L's backyard. Since arriving nearly twelve months earlier, I had become more of a soldier than I had ever been in my life, and it was all for a reason the future would soon reveal.

# UNCASING THE COLORS: RETURNING TO THE MILITARY

**N**early four days elapsed as I drove back across the country. My destination was Atchison, Kansas, a small town where I had spent my later adolescence. I left Atchison when I entered the Army and returned only to visit my mother or preach while a student at Central Bible College. Although rare, my visits to see Mom, Uncle Carl, my brother, his family, and a few friends and acquaintances were always enjoyable and gave me a chance to catch up on all the news.

One of my best friends that I made a point of seeing was Ken Watkins, the senior pastor of New Life Assembly of God. With his black motorcycle vest and dark, course beard, he looked more like a biker than a minister. New Life was a Pentecostal church with many wonderful people in its ranks. After arriving in Atchison from California, I contacted him by phone and we immediately began spending time together.

One day we stopped at the public library. As we walked among the bookshelves, Pastor Ken broached a subject that had been on his mind. "Jeff, I want you to consider working with me as an associate pastor. I would really enjoy working with you, but pray and do what you sense God wants you to do. Whatever you feel He wants is what you should do."

"I would like that," I said. "And I agree that praying about it is the right thing to do."

We continued walking past shelves of books until we came upon a large rack of magazines and novels which the library was trying to sell. I purchased a book by the famous Christian apologist, Francis Schaeffer, entitled *No Little People*. Knowing that Schaeffer was a legendary defender of the faith, I thought it might serve as good reading material later. Besides, it only cost a dime.

With God's leading, I eventually decided to become Pastor Ken's associate pastor. Not only a great friend, he was one of the most devout men I had ever known. Months passed and the opportunities to learn from him helped me to develop professionally and as a Christian. I preached, prayed, visited the sick in the hospital, and co-served at funerals and weddings. Serving with him instilled in me a greater respect and admiration for those who worked in pastoral ministry.

One evening when I was at my mother's house, I thought about how much I enjoyed serving as a pastor. As I reflected on how God might use me in the future, my mother returned from her job at the Eisenhower Veteran's Administration Center in Leavenworth, Kansas.

"Hey, I talked with a chaplain at work and he wants to meet you," she said. She had mentioned him briefly during a discussion when I was in college.

I brushed it off, thinking, "It's another attempt to convince me to be a chaplain." But my mother wouldn't give up. After a month of hearing about this chaplain, I decided to appease my mom and meet the guy. But I told myself, "I'll visit him, mainly because he probably has some cool war stories, but he's not going to convince me to become a chaplain."

A few days later, I drove the twenty minutes to Leavenworth from Atchison, and met Chaplain (COL) Gary "Sam" Sanford, a retired Army chaplain, for lunch. He told me about his combat tours in Vietnam and Iraq (Operations Desert Shield/Storm).

We met again many times over the next few months and discussed God, politics, and the military chaplaincy. Gradually, my hesitation for becoming a chaplain began to fade. Years of resistance were now eroding as a battle-tested chaplain, who had successfully served soldiers and earned their respect as a leader, told me how fulfilling it was to carry the cross, the Christian banner of faith, to the battlefield. On top of that, his experiences allowed him to continue passionately serving veterans as a pastor and a VA chaplain.

For the first time, I began to seriously consider the chaplain corps as a possible ministry. This new vision enveloped my life, both day and night, until I finally knew that it was what God wanted for me. Not only had He spoken in a whispering voice to my heart, but also through a consistent sense of peace that surrounded my soul. I had reached a surprising and definitive conclusion: God was indeed directing me to uncase the dusty old flag hidden in my heart and prepare it for a dramatic return to the military. But this time I would serve as a soldier of God.

Last but not least, it had been four months since the woman in Los Angeles had prophesied about my future. It appeared that the divine plan God had for me all along had come to pass.

"What exactly does a guy have to do to become a chaplain?" I asked Chaplain Sanford.

"It's a long process, but you will know it's been worth it when your soldiers appreciate you. First, you have to gain a few years of pastoral ministry experience, because you are a pastor to the armed forces community. Second, you have to get your ordination credentials. Then you will need an ecclesiastical endorsement from a denomination, an undergraduate degree from college, and a Master of Divinity from a theological seminary."

I spent the remainder of the year visiting seminaries, chaplains, libraries, and talking with other chaplains in order to study as much as possible about religious support to the military. One by one, the requirements fell into place and I edged closer to my new goal of serving soldiers. It was a difficult day for me, however, when I had to end my service at New Life Assembly of God in order to become a commissioned officer and enroll in seminary.

## BEGINNING SEMINARY

The United States Army requires its chaplains to earn a Master of Divinity degree before entering active duty service. I had earned a bachelor's degree in Biblical Theology from Central Bible College before venturing to California.

Now I was required to tackle the intimidating task of graduate studies. I searched out, applied, and was accepted into The Assemblies of God Theological Seminary in Springfield, Missouri.

To help pay for graduate school, I worked at a local hunting and fishing store called Bass Pro. Other positions I held included security guard, and line work at a battery factory. These jobs served to pay my bills; however, the honest-to-goodness ministry preparation for the chaplaincy came through my pastoral ministry at local churches. It was ironic that this occurred at Fort Leonard Wood, Missouri, the very place I refused to help minister at while in Bible college.

## MENTORSHIP

In the fall of 2002 during my military ministry, I met an Army chaplain by the name of Chaplain (CPT) Jeff Jay. He was also a graduate of the Assemblies of God Theological Seminary, and was serving on active duty as an Army chaplain. He allowed me to preach and serve Holy Communion to the soldiers on Sundays. He was one of the most dynamic leaders that I had ever seen. Better yet, he had invaluable experience which he was willing to share with me. This allowed me to see firsthand and better understand the possibilities of having a successful ministry within the military.

Along with the Fort Leonard Wood ministry, I also pursued civilian ministry. I served in assistant pastorship roles while helping Chaplain Jay at Fort Leonard Wood. The first was with Cumberland Presbyterian Church in Cumberland, Missouri, where I served during the first two years of graduate school. The second church was National Avenue Assembly of God in Springfield, Missouri, where I worked for the remaining year and a half of school. These ministries gave me great opportunities to develop as a spiritual leader because of the two pastors I worked with: Pastor Kevin Smith and James Cookson.

Both of these men taught me about leading a church and dealing with the inherent politics. Their congregations supported me, all the while knowing that my time with them would be finite. During that final phase of my life as a student and associate pastor, I stumbled across the path of someone who would change me forever.

# TANISHA

The day I met a beautiful, bright student named Tanisha marked the most important day in my life. Some acquaintances of ours introduced us and our first date was lunch at a Mexican restaurant near her school. Her stunning blonde hair and gorgeous green eyes nearly knocked the wind out of me. It was at a restaurant that I realized her personality matched her sparkling outward beauty. Tanisha was a Navy veteran, having served in the 1990s as a Hospital Corpsman. When I met her, she was in her final year of working towards a bachelor's degree in cell-molecular biology at Southwest Missouri State University.

A pivotal point in our relationship occurred during the unfortunate and untimely illness of my mom. In 2003, she was diagnosed with acute leukemia, a terrible and merciless cancer. I had been in military training for nearly three months. Upon completion of chaplain training in South Carolina and after my graduation from the Army's Airborne (basic parachute training) School, I returned to Kansas to meet with friends and family who were gathered at my mother's hospital bed. I answered questions about mortality and eternity for all who asked. Through these conversations, my brother gave his life to Christ. Later, I would offer Holy Communion to my entire family, one of the most precious moments of my life. Although my father declined, he later gave his life to Christ as well.

Throughout the rest of the day, we talked, thanked friends for visiting, and prayed with my mother. Two days later, as we prayed at her bedside, Mom grabbed my brother's hand and squeezed it, and at the same time turned her head to look at me. With one final glance on this side of life, she looked into my eyes and stepped across the bridge between life, death, and eternity. Witnessing my mother's hard-core faith endure under intense suffering was an amazing lesson in the importance of eternal life and the failing temporariness of this world.

A few months after my mother's passing, I proposed to Tanisha. A year later, we were married at Fort Leavenworth, Kansas. Not long after that, I finished my final semester of seminary. During graduation week, I received a telephone call from a military chaplain at the Department of the Army.

## FORT DRUM, NEW YORK

"Chaplain Bryan," she said, "we know you have assignment orders for West Point, but we want to know if you will be willing to give those up in exchange for an infantry unit at Fort Drum, New York. They're getting ready to deploy to Iraq and have no chaplain."

I asked, "Ma'am, would it be okay if my wife and I talk about it and get back with you within the next couple of days?"

"Sure," she said.

After talking and praying about it with Tanisha, we decided that the 10th Mountain Division was the choice we wanted to make. I called the chaplain back with our decision. I knew that it was almost unheard of to be asked by the Army about an assignment, especially considering that I was a junior officer. The request was quite respectful, and we were certain that the light infantry unit, the spearhead of battle, would probably need a chaplain more than anyone else. With God's help, I was ready to be their spiritual warrior.

During my last week of seminary, I took a final walk through the school and made my way to a special prayer room on the second floor. The small, peaceful meditation room was decorated with beautiful stained glass windows. I sat quietly and soaked in the ambience of the silent room. Detailed maps of missionary activity around the world were pinned on the walls, and national flags representing countries from across the globe hung near them. The room was a sanctuary, filling me with a sense of serenity—a much needed commodity in a future that would be marred with dark, enveloping war clouds.

Nearby on a semicircular wooden bench rested a small, well-used prayer journal. Scribbled on its pages were heartfelt messages from students. A note on one page read, "Lord, send me into the belly of the beast and let me face my enemy. Never let me do it for myself, but always for others." A Scripture from the book of Isaiah followed: "And the Lord said, 'Who will go for me? Whom shall I send?' And I said, 'Here am I, Lord, send me.'"

I was the one who wrote that message nearly four years earlier when I had first arrived at the school with a fresh drive to be a chaplain. That drive came from a deep spiritual hunger in my soul to serve soldiers in the worst combat scenarios because that was where they needed God the most. Much like a persistent hunger pang within my belly, the vision to minister to warriors would not subside. If anything, it actually increased as I thought about all of the soldiers fighting, perhaps dying, with little or no faith.

Less than six months after graduation from seminary, I faced the task of moving to New York, processing into my new unit, and deploying to combat. Tanisha and I traveled across the country and eventually arrived at Fort Drum. The next week was spent enjoying our final opportunities together before war. I spared no effort at balancing the challenging tasks of in-processing to Fort Drum, spending time with Tanisha, and meeting the soldiers in my new unit.

My journal that week read, "It's July and I have had a head-on collision with reality. The burden I carry feels as though it is a massive freight train resting squarely on my shoulders. I have begun in-processing to the 10th Mountain Division as well as processing for my deployment to Iraq with the 4th Battalion, 31st Infantry to Iraq - all within two weeks."

## A DIFFICULT GOODBYE

On the morning of 27 August, 2006, a day I had waited for all of my life, my alarm clock buzzed with a jarring sound. It was 4:40 a.m. and would be my last day in the United States for a long, long time. Tanisha and I packed my gear in the truck and made our way to my unit for transportation to the Wheeler Sack Army Airfield. Our anxiety increased with each passing moment. The tension became unbearable.

Saying goodbye to my wife was one of the most emotional events of my life. The buses were en-route along with a convoy of flatbed trucks for our equipment. As we stood waiting, Tanisha and I decided that we would appreciate the opportunity to be with each other one more moment.

The cool wind blew through the beautiful evergreen trees and the sunshine seemed especially bright. The gentle morning began to bring a positive outlook to the day as we did our best to savor each moment. The pending separation for war caused us to appreciate each other like never before. Other families stood quietly nearby, probably thinking the same things we were, waiting for the difficult moment which all military families must face.

Finally the clock ticked down and the voice of war called for us. We soldiers looked into the eyes of our loved ones and held them as if we'd never see them again. I hugged and kissed Tanisha, collecting each moment in my mind. We held hands one last time as we saw a long parade of yellow school buses roll over the hill toward us.

When they stopped, I took a deep breath and walked up the stairs of the quiet bus in front of me. Once onboard, I looked through the window to see Tanisha turning to walk away. I tried with all of my might to open one of the little windows that stood between us. I wanted to look into her eyes once more and tell her I loved her. I pushed until my fingers hurt, but the window wouldn't budge. My heart sank at the thought that I wasn't successful. But as the bus began moving I noticed that she turned to look at me one last time.

I pressed my palms against the dirty glass and mouthed the words, "I love you."

She smiled back and did the same.

I intended to treasure that last glimpse of her smiling face until the day I returned from combat.

If I returned.

# 5

# POLAR BEAR
# CHAPLAIN

The old, bus lumbered away from the area where our families had said goodbye and towards Fort Drum's Wheeler-Sack Army Airfield. As it did, I recalled the various events that had occurred throughout the previous two weeks. There was, of course, quality time spent with my wife before the send-off and the critical task of developing relationships with my soldiers and commanders. We had not even left the confines of the installation yet and thoughts of war were already wearing me out.

As the vehicle maneuvered along the worn-out streets of the post, I looked out the window and contemplated the moment. Thoughts drifted through my mind, including how well I might perform in combat. What would I see? What challenges to my faith awaited me on the other side of the world?

Would I survive?

Stories have been told of chaplains who deployed to combat soon after arriving at their new units, but a mere two weeks with my unit was maddening. I had expected to deploy quickly, but when the day arrived, it hit me hard. Nevertheless, I had volunteered for the assignment and was determined to honor that commitment, despite my fears.

Riding along that morning, I thought about how much personal time I had spent preparing to honor that commitment. I desensitized myself by watching war videos on the Internet. I spoke with soldiers who had returned from the battlefield. I also read articles about the combat operations in Iraq. One such article described the men whom we would replace, a battalion of infantrymen from the legendary 101st Airborne Division (Air-Assault). The article noted that the 1st Battalion, 502nd Infantry, would soon return home from a bloody tour inside Iraq's deadly Triangle of Death.

What had they experienced?

Deep fear began to creep over me as I sat on the bus and thought about the danger we would soon face. The smothering heat within the vehicle only worsened my anxiety at the thought of my decision to join the 10th Mountain Division during a war.

As I looked out the window at the passing road, several thoughts ran through my mind. "This isn't the first hardship I've faced; I can definitely handle this." "If I have any hope of making it through this, it will only be because of God's help." The tension within me was so high that fear fought to paralyze my will. I thought of that terrible day in 2003 when Mom died. At that point, I closed my eyes and prayed, "God, you know that I am not a quitter, but without your peace, guidance, and strength, I am going to be overcome by fear. Please help me! Amen."

## THE HISTORY OF THE 31ST INFANTRY

I looked toward the sky outside the dusty bus window for relief from the thoughts of battle. Bright rays of sunshine flashed sporadically through the trees, making me squint. Eventually I was able to relieve my mind by thinking about the incredible heritage that the soldiers in the 31st Infantry Regiment had earned throughout previous engagements. Now it was my turn and I would build on that sacred legacy.

"Climb to Glory," the motto of the 10th Mountain Division, the 31st Infantry Regiment's higher headquarters command, originated from the regiment's legendary history. From day one in the division, I appreciated the motto's spiritual application of "glory." It reminded me of how life is a journey—a climb to glory—in which people strive to reach great heights, just as the brave mountain soldiers did.

These soldiers often faced unimaginable odds, and yet they refused to surrender. Their proud history is demonstrated not only in the freedom of the world, but also memorialized by history on many of the world's famous battlefields, including Siberia, the Philippines, Korea, and Vietnam.

Everywhere they went, their chaplains went with them.

The 31st Infantry was activated in the Philippines in 1916 due to a need for an American force overseas. They immediately moved to Siberia where they earned the nickname "Polar Bears" because the soldiers often saw wild polar bears roaming the land. The unit was moved back to the Philippines not long after, but the nickname stuck. It was there, while facing overwhelming Japanese forces, that the regiment was overrun and taken into captivity. In their brutal captivity, the Polar Bears courageously endured the terrible Bataan Death March.

While imprisoned by their captors, many of the Polar Bears died of starvation, disease, and outright execution. Such was their pride in the unit that one of the last missions before surrendering Bataan was a secretive escort of the unit's colors and the 'Shanghai Bowl'. The silver punchbowl was a special piece of unit memorabilia, handcrafted from 1600 silver trade dollars during their 1932 expedition to Shanghai. Under the cover of darkness the night before the surrender, these sacred items were evacuated by barge to Corregidor Island, where they would remain buried for four years, until they could be recovered after the war. The Shanghai Bowl's rich history represented both the enduring tenacity of those who, at Bataan, fought to the last available bullet and endured imprisonment. It also represented the unconquerable will of the Polar Bears I would minister to in battle.[1]

Besides the flag and the Polar Bear bowl, other interesting artifacts reside with the unit at Fort Drum. The mascot, a 1,200 lb. statue nicknamed Big George, stands guard near the headquarters' entrance. Throughout the battalion, the polar bear image is captured on posters, coins, stickers, and hats. Further, the enlisted members have kept the polar bear image alive throughout the world by carving two-foot high, wooden polar bears, one of which has managed to deploy to places such as Afghanistan, Haiti, Djibouti, and Iraq.

---

1 Detailed regimental history is compiled by Col (Ret) Karl H. Lowe at 31stinfantry.org.

The bus and its pensive occupants now made its way through "the Old Post," the originally settled area of Fort Drum. Old Post now resembled a ghost town. I thought about the many 10th Mountain Division soldiers who made similar journeys on their way to whatever conflict or war called for them. From the Philippines in World War I and II, to the snow-capped mountains of Italy during WWII, the brave 10th Mountain troopers never hesitated to answer the call of their nation when it came to protecting freedom. Now, the specialized mountain warriors prepared to do it again, and I would be their chaplain.

## 26 JULY, 2006 – THE GEORGE EXPERIENCE

As the bus rolled on, I retreated deeper into my thoughts, trying to forget what lay ahead of me. In my short time at the post, many interesting experiences had occurred. One afternoon I was trying to locate some rifle marksmanship training ranges. I knew that the Polar Bear soldiers were somewhere in the backwoods of the fort, but exactly where was a mystery.

Before setting out to join the troops, I asked a lieutenant to draw me a map so that I could locate where they were. He gave me a hastily-scribbled scrap of paper that had stick-figure quality imagery. As I began the trek in my truck, I realized that road signs were not posted in many areas. After a couple of hours of aimless wandering, I ended up at a remote T-intersection.

I pulled my truck over to check my map. So far, I felt like I had discovered every dead-end road in the entire upstate region of New York. At that point I was aware that an attempt at deciphering the map was futile. Because of the vast, unmarked acreage of the installation, I knew I was in trouble. I hurled the drawing onto the passenger seat, threw my hands in the air, and rested my head on the steering wheel.

"Lord, help me! I'm lost." I prayed. "Please send someone. Amen."

Almost instantly, a large, green, military truck came blasting like a thunderbolt through the intersection and stopped in front of me. One of the two soldiers in the vehicle rolled down his window and asked, "Do you need some help?"

"Yes! More than you can imagine," I answered.

The driver jumped out of the truck and approached me. I disgustedly grabbed the map off the seat beside me, stepped out, and spread the useless sheet of paper across the hood of my truck. The Good Samaritan was a large, burly man with dark glasses, a five o-clock shadow, and a warm smile. After looking down at the map, he said, "You can follow me. I know this place like the back of my hand."

I agreed, but wanted to know who he was. "My name is George," he said.

I trailed behind the lumbering truck to the training area where my men were located. Before we went our separate ways, I got out and walked up to the vehicle to thank George. He stepped out.

After I said my piece, George asked, "Will you say a quick prayer for me, Chaplain?"

Answering in the affirmative, I placed my hands upon his helmet and prayed, "God please bless and protect George. I thank you for sending him to help me. Amen."

"Thanks for the prayer, Sir," he said, as he hopped back into his truck.

I knew that God had intervened on my behalf by sending George. The lesson that I would not forget was that even if someone drives aimlessly around the backwoods of life— to the point of becoming incredibly lost—God knows exactly where he or she is and will intervene in response to a faithful prayer.

As I watched the world outside the dirty bus windows, I wondered what had happened to George, what he was doing, and where he would eventually go. God had showed me through that brief encounter the importance of a military chaplain. Had I spent the day doing things other than searching for my soldiers, I might have never witnessed God's guidance for me as a chaplain and George might not have received his prayer.

## 31 JULY, 2006 – THE SCOUTS

As we continued zigzagging through the north-country post, my thoughts returned to my first week with the Polar Bears. I had spent each night thinking about how I could make positive impressions on the unit. I concluded that it had to begin with physical fitness. While each of the six companies stressed physical fitness as a priority, one group of soldiers undoubtedly stood out among the ranks.

They were a select group of warriors who were placed into a special team because of their exceptional strength and mental toughness. They specialized in reconnaissance, sniper marksmanship, and land navigation. Although all of the men in the battalion were tough, few could measure up to the extreme physical and mental demands of being on this specialized team.

So the day came for me to join the Scouts in their morning physical fitness training. My journal noted, "Six-mile run with Scouts! The ten mile run I had agreed to join them on was lessened to six." By the end of that run and the grueling six-minute per mile pace, I was exhausted. Just *thinking* about how fast they went made me tired. The actual run nearly killed me, but if I could handle—or survive—their sprint, my whole unit would know that I was serious about physical fitness for combat ministry.

## REMEMBERING WHY I CAME TO SERVE

As the beautiful canvas of an open sky passed over the bus, I recalled the days spent in the scorching heat of Fort Benning, Georgia; the grassy fields surrounding Fort Riley, Kansas; and the shuddering cold winters of Korea. Each experience forged me into a multi-dimensional warrior. Riding the bus, I mulled over God's destiny for my life. He had groomed me to serve as the combat chaplain of the 4th battalion, 31st Infantry Regiment. Now I understood why the Lord had directed me to serve in that capacity: I had a passionate love for the American soldier.

My life had come full circle. I was heading directly for the battlefield I had always dreamed about. I now knew that my actions were not about me, but the Polar Bears. The leaders of the battalion needed a thick-skinned soldier of faith who would be able to put the soldiers first in everything, and I was determined to be their man. The chain of command deserved someone who would take risks for their men. That was precisely the reason I was there.

Finally, the commanders demanded a loyal, motivated, and courageous warrior, one able to demonstrate excellence in every professional capacity, who would be willing to follow their team to the gates of hell and back.

That was exactly what I was ready and willing to do.

## THE POLAR BEAR SOLDIERS

The bus swung around onto another rugged road, and the centrifugal force threw me against the wall. I straightened back up, rubbed my arm, and looked out the window at the rows of empty WWII barracks. The soldiers who had once occupied them were the ones who deserved the credit for the 10th Mountain's legendary reputation. And like them, my men and I were soon going to face similar challenges. Perhaps I, and some riding with me, would pay the same price: never to return alive.

It was a terrible prospect to face, but as I considered it, I closed my eyes and quietly thanked God for the blessed opportunity to serve as their spiritual shepherd. I remember praying, "God, thank You for allowing me to be so fortunate. Help me serve these warriors with courage and bold faith in the name of Christ. Amen."

Now, only a few miles were left until the end of the bus ride. Soon, we would be dropped off at the airfield. I prayed yet again, "God, please have mercy on these brave men as they prepare to face whatever lies ahead."

## MY COMBAT JOURNAL

Beside me in the seat were a few important things I planned to carry into combat: my military-issue, camouflaged chaplain's kit; a small, gray digital Olympus camera; a tiny bottle of anointing oil; my brown Bible containing both the Old and New Testaments; two leather journals; and lastly, a ridiculously overloaded assault pack. Each of the items would serve essential functions in my deployment, but the journals would be the key to accurately telling this story, if the opportunity was to ever surface.

Before the bus ride ended, I scribbled down a few of my thoughts. Over the course of the next year, that little journal became my most private confidant.

My first entry actually took place on 13 July, 2006: "I begin this journal for pre-combat experiences as the chaplain of the 4-31 Infantry, 10th Mountain Division."

Followed by my personal signature, the entry was a reminder of my position as the unit's spiritual leader. I did that so that I would not be tempted to quit when we faced the worst. I could see the airfield at the end of the road; the worst of war indeed awaited us.

A sudden and annoying screech erupted from the brakes, sending me plowing into the seat in front of me. Seconds later, I realized that the dreaded moment, when we would step away from American soil, had arrived.

I slid off the seat, stood up with a deep sigh, grabbed my gear, and climbed off the bus, I felt one of the most nauseous feelings in my life. My stomach churned as I thought about how the next few steps could very well be among my last in the land that I loved. After we unloaded the bus, we waited inside a building near a runway for the go-ahead to embark on the flight toward hell.

# 6

# THE AIRFIELD, KUWAIT, AND THE FLIGHT INTO HELL

## 15 August, 2006 – THE FLIGHT TO KUWAIT

Former First Lady Eleanor Roosevelt once remarked, "You gain strength, courage and confidence by every experience in which you really stop to look fear in the face...You must do the thing you think you cannot do."[1] I knew perfectly well at the time I signed up to be a military chaplain that both opportunity and risk awaited me. And they did!

Before I had time to reflect on my fear, Lieutenant Colonel Infanti (LTC), the battalion commander, told me to say a prayer for the unit. As the unit commander, he was the leader who was overall responsible for everything in the organization. In the short two weeks up to this point, I learned a little bit about his reputation. Those he led commented on how diligently he managed his team. I increasingly realized that LTC Infanti was a man in a class of his own when it came to respect from soldiers. I gradually learned he was undergirded by a strong foundation of morals, faith, and respect.

General George S. Patton, Jr., said, "You must be a horse master: a scholar; a high minded gentleman; a cold blooded hero; a hot blooded

---

1   http://womenshistory.about.com/cs/quotes/a/qu_e_roosevelt.htm.

savage."[1] Nowhere could this be more relevant than in military training and discipline prior to war. There was no doubt in my mind that LTC Infanti, also known as Polar Bear 6, had ample reason for requiring many long hours of difficult training. The preparation pushed us to the point that most of us thought we would break, but I knew in my heart that the rigorous demands would pay off in discipline on the battlefield. Throughout it all, I had noticed that he and his command team were always in the front of the ranks, leading the way.

Standing with the unit at the airfield, LTC Infanti organized the entire battalion around himself in a half-circle and told them, "Everyone in the first three rows, take a knee. The chaplain is going to say a prayer."

I walked to the center of the formation and prayed for the protection of the soldiers. "God, You alone know what lies ahead of us. Grant us protection and inward assurance as we step forward to face our foes. Amen!"

After my prayer, LTC Infanti said to the group, "Listen up! You men have trained your hearts out and I'm proud of you. Real proud! You might not like me because of how hard I have pressed you in training, but that's okay because I did it for you, to keep you alive in battle. This will be the last time we, as a complete battalion, will ever stand together. Now let's go make our country proud, our families proud, the men that served before us proud, and ourselves proud. Polar Bears!"

The group dispersed then formed up in a line, which snaked its way across the Wheeler-Sack Army Airfield. At the front of the formation, a soldier held the American flag high; pride filled me as I saw the flag's beautiful streaks of red, white, and blue blowing in the wind. Slowly the line began to move forward as one by one, soldiers ascended the stairs into the enormous aircraft. It resembled a Boeing 747, but seemed smaller in size.

After climbing the aluminum steps, I turned and looked behind me. The line of personnel stretched back across the airfield as far as the eye could see. Pivoting back around, I boarded the aircraft. I made my way to the crew's microphone and made an attempt to ease everyone's stress.

"This is the chaplain speaking," I said over the PA. "Please get comfortable because in a few moments I will be passing around an offering plate."

1   Carlo D'Este, Patton: *A Genius for War* (New York: Harper Collins Publishers, 1995), 304.

Moments later, after walking back to my seat, I thought, "I sure hope this plane can take off because that joke sure didn't." Within minutes I felt the huge aircraft shake and shudder. Soon, we lifted off the earth and into the clouds. I was one step closer to facing my destiny. I was on my way to war.

### *17 August, 2006 - Kuwait*

After the plane landed in Kuwait, my chaplain assistant, Private (PV2) Dustin "Dusty" Boyd and I stood in the aisle with the rest of the troops. Dusty was a young, highly energetic soldier who had been assigned to me as a bodyguard. Chaplains are considered non-combatants according to the Geneva Conventions and are thus prohibited from carrying firearms. Personal protection of the chaplain is a chaplain assistant's primary job. Although we had only known each other for a few weeks, Dusty demonstrated that he was ready for the job by spending countless hours at Fort Drum's rifle training ranges. Now that the time for practice was behind us and the time for battle was at hand, we would see just how good a marksman he was.

The aircraft door opened, we looked at each other, and then walked out into the blinding light. A powerful shockwave of desert heat engulfed us as we stepped down the metal stairway and onto the enormous Kuwaiti runway. The blistering temperatures made me feel as though I had just entered an oven. I remember looking at Dusty and saying, "Wow! I've never felt heat like this in my life. This must be what hell feels like."

Large white touring buses sat at the edge of the airfield, ready to transport us through the next phase of our long journey to the battlefield. The windows were covered with small red and blue velvet curtains. Some soldiers said they served to hide the Americans from the Kuwaitis who would be offended by Westerners. Others believed the curtains' shielded Americans from snipers. Regardless, we sat comfortably in the shade they provided as our convoy snaked through the barren wasteland.

After a long ride through the sandy no-man's land, we eventually arrived at a remote camp. Under cover of darkness, we dragged our ridiculously heavy assortment of rucksacks, assault packs, and duffel bags to cots in a small city of military tents.

The next morning at 5:15 a.m., Dusty and I awoke, ate breakfast, and explored the enormous camp. We found small jewelry shops, trailers serving plenty of American-style fast food, and even a few Internet service shops. While scouting the amusement area, we saw Polar Bear 6.

"How are you guys doing?" He asked.

"Sir, I'm ready to get out of this place and get into the fight," I responded. I had trained for war, both as an enlisted man and an officer, long enough; it was time for action. I was as ready for the fight as I would be. I had no idea at the time how unprepared I would be in my own strength or just how sufficient God would be in His.

### 18 August, 2006 – Kuwait

When I was not counseling troops, I experienced brief bouts of intense boredom. Fortunately, my excursions around the camp usually turned into ministry opportunities. Not only did I encounter Army soldiers, but also service members from other branches, all of whom generally requested prayers to help them make it through the deployment, for their units, and for their family members back home. There was no shortage of opportunities to discuss life, death, faith, and God with the inhabitants of the camp.

One evening while in the camp's chow hall, I found a place to sit next to five Navy helicopter pilots. As I ate my dinner, one of them said, "Hey, Sir! We like having chaplains around the flight deck. Would you care to come over and hang out with us? Maybe say a blessing for our aircraft and crews?"

"Absolutely," I replied. When is a good time?"

"How about tomorrow?"

"My chaplain assistant and I will be there."

The next day Dusty and I ventured over to the airfield to find the pilots. Unfortunately, their aircraft needed unexpected maintenance, so we were limited to conversations on the ground. One asked for a prayer. "Chappy, how about a prayer?"

"Lord, I ask that you keep these flight teams and their awesome machines safe and flying. Bless them, their families, and their unit, Amen."

We eventually left and visited other flight crews scattered around the airfield, including a National Guard helicopter team. In the course of conversation, they asked us, "Do you guys wanna go for a ride around the desert, maybe even to the Kuwait-Iraq border?"

"That would be awesome," I enthusiastically replied.

Within fifteen minutes we boarded and strapped ourselves into their UH-60 Black Hawk helicopter. We flew around the desert with the doors of the aircraft wide open.

"Wow," I told Dusty with a beaming grin on my face, "This combat thing isn't so bad if you know where to find the fun!"

### 19 August, 2006 – Kuwait

According to my journal on this day, I learned a great lesson in humility. Major (MAJ) Mark Manns, also known as Polar Bear 5, requested my presence in the command center. We had built a great relationship in the short time we knew each other. This day, he wanted to talk to me about an issue involving Polar Bear 6 and me back at Fort Drum, just days before we deployed.

The matter he wanted to talk about involved my presence on a security team without my assistant. Before we deployed, my division chaplain had told me that I needed to state to LTC Infanti that I should never be separated from my assistant; LTC Infanti informed me that it might have to happen on convoy operations at some points. This was a definite dilemma because I was caught between two senior leader's opinions. One thought I should stand my ground as a chaplain and the other believed that a new chaplain had no place telling him how to run his battalion. In everyone's pre-deployment hurrying, the issue was sat to the side.

The executive officer, Polar Bear 5, remembered it in Kuwait and brought it to my attention. He thought that I had told Polar Bear 6 that I was not going to travel without my assistant. It was a simple misunderstanding, but I tried to explain, "But, Sir!"

The executive officer (XO) stopped me. "Chaplain, shut up and listen to me. You're a good chaplain, just don't go around telling the BC [battalion commander] what he will or will not do. You still have to prove yourself in combat; this is simply not a good way to do it."

"Okay, sir. I'll make sure it doesn't happen again."

He nodded, said "Alright," and then signaled for me to leave. I spent the rest of the day sliding back and forth between despair and assurance. The rebuke was meant as constructive criticism. Part of me believed that I had tarnished the hard work I had put in up to now. Another part of me kept returning to the words the XO had left me with before he dismissed me, about me being a good chaplain. Although I still had to prove myself in combat, his appreciation motivated me.

I thought about Psalms 13:18: "He who ignores discipline comes to poverty and shame, but whoever heeds correction is honored." The lesson that the Scripture brought to me that day in Kuwait was the importance of maintaining an honorable attitude when facing the frustration of criticism. With this in mind, I spent my day being productive rather than being filled with despair. As a seeming reward for my diligence, I discovered a phone tucked away behind the camp chapel.

### 20 August, 2006 – Kuwait

Amazed at the comfort of the hidden chapel annex, I called Tanisha. We talked until the early hours of the next morning. She told me about her life back in upstate New York, and I told her about my fruitless war against the cruel and unforgiving heat of the Middle East. I also told her about the long, exhausting hours of counseling, conducting death notifications, and gearing myself up mentally for combat.

"Make sure you take care of yourself in every way: mentally, physically, and spiritually, okay?" she said.

"Okay," I replied, thinking how drained I had become so early on in the mission.

I hadn't even stepped foot in the combat zone yet. That was the real proving ground. Although realistically it was only a couple of weeks away, it felt like light-years when I considered how weary I had already become. I wasn't about to waste precious time telling Tanisha about my exhaustion, however. Hearing her voice boosted my morale and recharged my energy.

Despite the opportunity to call home, the days still crept along, as did the threat of higher temperatures. After weeks of solving soldier's issues, spending days and nights with my troops on training ranges, and losing my battle with the sun, the illusion I was an unbreakable agent of the cloth began to fade.

The merciless heat baked my skin. It seemed that the more I tried avoiding it the more I felt its searing rays. When I wore my heavily-plated body armor and spent the day training with no shade, the heat was magnified a hundred-fold.

Enough was enough. I needed to figure out a way to better handle the stress or it was going to crush me. The best solution came through a personal resolution to practice self-care, a term understood by anyone who works in the healthcare field. It would consist of a better-balanced cycle of work, sleep, work, sleep, work, and sleep again. Having a reasonable ration of energy left over each day for the long, difficult fight ahead would be critical, not optional.

### 21 August, 2006 – Kuwait

As the days passed, I strived to equilibrate my duties with rest, but the prolonged anxiety of approaching combat was taxing. I knew that the sooner we crossed the border into Iraq and faced our foes, the sooner we would win and return home. In my journal I wrote, "Even though I am getting more rest, I'm exhausted. Being a chaplain is tough work. Although I wish that I had more energy, the kind I had when I was eighteen years old, I can't imagine wanting to do anything else. I know that I'm doing what God has directed my entire life for."

### 22 August, 2006 – Kuwait

Although the work was exhausting, I recognized the importance of my role as a chaplain. Even ministry in the late, quiet hours of the night seemed exciting. As I ventured through the walkways of the tent city, dry gusts of desert wind threatened to knock me down, but I would occasionally find a soldier sitting by himself who needed to talk.

One morning, I saw my battalion commander's personal element leave for Iraq. I looked down at my watch. The dimly-lit display read 6:30 a.m. The commander's decision, which he passed on to me in our battlefield update briefing a day earlier, was to keep me back with the larger portion of the unit. I wondered what they would encounter once they arrived. By the time the sun ascended the horizon, a third of the battalion was gone, making the place that had once been bustling with activity, appear like a ghost town.

At 11:00 a.m., I was required to attend a brigade meeting of all the chaplains and assistants. The briefing would bring me face-to-face with one of the most perplexing dilemmas in the chaplain corps: that of being ordered not to proclaim the name of Christ in public prayers. Back in the States, I had been told by numerous senior and retired chaplains that few chaplains, if any, had actually ever been told not to use the name of "Jesus" or "Christ" when they prayed in public. However, in our meeting, the brigade chaplain, my immediate, chaplain supervisor, let us know, in no uncertain terms, that using Christ's name in combat ceremonies would not be tolerated. We might offend non-Christians.

At one point, in his speech, the brigade chaplain looked directly at me. "Jeff, this especially means you. Do you understand?" I had no idea why I was singled out. I was never dogmatic about the issue in the past. I was deeply offended to be ordered to neuter my faith for the sake of others, especially when I was preparing to defend that freedom.

Shortly afterward, I spoke with LTC Infanti concerning the gist of the meeting. His reply was reassuring. "They will be *my* ceremonies, not the brigade chaplain's, so say what the heck you want to say." At that point my spirits soared because I knew my commander supported his, my, and our soldier's religious freedoms—the stuff for which we came to fight.

With the upturn in my morale, I wanted to make sure that the remaining Polar Bear soldiers, many of whom were Catholic, were taken care of. I turned my attention to arranging a Catholic Mass before departing for Iraq. While searching for a Catholic chaplain to conduct Mass for them, I learned that there were only six priests serving thousands of soldiers in both Iraq and Kuwait, none of whom were at this camp.

Having a streak of Irish stubbornness in me, I refused to give up when I was told, "Good luck on getting a Catholic chaplain. You're probably not going to find one and if you do, he probably won't visit here for another few months."

Another naysayer said, "Getting a priest to fly here is practically impossible because they are all in Iraq."

I told them both, "We will see about that."

I scoured the camp before locating a phone number for a priest named Chaplain (COL) Maholic. I contacted him with the phone I had found in the out-of-sight chapel annex one evening.

"Sir, I know that you must be crazy-busy but I have an important question to ask. I have about 600 infantrymen here with me, of whom nearly eighty-five percent are Catholic. They need a Mass before heading into a very bad part of Iraq in the next few days."

He said, "Meet me at the airfield at 1:45 p.m. tomorrow."

"Thanks so much, Sir," I replied. "I'll see you there and you won't regret coming."

I met Chaplain Maholic the next afternoon and escorted him to my unit's area of operations, telling everyone, "This might be your last chance to attend a Catholic Mass for a long time. Head over to the command tent in fifteen minutes if you would like to attend."

I had waited for him to arrive before dispatching several other soldiers to spread the good news. Soldiers came out of the woodwork, even from other units. Even though Chaplain Maholic stood upon an aluminum chair, I could barely see him because of all the soldiers. Many knelt, others stood, and some quietly listened at the outer edges of the crowd. The soldiers were grateful that a priest had come, but I was the one who was truly blessed. These men and women were simply enjoying the freedom of worship that they were about to defend, some even at the cost of their lives.

Later in the day, still filled with gratitude over the priest's visit, I received word that a grandmother of one of my soldiers had died. After ministering to the soldier, I asked, "Since you're not going back to the U.S. for her service, would you like me to conduct a small, personal memorial service just for you?"

He agreed and I rested my chaplain's cross and chalice upon a chest-high stack of packaged water bottles behind a nearby tent. I prayed, "Lord, I thank you for this soldier. I ask that you grant him and his family peace. The loss of a loved one hurts so badly. We trust you will help them during this time of tragic grief. Please bless and heal. Amen."

The soldier was grateful, saying, "Thanks, Sir! This made me feel better because it honors my grandmother."

By 6:00 p.m., and with the day nearly over, my final task was to attend an information update briefing. As soon as it ended at 9:45 p.m., I had to conduct a death notification for another soldier whose relative had died. I finished counseling the soldier at 11:35 p.m. Delivering next of kin (NOK) notifications was a duty I carried out frequently while in Kuwait. At one point, I conducted nine within a single day.

A few evenings later, I was walking back to my tent, thinking about sleep, when I saw someone from my battalion approaching.

"Hey Sir, can you pray for my team? We're leaving for Iraq in a few minutes."

I followed him to the waiting element and prayed a prayer of protection and blessing on their departure and mission.

The cluster of troops showed no reservations about their hope in a higher power, "Thanks, Chaplain! Keep us in your prayers because the real work starts once we fly into the Triangle of Death."

I said, "You're right about that and I will. More than that, I should be joining you in a day or two."

### 23 August, 2006 – Kuwait

I was struggling to keep my eyes open after the tiring night of duties. My goal for the morning was a briefing for the remaining commanders detailing a religious support plan for Iraq. It would begin with the following statement: "To conduct religious operations across a full spectrum of operations; to ensure the free exercise of religion; to assess the morale of the unit for the commander; and to provide spiritual, moral, and ethical leadership to the unit." My plan centered on providing religious services such as counseling, briefings as a staff officer to the commander's staff, and a substantial ministry to the troops on the front lines.

After the meeting, Dusty and I traveled to a nearby rifle range to watch our scout snipers hone their shooting skills. Returning later in the evening, I placed my gear next to my cot and walked to the center of the camp for chow.

When I came back to the tent, I realized that somebody had pilfered through my gear and stole both the protective throat guard and Kevlar crotch shield from my individual body armor (IBA). Angrily, I voiced my frustration, "Who's the wise guy that took my gear?" Everybody in the tent was going to know that some selfish, unrighteous, and now endangered thief stole my gear.

A nearby soldier offered his thoughts about it. "Somebody's definitely going to hell for this one!"

I said, "If I catch him, I'll send him there myself."

### 24 August, 2006 – Kuwait

The 24th of August, 2006, was a scorching, hot day at the mortar training ranges. As the temperature climbed to 125 degrees, all I could do to bear the high temperatures was to walk around and tell myself, "It can't be any hotter for me than it is for everyone else." Another thought struck me that if this place was hot, hell must be really, really blistering.

Later, we returned from the ranges and I spent some time with my friend, First Sergeant (1SG) Matt Eversmann. After I cut his hair with my electric clippers, we ventured to the camp's dining facility for dinner. Matt was a leader with an impeccable reputation and a heroic legacy from his role in the famous battle of Mogadishu, Somalia (portrayed in the 1993 film *Black Hawk Down*). Our friendship was not centered on his achievements, but rather his attitude toward life, family, and faith.

The soldiers of the Polar Bear Battalion respected Matt because he was a bold, integrity-driven, heartfelt leader. I knew him as a man who never demanded respect from others, but who influenced others by what he did. That is what many call "leading by example." Having the opportunity to serve as his chaplain was one of the greatest blessings I experienced. After a satisfying dinner, we walked back to our respective tents and retired for the night.

### 25 August, 2006 – Kuwait

One of the strange things about war is the certainty of bizarre and chaotic events. One day while I was walking through the tent city a soldier ran up to me and gasped out, "First Sergeant Eversmann needs you right now, Sir!"

"Okay, take me to him."

We blasted our way around tents, running furiously and jumping over tent tie-down cables in a way that would have made Jesse Owens proud.

Finally we made it to Alpha Company's area, and as we approached the entrance, I saw 1SG Eversmann and a group of soldiers near the back of the tent, all gathered around a soldier. The young man was bloody and tied to an aluminum chair.

My first thought was that somebody had killed himself.

"What happened?" I asked.

"Thanks for coming," 1SG Eversmann said. "This guy, whom you talked to earlier in the week, flipped out on us. He refused numerous orders to get off his cot, put his uniform on, and conduct his normal duties. After he was told that he would be reprimanded, he sat up and began punching himself in the face. We had to subdue him and tie him up using his boot strings [to keep him from further harming himself]."

I stood quietly for a minute and then walked up to the soldier. It was one of the most bizarre things I had ever seen. He sat in the chair, blood covered and soaking wet, motionless like a lifeless mannequin.

I said, "Talk to me, man. What happened?"

Finally he muttered, "I just want to go home."

With that I said, "Okay" and walked back to 1SG Eversmann, who stood by with a team of NCOs from his company and the company commander, Captain Brent Dittenber.

"I think we need to get this guy to the camp's mental health facility immediately," I said. "They can evaluate him all they want, but in my opinion, any guy who is willing to beat himself half to death rather than face combat doesn't need to be around weapons or people."

The soldier was later escorted by a couple of soldiers to a mental health team. He was shipped back to the United States and reassigned to a mental health facility. I never heard from him again. It was a sad and unpredictable welcome to war. I knew from that day on that my skin was going to have to be really tough if I was going to walk away from it all one day with my sanity intact.

### 29 August, 2006 – Kuwait

During the last few days in Kuwait, the 4th Battalion, 31st Infantry was leaving for Iraq in droves. My commanders stood firm on their decision to keep me with the trail element because it had the largest number of soldiers. With fewer and fewer troops to counsel, I sat in an empty tent and contemplated my plans for the memorial ceremonies certain to be needed on the front lines soon.

In my journal I wrote, "I learned a valuable lesson today: even with only a few soldiers around, issues of life still happen. Trial is not something relegated to large numbers of personnel. If only one man stands in the ranks, he will have problems. It's just life!"

At 1:00 a.m., I was awakened to notify a soldier that his wife had attempted suicide. After an hour of trying to calm him down, I was able to get his wife on the phone and help her find emergency counseling back in the states. I thanked God that everything worked out relatively well.

On my way back to my tent at 2:30 a.m., someone approached me and said, "Sir, we have a Red Cross message. Someone's grandma has died."

"Some nights are just really, really long," I thought. I was reminded of the words of the Apostle Paul in Second Corinthians 6:4-5, "We commend ourselves in every way: in great endurance, in troubles, hardships and distresses; in beatings, imprisonments and riots; in hard work, sleepless nights and hunger...."

### Leaving Kuwait – 31 August, 2006

I stood silently in what had once been my unit's command and control room. It was now nothing more than a lifeless shell of a building. There was no activity at all, except for a few pieces of paper blowing across the floor. The doors now just swung open and shut with the breeze.

At 12:45 a.m., touring-style buses lined the narrow road running through the middle of our nearly vacant portion of the camp. Those of us who remained loaded our gear into the underbelly storage compartments and climbed aboard. As we pulled away into the night, I watched as other buses rolled in carrying a new group of soldiers.

Our trip lasted throughout the night and well into the next day. As the hours passed, I peeked through the red and blue curtains occasionally to watch herds of wild camels and clans of roving Bedouins crossing the barren desert. Many burned and destroyed vehicles, possibly from the Desert Storm conflict in 1991, littered the landscape. It felt strange knowing that I was finally leaving Kuwait and inching closer to the historic land of Babylon: Iraq.

We arrived at the final stop before crossing into the country of Iraq: an airfield in the middle of nowhere. After cramming into the C-17 Globe-Master aircraft with the other troops, I tried my best to ignore the heat and prayed, "God, please provide some cool air and please give my legs some relief from the weight of this gear."

We flew out of the small, oil-rich country of Kuwait, and headed for Baghdad. The soldiers were quiet as they sat back and awaited their destinies. My prayer for cooler temperatures was eventually answered as our aircraft descended into the Baghdad International Airport (BIAP). With a frightening scream from the plane's hydraulics and a great thud from the plump tires, we touched down onto the Mesopotamian ground. The C-17 rolled to a complete stop, we waited for a few minutes, and the massive metal ramp slowly clanked its way open. The open ramp revealed a brilliant tunnel of sunlight. It was my first glimpse of the combat zone. I stood up, lifted my gear, and walked toward the light.

# 7

# FIXING BAYONETS: THE 10TH MOUNTAIN DIVISION'S MOVEMENT INTO THE TRIANGLE OF DEATH

The eerie bus ride from one Baghdad airfield to another led us through neighborhoods littered with razor wire, abandoned guard towers, bullet-pocked billboards, destroyed buildings, and abandoned vehicles. A new level of unease washed over me. The maze of ruined structures testified to how much destruction and despair could be brought upon a society by war.

In just the first few minutes after landing in Iraq, I witnessed more devastation than I had ever seen. Burned-out vehicles cluttered the roads, piles of trash littered the ground, and there seemed to be no people anywhere. I felt as if the jaws of hell stood open before me. Fear wasn't the only sensation I experienced; I was also exhausted from the long hours of travel. I fought off the weariness and looked around the interior of the bus, recognizing that my life was now more in jeopardy than it had ever been. The wreckage of a nearly destroyed civilization rested only feet away from my window and yet none of it resembled anything I'd seen in war movies I had watched as a kid. Hollywood's version of war centered on men fighting battles, with no thought of pain or fear. This desecrated, demolished landscape, and the carnage it represented, was real and one in which I could perish. That was a terrifying prospect to confront.

As we ventured through the city, we played the U.S. Army's age-old game of "hurry up and wait." It was a constant process of moving and stopping with seemingly no destination in sight. We shook our heads in frustration as a soldier joked about the pathetic possibility of dying in the buses rather than in a blazing firefight on the front lines.

Finally, we arrived at the airfield. I exited the bus and found an empty space on the hard concrete runway to lay down my gear and rest. We waited quietly in the dark hours of the night. Between the mental exhaustion, the physical fatigue, and the danger we would soon face, our fear birthed silence. We knew that this was the end of the line for buses and airfields. Our next stop would be inside a hornet's nest.

It was then that I heard the distinct sound of helicopter rotor blades.

They were coming for us.

## BAGHDAD – DAY ZERO, 2:30 A.M., FLYING INTO THE TRIANGLE OF DEATH

### 01 September, 2006

Our time had come. The brief quiet of the Baghdad airfield would soon be a thing of the past. Our next objective was hell and it was time to flip the adrenaline switches back on and shift any gears of doubt to courage.

As the sound of the approaching helicopters grew louder, someone yelled, "The birds are inbound!" We knew that it was time to do what we had trained so hard to do: retake the forbidding Triangle of Death from insurgents and give it back to the victimized people of Iraq. I fumbled about in the darkness, trying to gather my gear rather than someone else's. Heaving everything over my shoulders, I moved toward the group of aircraft which had just landed.

We scrambled into the powerful helicopters. Within moments, the pilots finished their pre-flight checks and signaled for us to hang on. Then, with a sudden shudder left and then right, the aircraft heaved off of the ground and into the black Iraqi sky. The pilots pitched, weaved, and rolled above buildings and trees in a constant defensive pattern. We pierced the thick clouds of smoke from burning trash, an odor which singed our nostrils. Aware that at least six American aircraft had been shot down since 2003 in the area, the flight crews wasted no time getting to and from their objective.

The CH-47 Chinook's rotor blades reminded me of a stampede of wild horses as they cracked, screamed, and whipped madly through the air. I tilted my head over the pile of gear that was crushing my lap and peered out of the open rear exit of the aircraft. Flickering lights below passed by like falling stars as we accelerated.

I thought about the possibility that we might be shot down by enemy gunfire. But, I had deep confidence in the crews who manned the aircraft, including the two crew chiefs that guarded each side of the helicopter with machine guns, ready to fire at any threat. The dim, tactical green lighting inside the cabin reminded me of a beautiful evening underneath a glowing moon. But the threats waiting for us in the darkness below were not comforting. Whatever safety we had on the flight would disappear within seconds of landing. Whatever waited for us at the other end of our flight was drawing closer with each passing moment.

I felt the helicopter circle as it made its descent. We looked into each other's eyes, wondering if it would be the last time, and prepared to step into one of the deadliest places in the world. Once we emerged from the helicopter ramp, we would have no one but each other. I gave a reassuring nod to my men, reminding them that God had indeed directed us to this point and would continue to be with us through it.

## BOOTS ON THE GROUND IN THE TRIANGLE OF DEATH

Rarely in my life had I sensed such deep fear as I did that night at Forward Operations Base (FOB) Mahmudiyah, Iraq. Although Polar Bear 6's Personal Security Detail team was already on the ground, my element was prepared to defend itself upon landing in case they were not at the landing zone. A torrential cloud of sand blinded everyone preparing to offload the helicopter as its wheels slammed into the hard ground. I ran out the back exit with my gear in my arms. Powerful gusts of wind from the aircraft's rotors overtook me, shrouding me in a storm of dust.

The hot exhaust from the helicopter's massive turbines seared my nostrils, leaving me choking on the fumes as I ran fifteen feet and plopped down on the ground in order to keep clear of the departing Chinook. Within seconds, it was gone. I could hear other flights, also carrying 10th Mountain fighters, approaching in the distance.

Attacks from small arms fire and incoming rockets did not occur. The vast darkness proved to be a great canopy for the remote camp which was situated nearly twenty miles south of the city of Baghdad. I stood up, flipped on the night vision goggles attached to the front of my helmet, and fell face first over some rocks and uneven ground as I tried to walk off of the landing zone.

Even though I could hear the helicopters in the distance, I sat quietly in a defensive position with the rest of the element. Once, we conducted a head-count of personnel, we began moving toward another friendly element that had landed nearby. Our two teams joined and then began a lengthy walk to a nearby hill littered with the pale silhouettes of tents. The hill was the central portion of the FOB Mahmadiyah.

I prayed as I made my way through the field, "God, thanks for not letting us die tonight, for the little energy I have right now, and for letting us get the ball rolling so that I can get through this."

In time we arrived at the FOB, a small base made up of sectioned tent cities. Situated in the muddy shallows of a large field, the base, which had once been known as FOB Saint Michael earlier in the war, rested on the outskirts of the highly dangerous, war-torn city of Mahmudiyah. Marines, Army, and Army National Guard units had been its cyclical inhabitants for years. The current focus was mainly on maintaining an eastern stronghold in the area, which left almost all of the western sections of the sector unmanned and uncontrolled. The westernmost border, nearly fifteen miles away, was flanked by the famed Euphrates River. Across the river was the deadly Al-Anbar Province, otherwise known as the "Cradle of the Insurgency."

The Triangle of Death was located in the southern farmlands of the Baghdad Province, the area recognized by historians as ancient Babylon. On a broader scale, the Sunni Triangle, which encompassed part of our area of operation, consisted of a larger collection of provinces dividing the nation. In contrast, the Triangle of Death was much smaller; comprising mainly farmlands located about twenty-five miles southwest of Baghdad City. It was in this "Southern Belt," as it was sometimes referred to, that we Polar Bears found ourselves. We were in the middle of nowhere—and outnumbered by thousands of militant Sunni insurgent forces. The region quickly became known as the Triangle of Death, or the "Graveyard of the Americans." Aside from IEDs (Improvised Explosive Devices), daily rocket attacks, assassinations, vicious mortar barrages, torture, extortion, rapes, kidnappings, shootouts, and devastating car bombings, it was not that bad of a place.

Since 2005, elements of the 101st Airborne Division had occupied the eastern city of Mahmudiyah. The "Strike" battalion of the 101st Airborne Division, legendarily known as the Screaming Eagles, moved into the volatile region. They were a 1,200-soldier entity, which included an armored company of mechanized fighting vehicles and tanks. They were a stout fighting force and considered brothers in battle with the 10th Mountain Division. This fraternity of the 101st and 10th Mountain had been established in 2002 during the mountainous battles of Tora-Bora and the Shah-I-Khat Valley in Afghanistan.

Looking for the 101st's chaplain team—our ministry counterparts—I walked through the small encampment with my chaplain assistant Dusty until we found their chapel. In it were Chaplain (CPT) Davis and his assistant, SGT Golden. We got to know each other over the next hour. After talking for a few hours, we rested. The next day we toured the remote FOB. There was a notable increase in outgoing flights for the 101st. It reminded me of an unending assembly line, as each flight dropped off my men and took theirs away. With the dwindling numbers of Screaming Eagles, it felt as if an angel of death had swept over the base and snatched the 101st troopers away into the night.

The Strike Soldiers had known that when the 10th Mountain Division arrived, they would at last be able to close the book on one of the most challenging chapters in their unit's history. It had been an indescribable twelve months of sacrifice for them. Now, after nearly a week of transitioning the units in and out of responsibility for the area, the time for the chaplain team to depart arrived.

Since there was nothing left for us to do for Chaplain Davis and SGT Golden, I lay on my cot at the chapel tent and Dusty rested on his, which sat on the other side of a wooden barrier. In the darkness, I stared at the canvas ceiling. The 101st ministry team had said their goodbyes earlier and now waited for their flight to arrive on the landing zone. Suddenly I heard the sound of helicopter rotors slicing through air. In only seconds, they were gone and I was alone. It frightened me to think that I was suddenly the only chaplain in the Triangle of Death. "Lord," I prayed, "I really need your wisdom and guidance now. Protect the men who have been here and those like me who are coming. Give me wisdom to lead these troops and to live what I preach, whatever happens. Amen."

## STANDING ON HELL'S HIGHWAY – 15 SEPTEMBER, 2006

Although the Screaming Eagles' chaplain team had left, a handful of their soldiers remained behind to show the 10th Mountain around the sector. Through these trips I was able to visit various checkpoints and battlefield positions my soldiers had began occupying. One evening I joined a small element of the remaining 502nd soldiers along with an element from my Bravo Company as they patrolled in vehicles through the farmlands to the city of Yusufiyah.

As we reached the center of the town, every light in the community blinked out.

I thought, "Holy cow, the whole stinking town is about to blow up on us!" The others with me shared the same sentiment. One soldier said, "I think we may be in for big trouble."

A leader from the patrol yelled over the radio, "If they haven't killed us yet they're probably not going to. Everybody just stay calm and keep your eyes open, just in case."

While moving through the cratered streets and alleys, we frequently changed speeds to avoid being struck by IEDs. As darkness shrouded everything, fear shot through my veins. I told myself, "If they're good enough to synchronize every light in this place, then they really know what they're doing." It was unlikely that a power failure caused the blackout. There had to be something more intentional behind the event—possibly an ambush awaiting us around one of the street corners.

We managed to make it through the village unscathed. After we passed though the last neighborhood, we made our way back into the country. We finally arrived at the farthest outpost the 101st had occupied, a fortified house known as the Alamo. It sat alone in a field, with a short driveway connecting it to the infamous Mullah Fayad Highway, a route known for its importance as a critical smuggling thoroughfare for Sunni insurgents. Declared "impassible" by American forces, insurgents daily maneuvered foreign fighters, rifles, and vehicle bombs from the Al-Anbar Provence into Baghdad City along the deadly highway.

Our humvees idled on the side of the road, as Dusty, several members of the patrol, and I walked carefully around the perimeter of the two-story brick building. Three jagged strands of rusted razor wire, placed as traffic obstacles, lay stretched across the road, while a couple of troops stood on the rooftop behind sand bags, manning two, large Browning M2HB .50 caliber machine guns.

I quietly asked one of the soldiers why the road was blocked. "Can't we travel up the rest of the road? Other than the car headlights at the other end, it looks pretty quiet. Can it really be that bad?"

The soldier bluntly answered, "If anyone goes past this wire, they're going to die. Anybody that tries to drive up the rest of the road will never live to see the other end."

Then he added, "One of our patrols tried to drive up there and was hit by such a catastrophic IED that the only thing left of the vehicle was a motor block, bolts, some scrap metal, and DNA from the crew. The recovery team sent to return the destroyed vehicle was also struck by IEDs. By the time the recovery team found the first vehicle, it was so badly disintegrated that it took three days to find any DNA samples from the soldiers who had occupied it."

The pensive soldier continued scanning the field. He resumed his story,

"We also had six aircraft shot down near this highway and have decided that it's too dangerous of a place. It's just not worth going up it."

Another soldier further explained, "Everything, including our recovery teams for the downed aircraft, was destroyed. There have to be IEDs planted every few feet under the road."

A few minutes later Dusty and I made our way to the rooftop. While visiting with the men there, I stared down the dark, quiet road, contemplating the lives it had claimed. I watched through my night vision goggles as vehicles moved along the northern end of the highway.

"Do you see those vehicles, Sir?" one soldier asked. "Some of them are going in and out of the Russian Thermal Power Plant. It's an insurgent stronghold."

"If we know the cars in the distance belong to bad guys, why don't we go after them?" I asked.

Never taking his eyes off the road, the soldier replied, "Since some of the people driving the vehicles aren't close enough to give our unit problems, the best thing to do is to ignore them."

"But I thought all bad guys are a concern to us," I replied.

"Maybe so, but if they aren't bothering us, then why should we invite trouble?"

I concluded that since the Sunni terrorists were able to maintain a thriving stronghold in the sector, serious trouble lay ahead for my unit. It was impossible for me to know exactly the magnitude of that trouble. But, the Polar Bears were ready and willing to face whatever challenge lay ahead of them. Even though our unit's first large scale victory was just ahead of us, the treacherous Mullah Fayad Highway stood in our way.

## TRAGEDY AT CHECKPOINT #142

The next day back at FOB Mahmudiyah, I walked around the perimeter of the urban outpost and visited the final few 101st soldiers who were manning the camp's defensive towers. I entered one of the towers, climbed a rickety ladder, and joined a couple of riflemen manning a machine-gun nest.

Surprised at seeing me there, one soldier said, "Sir, thanks for coming up here to visit. You're the only officer that's ever come to see us."

"Being with soldiers is why I came to Iraq," I said. "Are you guys doing okay?"

During my short time with them in the tower, they felt comfortable enough to share their frustrations dealing with the political climate, the burdensome rules of engagement, and a terrible tragedy which devastated their unit. One said, "It's too bad that the Army doesn't invest more troops in the Triangle of Death. We need more forces if we're ever going to win in this area. I just don't know if anybody believes we *can* win against these people."

A second soldier overseeing a pile of ammunition boxes continued, "Americans aren't even supporting us like they did when we first came over here last year."

The first one added, "These rules of engagement really stink. Once, we saw a small white car pass by here, on the road outside the wall. The men inside it were pointing AK-47 rifles at us through its windows. We called on our radio for permission to fire at them but were told not to because the occupants might have been part of an Iraqi wedding celebration, not insurgents." Changing topics, the young warrior added, "But that's not all, Sir. The worst thing has been the tragedy involving PFC Stephen Greene."

I soon realized the challenges my battalion would face. There was the fact that: 1.) The Triangle of Death had been written off as "uncontrollable" by many in the Army. 2.) Signs of degrading support for the war effort were becoming more apparent as the number of casualties mounted. 3.) The most barbaric crime in the conflict committed by American soldiers had just recently occurred in the area. Along with the 101st, the 10th Mountain would continue to face the repercussions.

In 2006, a small group of soldiers made up of SGT Paul E. Cortez, SPC James P. Barker, PFC Joseph V. Spielman, and PFC Stephen D. Greene, managed to get their hands on alcohol, which was prohibited in combat by order of American commanders. Against their own strict Muslim mandates, Iraqis provided the five soldiers at Checkpoint #142 with whiskey. Over a course of time, the troops reportedly began bothering a family near their position. Bolstered by liquid courage, the men made crude comments and obscene gestures to the family, including their two daughters.

One evening, after becoming intoxicated on a mixture of whiskey and American energy drinks, PFC Greene, the junior-ranking man on the team, effectively convinced his comrades to corral the father, Qasim Hamza Raheem; the mother, Fakhriyah Taha Muhsin; the five-year old daughter, Hadeel Qasim Hamza; and 14-year old Abeer Qassim Hamza al-Janabi, into their house as prisoners.

The soldiers took the 14-year old Abeer Qasim Hamza into a separate room and gang raped her while Greene shot the remaining family members to death in another room of their home. He then raped Abeer Qasim before shooting her in the back of the head with his military-issue shotgun. Upon leaving the scene of the grisly murders, the men burned the bodies and fled the house.

Following the horrible atrocity, the soldiers returned to their guard post as if nothing had happened. They cooked chicken wings on a makeshift grill and concocted an alibi for the murders; they would blame it on insurgents. Rumors quickly spread throughout the Iraqi community of the murders, along with whispers of revenge on the Americans who had perpetrated the crime. When questioned, the team of perpetrators claimed to know nothing about the incident, other than suggesting that insurgents might be responsible.

By the time the truth came out, it would be too late. A few months later, another element of soldiers assumed control of the checkpoint: SPC David Babinau, PFC Kristian Menchaca, and PFC Thomas Tucker. Late one evening, nearly twenty Iraqi men from an affiliate group of Al-Qaeda, known as the Mujahedeen-Shura-Council, came out of the darkness and surrounded the soldiers.

Within moments, SPC Babinau was killed and thrown over a small construction bridge and into a nearby canal. PFCs Menchaca and Tucker were captured, gagged, and tied to the back of a truck. They were dragged several miles to a house in Rushdi Mullah where they were filmed while being viciously tortured and mutilated. The men were eventually beheaded, burned, booby-trapped, and discarded in a field.

The small collection of Screaming Eagles left at FOB Mamhudiyah spoke of their frustrations of being perceived by the world as criminals because of the actions of a few. They knew that their unit was not going to be remembered for its sacrifices, but rather for the rape and murders. Not only did the event undermine the unit's overall efforts, the disastrous political scouring from the media left the unit's real heroes unsung: the thousand or so Screaming Eagles who served with impeccable valor.

## BLESSING A SACRED HELMET FOR THE SCREAMING EAGLES

The soldiers I spoke with in the towers departed Iraq less than a week later and the only remaining element of the 101st was the battalion commander, LTC Kunk, and his security team.

Before the chaplain team had departed, they left me an interesting array of gear in a black, plastic foot locker that sat in the corner of the chapel tent. In the box were three pairs of tan combat boots and three helmets, used for memorial ceremonies.

The same week, another unit, the 2nd Battalion, 15th Field Artillery Regiment, moved into FOB Mahmadiyah in order to serve as our brigade's indirect fire-support entity. Their chaplain, Rich West, and his assistant, PFC Cobb, had no memorial boots or helmets so I gave them one of the sets that I had inherited. I kept one helmet and the other boots for myself but this left me with a dilemma: what to do with the remaining helmet, the one with the black, heart-shaped patch on it.

My heart rebelled at the idea of turning it in to a supply office because it had been used as a platform item in the Strike Force battalion's memorials, including the one for the tortured soldiers. Someone would surely rip the unit patch off and reshelf the sacred item for redistribution to other soldiers who would know nothing of its significance. After thinking about it for a day, I decided to give the helmet to someone who would appreciate and safeguard it forever: the battalion commander, LTC Thomas Kunk.

I had come to know LTC Kunk through small convoy trips to outposts during the transfer of authority between the units. The respective battalion commanders, their corresponding security details, and I would visit LTC

Muhammad, an Iraqi Army battalion commander, and drink chai tea while discussing the positive aspects of our joint military relationships.

It was after one such trip that the moment presented itself. I spent some time with LTC Kunk after returning from one of the trips. While walking to lunch, he said, "Yeah, Chap, You've got to be careful out here. I think I've been hit by IEDs at least thirteen times; it's a pretty crazy place." After finishing lunch, I walked back to the chapel, retrieved the sacred helmet, and ventured to his portion of the camp. I found him smoking a cigarette behind a tactical command and control building. I held it behind my back until I respectfully talked to him about it first, thinking maybe he would not want it. His appreciation was evident as he took the helmet from me. After staring at it for a few seconds, he said, "You guys always amaze me."

"Sir," I told him, "it's a real honor to be a part of your team, even if we wear different patches and come from different places."

He said, "I appreciate all of the work you 10th Mountain guys have done in this war and I hope to see you again one day. God bless you and your men, Chap!"

With that, we stood in silence as he looked back down at the helmet. We both walked away, and as we did I thought about the hallowed connection between soldiers when it comes to their fallen heroes.

The next day, LTC Kunk and his last few remaining soldiers officially handed over the reins of the rural FOB to my unit and flew out of the sector. Polar Bear 6 wasted no time; he gathered as many soldiers as possible in an old office and said, "Any delay in fighting will be disastrous." Reflecting some tactical wisdom from General Patton during WWII, he said, "We will attack, attack, and continue to attack!" After a moment of silence, he added, "Pack everything up. We're all going west--right-into the places that others said we could never go and directly into the areas that they told us we'd never control."

My commander's directives concerning our upcoming mission to repossess the "uncontrollable" Triangle of Death were followed by a personal address to me: "Chaplain, I hope that you're praying for us every day."

I said, "Yes Sir, you can count on that."

With that, he turned from me, looked at the crowd gathered in the old office of the former factory and said, "We're going to move west soon. When the bad guys try to stop us, they will fail. It's not going to be easy, but we will keep pushing them until they are destroyed. We'll gain control of the land they've terrorized since the beginning of the war, and when we've recovered it, we'll give it back to the people who rightfully own it.

Immediately after he finished speaking, I walked back to my chapel and prayed, "God, please give us success and crush our enemy. As we get ready to stir the hornet's nest, protect us and grant our team victory. Amen." I then began packing my gear for Task Force Polar Bear's first major battle.

# 8

# THE 10TH MOUNTAIN DIVISION'S FIRST BATTLE INSIDE THE TRIANGLE OF DEATH

Shortly after that meeting, I learned that my chaplain assistant was being transferred to another 10th Mountain Division unit in the city of Baghdad. His replacement, SGT Stephen Tennant, was a monstrously large guy with tattoos of flames etched across his arms. SGT Tennant was from Ohio, and had always wanted to serve with a front-line infantry unit. Now he was being given that chance. From his first day in the area, he was ready to storm the battlefront, and that is exactly what we did. I told him that I was a hard guy to work with because I moved fast and felt it was a chaplain's duty to run toward chaos. But I also noted that I would never expect him to go anywhere I wasn't ready to go, and that I would never hold him to a standard I wasn't ready to demonstrate first.

"How ready and willing would you be if we were to catch a convoy to the front line right now?"

"I'll go anywhere, anytime, Sir," SGT Tennant responded.

With that, I said, "Good, because I have seats in Polar Bear 6's convoy and it leaves in about twenty minutes."

We loaded into one of the vehicles in the battalion commander's convoy and departed. Eventually we found ourselves at Patrol Base Yusufiyah. It was a small camp built by a minuscule team from the 101st that had made its way into Yusufiyah, one of the most volatile cities in Iraq. Thick clouds of dust enveloped our vehicles as we pulled into the camp, comprised mainly of an old factory. After we parked, our small entourage walked with the men who had inhabited the old facility. They made up a mixed crew of Iraqi soldiers, as well as American troops from the 101st and 10th Mountain.

We sipped chai tea with the Iraqi army leaders and met with some of our men to discuss the approaching mission of bringing the task force there to control that area. For nearly forty-five minutes, our teams discussed how "crazy" the place was. One said, "We were in a three-hour firefight a few days ago. The bad guys were shooting at us from rooftops throughout the neighborhoods just outside our walls. They were everywhere."

As we ended the meeting and walked back to our vehicles, 1SG Eversmann asked me, "Hey Sir, can you come back out and serve us communion soon?"

"As soon as I get back and get my chaplain kit I'll be back."

Another soldier asked, "Hey, Chaplain, I was just wondering what God thinks about us killing bad guys?"

"I really think he understands the difference between needed and needless, justifiable and unjustifiable. Your job here involves doing it for a greater good."

Since our Yusufiyah soldiers were the tip of the battalion's spear, most of them wanted to spend personal time with me, especially since the task force's initial battle movement was only days away. This was challenging, for there were nearly a hundred of them and only one of me. The fairest thing I could do was to keep moving around the area and visiting as many soldiers as possible. However, I felt guilt over the fact that I assumed some would die in the approaching battle.

I wanted to participate in the forthcoming mission with them, but when asked, my commanders wanted me to stay at the Yusufiyah aid-station.

"We don't want you to go this time," they said. "The task force casualty collection point will be where we need you most. From there you can cover any casualties."

I concluded that my immediate ministry would be focused on talking with the men before they began their assaults, being with the casualties during the operation, and debriefing the troops when they returned to Yusufiyah.

I returned a couple of days later to visit the band of anxious riflemen. They were going to be important players in a mission scheduled for later that night. Bravo, Charlie, Delta, and Fox Companies also trickled in for the event as well. They would all converge at the primitive encampment to take part in Operation Polar Rock Blizzard, the unit's first large-scale combat operation. The courageous collection of warriors waited for their opportunity to stand face-to-face with the enemy, unaware that when they did, they would change history by shifting the balance of good and evil in the Southern Belt farmlands of Iraq.

Some of the regiment's Scouts, made up of reconnaissance and sniper teams, asked me to pray over their teams and sniper rifles. One walked up, handed me his M-24 SWS rifle with the request, "Chaplain, can you please pray over this and my cross necklace?"

Another asked as he handed me his enormously long M-107 .50 caliber rifle, "Me too, Sir, will you pray over mine?"

I quickly told all of them, "Absolutely! Everybody gather around, there's plenty of room." I blessed the men with anointing oil, then placed my hands on the soldiers and their weapons, and prayed. "Please Lord, protect these men and make their rounds lethal and their steps safe. Amen."

Afterwards, they said, "Thanks for the blessings, Chaplain. We appreciate them."

By the time the assortment of hunter-killer teams were ready to move forward into the final staging area, I had prayed over their entire platoon. Bowing their heads in reverence to God, I blessed them. As the scouts reconfigured their gear, they stepped away and into the darkness outside of the tent. I bowed my head for a moment as the silence enveloped the small structure. With a final glance around, I too, stepped out into the night.

This assortment of troops would conduct precision combat operations from air and land in order to kill designated enemy personnel. Five massive M-1A2 Abrams Main Battle Tanks operated by soldiers from the 4th Infantry Division would provide firepower in support of the infantrymen over the three-day operation.

Many elements of the task force would march through toxic, water-filled canals which flourished across the farmlands, along bomb-laden roads, and in marshy fields surrounded by enemy snipers. No matter the dangerous elements or terrain, the soldiers of Task Force Polar Bear were ready to destroy those responsible for fueling Iraq's devastating insurgency. They were intent on bringing serious pain to their opponents, and it would come by means of an alarmingly violent and quick attack. The goal was to unfold a carefully calculated *Blitzkrieg*-style raid on numerous terrorist hideouts, leaving the enemy in as much confusion as possible. If the mission succeeded, any remaining enemy forces within the Triangle of Death would lose tactical initiative. Simply put, they would be forced to focus on regaining resources and morale.

I prayed fervently, "Lord, please send an Angel of Death on our enemies tonight. Break the will of the bad guys and annihilate them. Watch over our Polar Bears and bring them back safe. And give me strength to face whatever happens. In Christ's name I ask this, amen."

While waiting for the helicopters to arrive for the complex air-assault mission into the heart of the sector of terror—the Mullah Fayad Highway and the numerous villages connected to it—I suddenly realized I had been dragging my gear around with me for almost an entire day. I decided to find a place to leave it for the remainder of the week. The medics, nicknamed the Witch Doctors, allowed me to share some of their living-space at the task force's aid-station. I left my gear there on a cot they provided, which would serve as my bed for at least a month. I immediately set out to find any remaining troops before the night's dramatic mission commenced. Just then, the piercing sound of aircraft came from nowhere.

Operation Polar Rock Blizzard had begun.

## THE BEGINNING OF THE FIRST BATTLE

### *2 October, 2006*

Throughout the long tiring night, the soldiers of the 31st Infantry waged an all-out offensive against militant forces in the Mullah Fayad, Rushdi-Mullah, and Al-Taraq areas of the Triangle of Death. They walked without rest along enemy-controlled roads, raided houses occupied by insurgent loyalists, and sealed off strategic roads with well-armed vehicles.

Unfortunately, luck would last only so long before it was replaced by the horror of war. I had stayed up with 1SG Eversmann during the mission's kickoff, listening to vital communications over a shelf of radios inside Alpha Company's tactical command room.

By the next morning, I sat next to a young soldier monitoring the radios and listened intently. According to my journal, "Things hit the fan in almost perfect synchronization as our men maneuvered their way around the battlefield to their objectives."

Abruptly, the soldier and I heard a loud message from Alpha's 3rd platoon sergeant. "Immortal 7, this is Immortal 3/7, over. Immortal 7, do you copy, over?"

The soldier ran in to get 1SG Eversmann while I stood by the radios. He came in and said, "Immortal 3/7, this is Immortal 7. Go ahead, over."

"Immortal 7, IA 6's [Iraqi Army commander LTC Muhammad] convoy has been catastrophically hit. Vehicles are destroyed. Standby. Over!"

1SG Eversmann responded, "Immortal 3/7, this is Immortal 7, I need a SITREP of IA 6 and his team, over."

What we heard next stunned us.

"Immortal 7, this is Immortal 3/7. All of them are KIA [killed in action], over!"

1SG Eversmann and I stood in silence looking at each other in complete shock. I wondered how we were going to deal with all of the Iraqi soldiers after such a tragedy. How would we tell them? 1SG Eversmann was not only thinking the same thing, but also wondering how we were going to inform their remaining leaders.

The soldier who had been monitoring the assortment of radios continued doing so as Immortal 7 and I hustled to where the battalion command team had been assembled and notified them of the tragedy. Everyone stood in silence as the terrible news was conveyed. The frightening reality of being inside the enemy's house was something we had already come to grips with, but now we realized things were only going to become increasingly difficult the more we invested ourselves in the fight.

Since the Iraqi soldiers had limited means of communication, Polar Bear 6 told 1SG Eversmann to notify them. Although I was not with 1SG Eversman when he told them, I was back at the Alpha radio room. I remember hearing the Iraqi soldiers wail loud Arabic prayers together. They also threw in a few high pitched curses at the Ali-Babas (evil men in Arabic).

Killing LTC Muhammad and his team was not enough for the enemy. They also targeted innocent civilians: mortaring, shooting, and even setting off deadly IEDs on the local populace. The terrorists had learned quite well from Saddam Hussein the terrible skill of punishing the innocent in order to influence their enemies.

Our combat medics did everything possible to help the brutalized victims who were being brought in to our camp's aid-station. I helped the medics carry the mangled bodies of Iraqis and Americans as the fight progressed.

I remember seeing one teenage boy who had been struck by an insurgent rocket. His blood poured out on the ground, an uncontrolled fountain of red as his body bounced up and down on the stretcher. I helped carry him to an American medical aircraft. One after another, we moved people around in an assembly line of desperation and hope.

After repeatedly filling helicopters with casualties, I held back my tears as I saw a small Iraqi boy who had been shot by the enemy. His blood dripped across the floor while his little limbs flailed with each step from his carriers. When he died, so did any remaining compassion for our enemies. Our world had transformed into a carnage mill, generating casualties by the hour and consuming any life that dared come in contact with it.

Back in the radio room, reports came in from our infantrymen that an MIA2 Abrams tank had been struck by an IED along an old bridge near the Mullah Fayad area. The blast damaged one of its wheeled tracks, completely disabling the large machine. Within half an hour another tank arrived to provide security until the tank could be fixed and returned to the action.

Helicopters poured into Yusufiyah throughout the week to pick up reinforcements for the battlefield, carry casualties to Baghdad, and transfer supplies between the fighting teams. The train of support kept moving and the enemy's likelihood of thwarting our efforts lessened. But the fight was far from over; the price we would continue to pay would be measured in blood and lives. I thought, "I hate war. The cost is more painful than I could have ever imagined."

One brave soldier, 1LT John Quilty, paid that price. He was a rifle platoon leader who had been leading his patrol along the Mullah Fayad Highway when he stepped on a buried IED. The explosion instantly threw him into the air as if he were weightless. His men, including a combat medic who had been near him, immediately treated him with bandages and tourniquets. Although he lost his hand, he lived and was returned to the United States.

In another area, SPC Satieon Greenlee, a gunner in an armed convoy, was shot in the head by an enemy sniper. He had been with one of the battalion's personal security detachments (PSD) that had pulled over on the side of a road for some American's who were in need of help. SPC Greenlee tragically died while helping others.

As time marched on, violence continued to reign. PFC Thomas J. Hewitt, a member of the troop attached to our taskforce from 1st Squadron, 89th Cavalry, was hit by an IED during a strike on his team. During the attack, one of his legs was seriously wounded. My men rushed him to the Witch Doctors' aid station, also known as the SGT Hunter Aid-Station (named by a small team of 101st soldiers in the past). Hewett was eventually returned to the United States. I prayed for him daily and our commander talked about his status during briefings. Sadly, after fighting courageously for his life in the United States, he died. Our spirits were crushed as another 10th Mountain Division hero was taken from us.

Within hours I returned to Alpha Company's radio room, I heard multiple radio messages echoing the victorious seizures of all battlefield objectives.

It was a relief to hear the calls for the end of the first mission because our unit was exhausted.

## ASSESSING THE FIRST BATTLE

### 3-10 October, 2006

The objectives that had been set out by the task force were now met. I couldn't wait to see the men at the front-line outposts. I traveled with Polar Bear 6's convoy to visit them. As we rolled through the ravaged countryside, the tension that hung over me was almost intolerable. Second by second, moment by moment, the thought of being killed by an IED went through my mind as I looked out the dirty little window of the vehicle.

Destroyed American vehicles littered the highways leading to the main objective areas, including one semi-trailer supply truck that rested thirty feet in front of its skeletal undercarriage. Doors open and windows shattered, the large vehicle sat deathly still, a mute casualty of a devastating bomb.

"This land is an incredibly primitive place," I wrote later in my journal, "with death and destruction everywhere I look."

We weaved left and right as we sped along the highway, dodging IED craters every few feet until we pulled into a village known as Al-Taraq.

There, at Al-Taraq, Polar Bear 5 and I walked through its perimeter area with some of Charlie Company's troops. The short trek along an old dirt road led us to a series of canals filled with disgusting green-and-brown colored water. Upon closer examination, we realized we were looking at quarter of a mile of unburied weapons caches along the canal road. The ditches were filled with rusty rifles, mortar rounds, ammunition, cell phones (for bomb activation), rockets, and a multitude of other things helpful for killing people. The Charlie soldiers had found them and placed them along the road for us to see.

Back at the main house, located next to a mosque, were a couple of large 250- and 500- pound aircraft bombs, along with a small white car with its rear seat missing. This was probably intended to be a vehicle bomb. As I stood with the team looking out over the fields, I noticed six-foot-high piles of donkey dung.

I asked my XO, "Hey Sir, do you think someone might have hid weapons in those piles of donkey manure?"

"That's a good idea, Chaplain." He told a lieutenant, "Have some of your guys check out those piles of crap."

Nothing was in them and after about thirty minutes of checking the place out, we loaded into our vehicles and continued driving along the Mullah Fayad Highway until we reached Rushdi-Mullah.

Once there, we walked into a rock-fabricated house which sat at the edge of a large field. According to our intelligence teams, it had once been an important torture house for Al-Qaeda. My stomach tightened as I thought about the people, including three Americans (Menchaca, Tucker, and Babinau), who had reportedly been tortured in it. Once a site of the worst kind of brutality, it now housed the leaders of 4-31's Bravo Company.

I asked 1SG Wilson, their senior NCO, "Hey 1SG, do you care if I hang out with the guys?

"No Sir," he answered. "I don't mind, they're out by the back of the house. A few others are pulling guard shifts on the rooftop."

I walked out and around the house to find a collection of exhausted grunts resting next to a wall. They were a proud band of mostly young warriors who had walked, ridden, or flown for nearly three days into one of a handful of locations that my unit was told they would never infiltrate, let alone secure. These Polar Bears had done the impossible as far as many outside of the Triangle of Death were concerned. I was proud as heck of them.

PFC Rivera, sitting on the ground with his team members, smiled and called out, "Hey Sir, do you have a cross with you that I can have?"

"No. I'm sorry," I said.

Rivera then replied, "How about the one on your uniform?"

At that moment I knew he had me. As important as my uniform crosses were, how could I refuse a guy who had just spent the last three days marching through hell? His clothes were soaked with filthy water from the canals and stained with mud and blood.

"All right," I said with a smile.

I took the small, black cross off of my uniform and gave it to him. His smile widened even more as he looked up at me.

I smiled back.

An NCO named SSG[1] Smith had been standing nearby, watching us. In appreciation he said, "Hey, Sir. If you didn't come to Iraq for anything else, you at least came here for us. Thanks! You're an encouragement to my men and me."

Another soldier asked, "Sir, can I talk to you for a second?"

"Sure," I said as the resting line of men all smiled at me.

"Sir, I was LT Quilty's radioman. He lost his hand the other day on the walk out here because of an IED. My job was to walk behind him and cover

---

1    NCO and SSG are acronyms for Non-Commissioned Officer and Staff Sergeant, respectively.

all radio communication for him. When he was hit, his blood flew all over me. I'm okay, but can you say a prayer for me to be strong, and for these other guys?"

I took a deep breath and with all eyes closed, prayed, "God, please bless these warriors. Grant them strength and peace during this crazy time and let their efforts and sacrifices this week never be forgotten. Amen."

After nearly an hour with the exhausted men at Rushdi-Mullah, an enormous boom ripped through the countryside. As the echo reverberated in the distance, LTC Infanti, who had been standing near the front of the house talking to some men, yelled, "Get in the vehicles! We're leaving right now!"

A one-vehicle team from Charlie Company, intending to park on the road and monitor the area, crept along the canal road.

Boom!

Their vehicle had been hit by an IED so powerful that it blew the vehicle's entire front end off the frame and implanted it deep in the dirt. Several soldiers from the team were seriously wounded.

It took less than fifteen minutes for us to race down the highway. As we neared the site of the explosion, I looked through the front window and saw two, black, AH-6 Little Bird helicopters flying circles around a medical aircraft to provide protective fire, if needed. The group of aircraft flew away after they recovered the casualties.

I stood in awe of the damaged machine that sat motionless on the road. The doors lay on the ground and blood splatter covered the cabin of the vehicle. I felt pain for the wounded men who had once occupied it, along with fear that another bomb under the road could explode. It was then I grasped just how intelligent and mobile the enemy really was. We had taken their property in the villages and some had fled, yet I sensed they were watching us from everywhere. I took a deep breath while thinking about how we had just walked on this very spot less than an hour before.

A short while later, our convoy traveled back to Yusufiyah, where we learned that many other dramatic events were unfolding. Although Operation Polar Rock Blizzard was officially over, the insurgents decided to retaliate. Alpha Company's new battlefield position, 155, came under a withering attack from three enemy machine gun teams. They approached from different sides of a field, surrounded the small building housing our men, and began pummeling it with gunfire.

A platoon, led by SFC Del Rodriguez, responded with amazing courage and ferocity. They called in mortar (indirect fire) support, AH-64 Apache helicopter gunships armed with lethal Hellfire missiles, Scout sniper teams, and even two British GR-4 Tornado jets for support. The fighter planes came screaming overhead, strafing the militants with blazing firepower from their 27mm Mauser cannons. The helicopters pounded away at the insurgents and the snipers systematically took them out, one by one, with their long range, Barrett M-107 sniper rifles.

We heard the action over the radios as we were pulling into Yusufiyah. Our convoy immediately turned around and headed to BP 155. As we arrived, I asked to be dropped off with the snipers standing behind the dirt mounds on a nearby road. As I watched, I pondered the blow the enemy's morale had to have taken. Certainly their hope in defeating us in a direct fight had to be waning.

SFC Rodriguez was awarded the Army's Silver Star award for heroic action in commanding the defensive actions that day.

As the firefight at BP 155 ended, fighting elsewhere ensued. I hoped the presence of a chaplain would encourage the men, so I spent the rest of the day canvassing the battlefield's many outposts. I welcomed the exhilaration brought on by firefights, but the pain of seeing team members hurt or killed transformed that exhilaration into vengeful anger. I wanted to make sure the men had someone to talk to about it.

The pace of it all became incredibly difficult to continue as incidents sprung up everywhere. The sheer numbers and the intensity of the battles increased as the insurgents became more desperate. They had ruled this nation and kept it in bondage for years; they had no intention of giving up their power. They could lay down their weapons and work with us, which was unlikely, or they could die fighting us. The choice was theirs.

As the months passed, the 10th Mountain Division pushed further into the bloody Triangle, brutally pounding its foes into retreat. The more the 31st Infantry invested its blood, sweat, and tears into the arduous fight, the more unacceptable defeat became.

# THE BLOODY BAGHDAD CSH

The number of IED, rocket, and small-arms attacks multiplied greatly over the next few months. I began noticing a significant hardness in my mind because of such sustained saturation in the brutal environment. I had seen many men suffer, and I suffered with them. I had sensed the fear in brave men who faced their mortality and I quivered with the same thoughts. I felt myself cycling through the feelings of insanity often associated with war, but I knew I'd never quit because that would mean giving up on my comrades. As long as a chaplain was near them, they could sense faith and mentally survive anything. But as the chaos escalated, I witnessed an entirely different area of the battlefield, one far away in an unexpected place.

Back when the battalion was staged at Mahmudiyah, I had made a few brief visits by helicopter to the 28th CSH (Combat Support Hospital) inside Baghdad's well-fortified Green Zone. It was the United State's Army's medical epicenter. The soldiers I visited during those first few weeks often returned to duty days later. But as the violence increased on the battlefield, the severity of the casualties did as well. During the winter, I was thrust into a heart-wrenching ministry.

The weather in Iraq turned cold and the spirit of Christmas rang through the hearts of the Polar Bears. I had somehow managed to conduct Christmas services at every battlefield outpost in the Triangle of Death over a two-month period. Because of the onslaught of IEDs and small-arms attacks against our convoys and patrols, my personal faith and determination were tested like never before. I fought for my sanity every day as the number of men I had come to know and care for gradually decreased. One platoon in Delta Company often found themselves facing six IED strikes a day.

I asked God, "Are You sure that you have the right guy for this? I care far too much about these men to keep losing them."

As I returned from the nearly four-week cycle of Christmas visits, I began preparing for an evening Christmas service at Yusufiyah. In the middle of the event, a soldier came running in, frantically shouting, "Sir, the battalion commander wants to see you immediately! We've got something serious going on!"

Calling a quick end to the service, Steve and I ran as fast as we could to the tactical operations center (TOC). We had not even thought about resting that day because of the importance of the Christmas service to our men. Soon Steve and I regretted it because we were running on mental and emotional fumes from the lengthy trips over the past month.

I ran into the room, almost tripping over a couple of aluminum chairs. Polar Bear 5 informed me that a vehicle patrol from Bravo Company had been struck by an IED. Additionally, SGT Luke Shirley from Bravo Company had been wounded by a pressure plate IED when his platoon dismounted their vehicles for a search of the area. Polar Bear 6 then approached me. "Chaplain, be ready to fly out of here in fifteen minutes. I redirected a helicopter to come get you and take you to the CSH."

In my previous trips to the CSH, I often traveled by ground vehicles. This time I would fly in a UH-60 Black Hawk helicopter. Due to erroneous information about seat availability on the bird, SGT Tennant remained behind. The helicopter swooped down onto the ground and picked myself, an NCO, and SGT Shirley's brother up.

After about a twenty-minute ride, we landed behind the combat hospital on a small, discreet landing pad. The other two men and I stepped off and away from the helicopter. Next, we began looking for an entrance to the trauma center.

I almost ran into a group of soldiers who were standing around another helicopter. I thought about how strange it was for a group of soldiers to be having a formation after midnight. But seconds later, reality dawned. They were preparing to load body bags containing American soldiers into their UH-60 Black Hawk helicopter.

I directed my comrades to come to a halt, salute, and respectfully wait until the soldiers were finished. Then I led the team away from the landing zone and into a nearby emergency room door.

This specific military trauma hospital was the inspiration for a PBS television documentary in 2004 called *Baghdad ER*. The documentary showed the reality of battlefield casualties in Iraq. When I had watched it on television, I wondered if I would one day see the bloody hospital first hand.

Operated by a remarkable team of doctors, nurses, and staff, this battlefield stabilization center dealt with the most critical injuries imaginable. Tonight, as fate would have it, I found myself, for the first time, in its Intensive Care Unit (ICU).

Once inside the CSH, we weaved our way through what seemed like miles of hallways and corridors, finally arriving at SGT Shirley's bedside. I felt a shock run through my body and fought to avoid staring at the amputated stumps where his limbs had once been. Moments earlier, his right arm and right leg had been surgically removed.

The doctors told me, "When you go back, tell your commander that the quick, decisive action of your medics—whoever they are—saved this soldier's life."

We sat next to SGT Shirley for two days, not eating or sleeping, while he tenaciously fought through his pain. My stomach growled from hunger and my mind felt numb from exhaustion and the shock of seeing the room filled with severely wounded men. But those things seemed frivolous when I considered what Luke and the other heroes in the surrounding beds were going through. I simply couldn't find it in myself to complain, even to myself. SGT Nicholas McCoy, an American soldier from the 501st Airborne Infantry Regiment, lay nearby. His entire body had been perforated with shrapnel from an IED. We spoke a couple of times before his energy eroded and he stopped talking. He rested next to two Kellogg, Brown, & Root (KBR) civilian contractors who had been wounded in incidents of their own. They both had reportedly been involved in unknown explosions and their entire torsos had been split open. Although they could not talk, I quietly spoke to them. I said, "You guys aren't alone and you've got some great doctors and nurses here to take care of you. I'm a chaplain and I'm going to wait here with you as long I as can. God bless you."

It was a horrible setting where the faith of a chaplain was vital, not optional. Pain and suffering filled the room. The injured needed a chaplain who could hurt with them.

On the other side of the room lay two insurgents, only feet from the Americans. I tried to ignore them, despite the enormous anger welling in me. They had accidentally injured themselves when the bombs they were preparing exploded prematurely. When I realized that they were being given the same treatment as my men, I was incensed. I couldn't comprehend how these enemies could ever be released to go back to their lives as terrorists.

Wasn't aiding and abetting the enemy treason? I could not believe that someone from my own nation would offer mercy to a merciless enemy. I felt betrayed by my country. I knew that these men would return to kill others like me if they had the chance. In the battle for the Triangle of Death, the enemy fought for an ideology, something not easily altered.

As I looked back over my shoulder at the American heroes lying in beds hanging on to their lives, I thought, "This is one of the worst things I've ever seen; it's going to bother me for the rest of my life."

Then I asked myself, "Whoever said that war was supposed to be fair? If I found such a person, I think I'd punch their teeth though the back of their head right now."

Almost three days later, my commanders came for me with an armored convoy. SGT Shirley was being evacuated for an eventual return to the United States and I needed to return to our area. On the ride back I contemplated the traumatic experience and prayed that God would help the wounded Polar Bears and grant me a few minutes of relief from it all.

When we returned to our patrol base, the battalion was preparing for its next major offensive through the sector.

While I had been in the hospital, Yusufiyah had come under a fierce attack from enemy fighters. The insurgents were unable to overrun our urban patrol base, but the incident signaled to us that many motivated and well-organized insurgents remained in the area. With that knowledge, my commander's intelligence teams sifted through their mountains of information to decide what our next objective should be. After careful study, the command team chose to seize the enemy's most significant safe haven. The selected target was Qarghuli Village: a refuge for Baath Party loyalists, Sunni leaders who masterminded terror throughout the region, and the home of a complex cell of Al-Qaeda operatives.

# 9

# AL-QARGHULI:
# OBSERVING FROM
# A DISTANCE

I watched the beautiful and isolated village from behind a wall of sand-bags on the roof of Battlefield Position #132. Thinking about the land surrounding me, I wondered how the place considered by scholars and archeologists as the Garden of Eden had become the modern-day war zone of Iraq. From behind my olive drab binoculars, thoughts of snipers occupied my mind as I scanned the Euphrates River Valley for militants.

The beauty of the area's lush, tropical vegetation nearly hypnotized me as it swayed back and forth in relaxing rhythm to the wind. An amazing history accompanied the great beauty. The patriarch Abraham had likely passed through these very fields on his way to Canaan. The Assyrians had ruled the world from here and later the Babylonians would build their vast kingdom.

Clusters of palm trees stood sentinel over nearby houses, but the peaceful splendor of the quaint community was a facade. Behind the beauty rested a terrible culture of organized crime and political terror. A merciless monster known as the Sunni insurgency waited for the opportunity to destroy the nation of Iraq.

Hidden in the houses of Qarghuli lived the financiers and decision makers of Al-Qaeda, as well as their fighters. They held allegiance only to Saddam Hussein and his Baath Party loyalists. Once the coalition forces captured Saddam Hussein, a power vacuum swept over the country, causing the Sunnis to retreat into the rural Qarghuli community.

In the upcoming weeks, Delta Company would move troops to the southern portion of the city to gain a control point from which they could operate. Snipers frequently targeted my men, sometimes hitting them. One day, a sniper shot out the window of a vehicle where I had been sitting only moments before. Along with the sniper activity, devastating IEDs would explode throughout the village, wounding many soldiers.

In an effort to curb future violence, we had talked with the townspeople during initial reconnaissance missions. Our men explained to the villagers that, "We came here to stop terrorists, not to interfere with anyone else. We want your help. Will you work with us by stopping the unnecessary killing of our troops in the region?"

In response, the community leaders told us, "We will not help you and we are not responsible for anything that happens to your men." In essence, their refusal to detour insurgents and work with us was a declaration of war on my task force. Regardless, we tried to approach the situation with as little violence as possible.

Following almost every meeting, sniper fire and IED attacks would skyrocket. The number of attempts to kill us tripled. I believed that the enemy was going to clash with us on a larger scale over time because of their intense hatred and their skillful organization. If their assumption was that we would eventually seize their village, it was correct.

The tension between the Qarghuli tribe and the 10th Mountain continued to smolder. Many Americans sensed a pivotal collision at some point in the future. A catastrophic event was bound to happen. The villagers were organized, patient and waiting for us to make our move. As they continued striking us with roadside bombs, they knew it was only a matter of time before we would reach our limit.

They were absolutely right.

# EXAMINING THE SEVEN SECTIONS
# OF THE VILLAGE

Qarghuli Village consisted of seven distinct areas which were critical for understanding: the north, south, east, west, the IED-saturated Malibu Road which zigzagged through the center of the village, and the land to the west of the Euphrates River. The last area was recognized as the Al-Anbar Province which was nicknamed the "Cradle of the Insurgency."

By far, the most strategically important terrain feature of the area was Route Malibu. The main thoroughfare through Qarghuli Village, it was a gauntlet filled with all manner of explosive devices. Consisting of a single lane of dirt and concrete fragments, Route Malibu began as a main road on the south end of the village and ended at the northernmost point. Six-to-seven-foot dirt embankments lined both sides of the semi-asphalt passage throughout the village.

The road was a perfect path for canalization, a situation where troops are required to travel along a certain route that sets them up for a deliberate attack. Lush, thick, vegetation; palm tree groves; and orange groves concealed rows of houses and their inhabitants from the road. Route Malibu was the deadly exception to the American description of Iraq as a war without front lines. It absolutely was a front line; it was a passageway into a sanctum of devils.

The daily need to move through the area became one of the most terrifying things I encountered in combat. Every time I traveled, I was certain that I would be struck by roadside bombs. I prayed every moment I was in a vehicle that God would protect us from the large 250-lb. and 500-lb. explosives buried with the express purpose to disintegrate us.

One day, the lethality of Route Malibu became clear. A convoy I was riding with was hit by an IED, wreaking havoc on the vehicle I was in. We managed to creep the truck along with flat tires and a significant portion of the front missing, until we arrived at an American outpost.

By the grace of God, though many of the convoys I traveled in didn't make it though the Malibu gauntlet unscathed; none of us were seriously injured.

The next major terrain feature was the legendary Euphrates River. Supposedly the Greeks named it Phrat, meaning "fertilizing" or "fruitful," because of its life-giving qualities. The Euphrates served as the region's most critical water source, but also doubled as an escape route for militia fighters who would attack us and flee. The boundary it represented caused us much frustration because we could not cross the Euphrates in pursuit of the enemy. That was the United States Marines' territory, and as such, we were ordered to disengage the enemy at the river's edge—perhaps so as not to step on the Corp's toes. Unfortunately, they were too far away in other sections of the massive province to police the area.

The rule failed to last. After repeated attacks by enemy forces from the river, we were forced to raid sites on the other side where the attackers fled. One surprised detainee, whom we captured in a lightning-quick boat raid, exclaimed, "How did you get here? Usually I hear your helicopters, hide my weapons, and go away."

We never told him about our boats.

The northern section of Qarghuli Village contained the most houses and inhabitants. High above its trees, a giant smokestack from the multi-story Russian thermal power plant protruded into the sky. The Russians had built the plant in exchange for Saddam Hussein's pledge of loyalty. The power plant was capable of supporting a large portion of the southern Baghdad territory, consisting of an area of nearly 300 square miles.

The plant now stood abandoned, with coffee cups still resting next to blueprints. What happened to it was a mystery. Now, the power plant was an insurgent sanctuary. In the early phase of deployment, Special Operations Forces, along with paratroopers, raided the power plant. Their efforts were highly successful—they destroyed the biggest vehicle-bomb factory in the country. They also paid a high price, taking so many casualties that their helicopters were overfilled with the wounded.

The commandos and the airborne troops did not remain in the power plant as an occupying element; theirs was a precision strike. The raid brought havoc on the enemy and later allowed a small element of riflemen from the 10th Mountain Division's 2nd Battalion, 14th Infantry (the Golden Dragons) to successfully occupy the structure. The small contingent of Golden

Dragons was not large enough to completely fortify the large facility, but enough to signify a vigilant presence.

Anticipating the mission of entering the village, I visited the southern tip of the village every couple of days. The location for the thrust into the inner portions of the village would begin near an intersection consisting of two roads: Routes Sportster and Sportster Extension. Near the crossing were five American outposts: 132, 142, the Water Treatment Facility, the Saddam Hussein Bridge, and a compound known as JSS (Jurf-al-Sakhr).

As a grisly reminder of the death we faced daily, a large, cemetery overlooked the southern section from an elevated field of dirt.

To the west, swampy marshes edged the Euphrates, lined by fields, dirt paths, palm groves, and small houses. Vegetation concealed most of the river, but the view from the outpost's rooftops allowed me to sit and watch the historic waterway, the barren desert just across the river inside the Al-Anbar Province, and the tropical countryside. The view never got old.

The remaining portion on the village's east side consisted of farm houses, fields, and an ominous road known as Route Caveman. Caveman was not considered a direct element of the village because it wasn't located immediately in the path of our mission. I walked with the first dismounted patrol there, and was warned by a local, probably in an effort to scare us away, "You will die. There are many large bombs still buried from the invasion [2003], intended for the big American tanks. They never came through here. Now they wait for you."

## EXAMINING THE DANGERS OF QARGHULI VILLAGE

Back in 2003, M1A2 tanks belonging to the Army's 3rd Infantry Division rolled through the Euphrates River Valley en-route to Baghdad. Passing through farmlands, they skirted the roads along the Euphrates instead of driving directly through some of the villages. Thus, countless 250-lb. and 500- lb. aircraft bombs hidden underneath Route Malibu were never detonated. We would not be as fortunate because we were not just passing through. We would have to take the direct route right into hell.

Initial operations for the 10th Mountain soldiers involved raids and reconnaissance patrols, which were conducted frequently to locate the bomb makers, operators, and other essential information regarding the area and the people. But activities as simple as foot patrols or convoy operations involved tremendous risk. Sometimes we were spared because of exposed trip wires and poorly concealed artillery shells. Occasionally, the soldiers would even catch the IED operator preparing his weapons in the reeds or near a house and kill him.

Even though the patrols around and into Qarghuli Village were extremely risky, I took part in them as often as possible, sometimes five or six times a week. I wanted to show my men that faith on the front lines was nothing to laugh at. I was terrified every time I went out with them, but it was on those daring missions that faith became even more real to me. I quietly told one man during a patrol, "I've learned how to pray out here like I've never prayed before."

My fear centered on the fact that I never knew who the enemy was, especially since he rarely wore a uniform and conducted most of his intelligence gathering without weapons. A smiling farmer, waving his hand as a salutation, might be the man who planted the bomb intended to strike my vehicle.

During raids, some locals did provide us with important knowledge, "We know where the bombs are. We will help you."

Searches later revealed critical information that saved many lives. Other times it was clear that misinformation had been given to us in order to lure us into an ambush. To Americans, trust was a sacred thing because it meant the difference between life and death. Most of the locals had unhesitatingly betrayed us with their unwillingness to stop attacks and join us in the struggle against the terrorists.

## UNDERSTANDING THE QARGHULI TRIBE

The Qarghuli tribe facilitated terrorist activities across Iraq from their rural community. They financed, organized, and armed fighters to fuel the flames of violence in their multi-faceted battle against Shiite Muslims. The tribal sheiks and their families kidnapped, tortured, and murdered enemies without mercy. Justice was something they administered through Fatwas (legal directives in Islam).

Like an organized mafia family, the elderly men at the top of the patriarchy made the final decisions for the village. They walked through the village like angry zombies. Generations of sons sat back and drank tea while their wives labored though cooking, selling items, digging ditches, farming the land for food, fixing automobiles, and fetching and carrying things for neighbors throughout the town in the heat of the day.

The first time I saw the assortment of locals, I thought, "I can't believe how evil their eyes look." The ones I came in contact with on patrols gave me goose bumps. Their expressions reminded me of the stereotypical Hollywood serial killer: deathly still with cold, hardened demeanors, glaring at their victims.

I asked an officer in my unit where such sinister people had come from.

He said, "I heard that they are originally from Turkey. The Russian workers at the former power plant were responsible for the blond haired, blue eyed children playing around the city."

Once, I travelled near Qarghuli Village in a humvee and saw a young boy beating a smaller girl over a toy. It appeared to me that life and respect were concepts reserved only for self-benefit, which is why they made such formidable enemies. Had there been a uniformed enemy in the area that had overtaken the village with force, I might have felt sorry for the local population. There wasn't though, so my dislike for them boiled.

## CONDUCTING A RAID

*8 November, 2006*

On 8 November, 2006, I wrote in my journal, "While with Delta Company, I woke up at 3:00 a.m., shook off my sleepiness, and prepared my gear for a dismounted patrol/raid into Qarghuli Village." At this time of year, Iraq was bitterly cold. The soldiers tried to keep warm with small bonfires inside the old, abandoned Water Treatment Facility. All of the windows had been broken out over time due to gunfire or vandals, and some had been replaced with green, overstuffed sandbags while others served as avenues of ventilation for the bonfire.

As a frigid breeze swept through the windows and into the building, SGT Tennant and I performed a humorous series of jumping exercises to stay warm. I remember thinking, "We may look like idiots to you guys, but at least we're warm."

Following our attempt to warm up, the soldiers of Delta Company finished their preparations for the mission, including pre-patrol communications checks with radios, and of course my favorite, the pre-patrol prayer. I asked God for protection. "Please watch over us and keep us safe. Cause any attempts by the enemy on this mission to fail. Grant us success and bring us back safe. Amen."

I donned my heavy, body-armor vest and my muscles ached under the weight. Other Polar Bears did the same, double-checking their gear, knowing that once we started the patrol it would be too late to come back. Fifteen minutes later we stepped out into the cold, moist night.

The brilliant moon illuminated the rural farmland. As we walked silently past the outpost's razor-wire perimeter, we ventured into a thick fog that was drifting over a field of tall reed stalks. My heart pounded with fear and I prayed for God's protection with every step. We gradually made our way onto a deserted road covered with bomb craters. I thought, "Holy cow, Lord! I'm trying to trust you; please keep this crazy road from exploding and killing everyone."

Continuing on with the foot march, we saw in the near distance that every house light in the village was dimmed. Vehicles were absent from the streets. Even the animals were silent.

I thought, "If everyone is sleeping, maybe we won't die after all."

We had made it along a road, through a field, and now we began hustling across Route Sportster Extension toward the Qarghuli Cemetery. It was a plot of land about the size of a football field situated on a small hill. The cemetery was full of shallow graves, some of which were dug up by scavenging animals. Countless human bones covered the ground. I stepped over human bones, rocks, and pieces of broken cemetery architecture.

I stopped suddenly. Six feet in front of me was a large, 120mm mortar round protruding from the ground. The instant my mind registered the danger, one of the soldiers in front of me kicked the round.

His carelessness could have killed everybody near him, including me.

Anger swelled inside me. I did not let it out, because I was worried about compromising the patrol.

"When we get back to the patrol base later," I thought, "I am going to knock the daylights out of this guy."

After calling in map coordinates to Delta Company's radioman at the Water Treatment Facility, we reached the next phase of our mission: entry into the main portion of the village. It was then that I whispered to Steve, "If the stuff hits the fan here, we're surrounded by an entire city."

Shadow by shadow, house by house, street by street, we combined as much speed and stealth as possible in our movement toward the houses of suspected enemy leaders. Everything had been going reasonably well when all of a sudden, clank! I quietly asked Steve, "What the heck was that?"

A soldier had accidentally knocked a metal bucket off a tree stump, startling some animals in a nearby yard. I tried to restrain myself from laughing out loud.

When we reached a small brick wall, the patrol leader halted everyone. Instantly, out of nowhere came a blaring 5:00 a.m. call to prayer from one of the local mosques. A soldier quietly chuckled, "Here we go. Now the whole village is going to go *Black Hawk Down* on us!"

Another one whispered, "Heeeeeeeeeerrrrreeee commmmeeee theeeeeee Americannnnnsss!" I was sure that the interpretation was wrong, but it was funny and that eased some of the tension.

Some troops knocked on doors of the target houses and others waited in the darkness. I whispered, "What kind of stupid rule is this? When did we start knocking on doors? Whatever happened to kicking the stupid things in?"

A soldier kneeling next to me said, "Sir, give it a second. There's a reason why. Just watch."

As the door slowly opened from the inside, rifles greeted the surprised occupants.

Once opened, the residents were questioned by our interpreters about enemy activity in the area. Within the next hour, our team searched seven other houses. It would be the only time in the deployment in which I gave candy to mothers and children, who were allowed to sit away from the questioning of their fathers. I remember one mother smiling at me and patting the top of her head in appreciation of the candy for her children. After this mission I felt the act was too personal and the risk of interacting with a suicide bomber was too high.

The men displayed entirely different attitudes and mocked us in Arabic.

I thought, "What the heck is this? Why are we letting these guys get away with this nonsense? My questions were answered as I watched our interrogator, who was a female soldier, yell "Shut up!" The men sat silently down on the ground, their eyes opened wide with surprise.

Shortly after 5:00 a.m., the patrol's leaders considered the mission complete and turned the team around for its trek back to the Water Treatment Facility. The team of raiders carefully began making a way out of the village as the sun ascended. As we walked toward an intersection, our machine gunners quietly swung their weapons around, scanning the area for threats. As things go in combat though, trouble was not far away.

Three men on our team tried to signal a small truck coming near the intersection to stop, but the drivers would not comply. After hand signals and shouting in both English and Arabic, a rifleman fired a warning shot.

Still the men refused to stop, at least not until the bullet ricocheted off of something, made its way to (and through) the vehicle's door, accidentally hitting the driver's leg, and barely missing the passenger's head by less than an inch. The truck stopped immediately at that point.

I was laughing so hard, I almost fell over. Another soldier, who was also laughing said, "Serves them right, Sir! They should have stopped when we tried to do it the nice way." The awakening locals had clearly been made aware of our presence and came out into their yards to watch us. As we began making our way back to the Water Treatment Facility, I saw three middle-aged men standing next to a donkey in a yard. They stared at us with looks of unbridled hatred. Their malevolent gazes followed every step we took. I could tell by their dirty looks that things were going to get crazy.

## TAKING CASUALTIES IN QARGHULI VILLAGE

### Late November, 2006

A lot of activity took place during the following weeks, and it was exactly as I had expected: enemy hit and runs, guerilla-style warfare, elevated sniper activity, increased vehicle-borne improvised explosive devices (VBIED), and more complex strikes made on small elements of men.

Rumors circulating about kidnappings of Iraqis and Americans in the area made everyone feel uneasy, so Steve and I increased our visits to the battlefield positions. We shadowed the units, providing a presence of faith as they engaged the enemy.

One experience involved a dismounted patrol through the city of Rushdi Mullah with Bravo Company on 15 November, 2006. It was as terrifying as it was successful. The city was hauntingly silent and the people were over-cautious about something unseen. After a tense patrol, we analyzed important information about the insurgents in the area. The Polar Bears had cleared the enemy out of Rushdi Mullah, but knew from the way the locals were acting that something sinister was likely to happen soon.

On 20 November, 2006, Steve and I visited BP 147 in Al Taraq which came under an attack involving mortars and machine guns. The incoming projectiles flew in and crashed around us. I heard flying shrapnel (a chunk of metal from an incoming shell) pass over my head. Unfortunately, the attackers were so far away, we had no chance at catching them.

Later the same day we moved down the road to position #146, which was south of #147 by a quarter of a mile. Once again, we came under attack. Steve and I had been on the rooftop when we saw mortar rounds landing in the field next to the house. I noticed an Iraqi army soldier standing on the same roof I was on, talking on a cell phone; I wondered if he had called in the indirect fire. I later spoke with an American who worked with the Iraqi army on a daily basis.

"This really worries me. I have been in numerous incidents in which Iraqi soldiers were using phones while on the rooftops of our outposts. Each sighting coincided with an attack."

"There's nothing I can do," he said. "They don't fall under American rules. I can't take cell phones away from Iraqis."

Another incident happened at outpost #147, Bravo Company's strongpoint. A small group of unknown Iraqi men arrived at the gate and demanded that the property be turned over to them. Our battalion knew that #147's two houses had served as torture locations during the 101st Airborne Division kidnappings. My men refused, "If you want it, then come and get it."

The men did in fact come back to get it. Their method of doing so involved a barrage of highly explosive rockets and mortar rounds. As the projectiles flew into to the small yard, machine-gun fire ensued. It was at this point that the scrambling Americans noticed a truck on a nearby street racing toward them.

They knew the vehicle was probably filled with explosives, intended to blow down the walls of the outpost. The soldiers fired every weapon available at the attackers. On the rooftop of the main house, a medic named Nicholas "Doc" Rogers rushed to an unmanned M240B machine gun and opened fire on the insurgents. While defending his team, enemy gunfire struck him in the throat, killing him. Because of Doc's actions, the speeding truck, which had indeed been carrying explosives, was violently blown off of the road.

Meanwhile, I waited with Delta Company at the edge of Qarghuli Village, listening to the firefight at Rushdi Mullah on radios. While listening for the official outcome to be broadcast, we discussed the battle. Suddenly, terrible news came forth of "Doc" Roger's death. I knew immediately that my priority was to move to Bravo Company's post and help. Within the hour, I caught a ride in a convoy to Rushdi Mullah and spent the next three days with them as they mourned the tragedy. When I saw that they had regained their focus, I returned to Delta Company's area.

On 25 November, 2006, the day arrived for Task Force Polar Bear to move into and seize the southern portion of Qarghuli Village. In an attempt to stay centrally positioned for casualty collection, I remained at the Water Treatment Facility with a third of Delta Company as its other elements stormed the village in the late hours of the night. Using the darkness to their advantage, the raiding force quickly extinguished gunfire that erupted from several neighborhoods. The task force secured two houses as critical command, control, and area over-watch positions. Firefights would occur intermittently throughout the week, but they were just another hazard in seizing control of Route Malibu and the neighborhoods surrounding it.

Following the infantry teams into the town were EOD (Explosives Ordnance Disposal consisting of Army, Navy, and Air Force technicians.)

They operated in five distinct vehicles: the Joint Explosive Ordnance Rapid Response Vehicle (JERRV), the Buffalo (basically, a bulletproof, 38-ton Mack truck), the Cougar (personnel transport), and the Husky and Meerkats (elongated vehicles equipped with X-ray machines underneath it to scan the surface of the road for buried explosives).

The EOD party stopped for a few minutes at the Water Treatment Facility until cleared to move into the city for IED removal. While there, I prayed with them. "God, please keep these men safe and give them success in keeping everyone else alive. Amen."

"Thanks, Sir. We always appreciate a prayer."

Within minutes, they received clearance and ventured out to begin ordnance removal for the soldiers fighting in the neighborhoods. That was when the reality of the struggle in that area again came to light.

At the southernmost section of Qarghuli, on Routes Malibu and Sportster Extension, simply making it onto the roadway was a death defying act. The EOD team crept past the Water Treatment Facility along Route Sportster and onto Malibu, carefully scanning the crater-covered road leading into the ominous village. Suddenly, a massive explosion ripped the Meerkat apart, tearing its frame and sending fragments of the machine flying. A security element which was attached to the demolitions clearing team called for an immediate medical evacuation aircraft for the technician who had been driving the vehicle. He was airlifted to Baghdad; miraculously he survived. For the soldiers left behind, including me, the incident stirred the grim fear of death and disaster.

On 26 November, I sensed fear as I joined Polar Bear 6's Personal Security Detachment (PSD) in a convoy mission from Yusufiyah to the new front-line inside Qarghuli.

I said a prayer as we prepared to drive away. In my journal that day I wrote, "After an early morning meeting with my battalion's commanders, I joined Polar Bear 6's convoy to visit the men fighting inside Qarghuli Village."

After logging every passenger's name, the PSD commander, 1LT Michael Johnston, joked with Steve and me about a Christmas tree we had stuffed in his trunk. It was the only one in our inventory and we were taking it to the front-line troops. He said, "If that thing gets blown out of the trunk, we aren't going to stay around to pick up the pieces."

We laughed as we climbed into our vehicles. It was then that I noticed Scarface, the commander's interpreter. His dark pair of sunglasses and black, baseball cap, caught my attention as he looked directly at me before getting in a vehicle. On his body armor was a red, white, and black Iraqi flag pin. I pondered how well he looked momentarily and then thought, "It's a really nice morning out here today. I hope we don't die."

It *was* a beautiful morning. The heat of the sun kept the humidity low and a breeze blew through the palm trees. Our radios were reasonably quiet, no enemy activity was being reported, and our team was alert and prepared for anything.

Loaded up, we traveled until we reached the Water Treatment Facility at the edge of Qarghuli Village. Polar Bear 6 decided to stop at the complex so he could speak with the troops there. I talked with a few of the guys for a short time before hearing 1LT Johnston telling everyone that the trucks were about to leave. Steve prepared to climb into one vehicle and I was getting ready to step into another—the rear, passenger side of PB6's. Suddenly, PB6 stepped in front of the door, smiled, and said, "Chaplain, where do you think you're going?"

I said, "Sir, we're heading up Malibu with you so we can see the guys who are making their way into Qarghuli."

He smiled at me through his dark ballistic glasses and replied, "That road is real bad. Why don't you and your assistant stay here tonight? You can catch a ride with someone tomorrow when it is a little bit safer."

I responded, "We were hoping to see the guys today, Sir. But if you want us to stay here, we will."

In his enigmatic, Godfather-style demeanor, he smiled. As LTC Infanti stepped into his seat, he looked over his shoulder and said, "You're really easy to work with, Chaplain!"

"So are you, Sir."

Steve, who was waiting at the door of his vehicle, walked back to where I was. We stood in place and watched the convoy as it drove out the perimeter and onto the southern portion of Route Malibu. Within ten minutes, we heard a roaring explosion rip through the neighborhoods and felt the ground shake as if an earthquake had struck. A massive black plume of billowing smoke filled the bright sky and we looked at each other in total shock. Steve and I sprinted to the tactical operations room and listened intently at a table covered with radios for information about what had just happened.

I told the operator, "I think that was LTC Infanti's convoy that just got hit!"

The radios quickly became overwhelmed with chatter between the convoy and the battalion. The operator verified, "Yes, Sir. It was his. We're waiting on further information from the guys there."

Steve, me, and a team of medics grabbed body bags, medical supplies, and ammo as we waited for permission to respond as a quick response team (QRF). As I ran to the vehicles with arms full of gear, an Iraqi Army soldier walked by. He was talking on a cell phone, and I wondered if it was a call made by him that caused the catastrophic attack on our team.

As we ran back to the radio room to get approval to go to the crash site, somebody at the wrecked vehicle radioed in. "This is Polar Bear 6's convoy. We've just took a massive hit from an IED. One vehicle's completely destroyed. It's upside down and in a crater. We've got one KIA [killed in action] and three WIAs [wounded in action], over!"

At that moment, everyone who had been talking on the radio network stopped in a moment of shock. I quietly prayed, "Please, God, don't let anybody else die."

Just then, "Polar Bear Mike, this is PB6's PSD. All crew are WIA and Scarface is KIA. We're requesting immediate medical evacuation at this time, over!"

Instinctively, we rushed to the trucks parked at the Water Treatment Facility, prepared to drive away when we heard more startling news over the vehicle radios. Someone at the crash site reported, "We can't have your response force come. Somebody just dropped some IEDs on the road. We're trying to establish security out here at the destroyed truck."

Someone else relayed, "We have a MEDEVAC inbound and its five minutes out, over."

While the other trucks in the convoy sat in a defensive posture along the road, parts of the battalion commander's vehicle littered the ground. A couple of the nearly 400-lb. doors had been blown off the truck. Half of the vehicle was completely gone. Scarface, who had been sitting behind the BC—in the seat that I would have occupied before LTC Infanti stopped me—was killed. Infanti himself was thrown from the vehicle and now lay on the road in shock, tended to by his combat medic.

The soldiers of the battered convoy were doing all they could at the incident site to keep the situation under control. I continued waiting with the quick reaction force, but the authorization to move out never came.

Out of nowhere, an American jet blasted overhead to ward off potential attackers and provide time for the medical aircraft to arrive. As it did, the helicopter pilot warned, "You guys are going to have to clear up some more of that road before I can bring this thing in!"

The Polar Bear soldiers cleared debris away for him to land despite the threatening security situation. The UH-60 Black Hawk lowered, received the casualties, and disappeared back into the sky.

Our investigators concluded that the buried ordnance that had exploded under Polar Bear 6's vehicle consisted of two Italian anti-tank mines and the two 80-lb. shape charges (homemade explosives). Amazingly, PB6, his driver, and his gunner survived and within a week were released from the CSH to return to duty. Although Polar Bear 6's back was later found to be broken, it never stopped him from doing his job.

God never revealed to me exactly why Scarface died so tragically, but it was clear that the Divine had not only worked on behalf of my battalion commander that day, but also for me.

The terrible incident was not the last catastrophic challenge our battalion would face. Nearly every other day somebody was wounded or killed by snipers or IEDs. One such soldier was SGT Christopher "Chris" Messer: a humorous, friendly, and strong leader.

I first met Chris through a request from his company commander, who was at the JS Bridge.

"Hey Sir, can you visit one of our outposts out here? We have a guy at BP#132 named SGT Messer whose platoon has taken a lot of hits over the last few weeks [Messer later told me that he had been getting hit between five and six times a day by IEDs]. It would be a great help if you could talk with him."

"That's why I'm here."

Not long after I arrived at the desolate checkpoint, I dropped my assault pack off in the small fortified house, and climbed a ladder to join Messer on the roof as he watched the roads and fields with a pair of binoculars. I spent the remainder of the day listening to him tell me about the challenges of war from his perspective.

"Yeah, Sir," he said, "I won't make it out of Iraq. I'll be killed by an IED."

"You can't talk like that, man." I said. "Everybody knows that dying is a possibility here, even me, as the chaplain. But believing that it's certain means you have a real bleak outlook every day. Living under fear crushes your hope and that's something that you really don't want."

I thought that maybe excess trauma influenced him to say the things he did, but Messer was already a proven combat veteran from the Battle of Fallujah, having served a tour with the 1st Infantry Division a couple of years earlier. He had sustained injuries then, even earning a Purple Heart. Why would he believe he would not make it out of the Triangle of Death?

Over the next few months, our friendship grew stronger. I took part in many dismounted patrols with his platoon and even rode to Baghdad with them. During that trip, I scared him when I took a photo of the giant sword monuments. He thought the flash from the camera was an IED explosion. Shortly before Christmas 2006, he committed his life to Jesus Christ, laying his eternal hope in the hands of God. Whenever Chris would visit the battalion's main camp, he would find me wherever I was. This led me to think, "He has me locked in his radar because he can find me anywhere." Visit after visit, we sat in vehicles together during his guard shifts, on rooftops while he scanned the area for the enemy, and on cots at night. All the while he reiterated his fear of dying from an IED.

The last time I saw Chris was in one of the platoon's vehicles on Malibu, in front of Battlefield Position #151, at 2:30 a.m. We sat in the truck and I stared past the paper photo of Christ which he had positioned near the windshield. I looked around the dark neighborhood, scanning the road and the fields as we talked. Unfortunately, I had to attend a meeting back at Yusufiyah within a few hours. Otherwise, I would have stayed a couple more days with him and the men at the rural position.

Momentarily, Fox Company would be sending a supply team through the area and I would ride back with them. I could see their blinding headlights as they pierced the darkness about a quarter of a mile away. Soon I could make out the rumbling of their engines as they approached. I put my hand on Messer's shoulder, tried my best to look through the darkness into his eyes, and said, "You are an awesome guy. I really mean it. I would never just tell somebody that if I didn't."

His smile illuminated the dark humvee. "Thanks, Sir. I think you are, too."

I then told Chris, "The chaplain loves ya man!" I opened the heavy door, stepped out onto the road, and prepared to join the convoy of approaching trucks.

Not long after that evening, on 26 and 27 December, I wrote in my journal about "my worst days," "my most personally challenging moments in combat," and "the darkest days in which I struggled for my faith." On 26 December, Messer and his platoon set out on a foot patrol through Qarghuli Village to search for enemy weapons caches. While they walked through a field located just meters from Route Malibu, they found a cache. To provide clearer access to the stash of weapons, soldiers set fire to the reeds enveloping the area. However, the blaze spread too close to the cache, causing ammunition to explode in every direction.

The team decided that the best choice would be to return home and come back the next morning when the fire was out.

On the 27th—Messer's fourth wedding anniversary—the team walked back to the cache site, crossing the same field they had the night before. Somebody from the village had been watching them during their evening mission and surmised that the platoon would return to retrieve the weapons. As the men neared the site, a blinding flash and deafening roar ripped through the dawn, instantly killing PFC Nathaniel Given and wounding Chris Messer. Given suffered from fatal shrapnel wounds to his head. Chris lost everything below his waist. He fought for life in the confines of a UH-60 Black Hawk medical helicopter. For nearly twenty minutes on his flight to the Baghdad CSH, Chris struggled with all he had before slipping into eternity.

I learned of the incident later that morning after finishing a meeting at Patrol Base Yusufiyah. Someone came up to me while I was walking around the camp and said, "Sir, someone needs you in HQ."

When I entered the command and control center, a soldier said, "Chaplain, there was a terrible incident this morning." Before he could finish, I looked down at the piece of paper in his hand. It read, "PFC Given KIA. SGT C. Messer WIA."

I felt as though someone had ripped my heart out of my chest. The officer said, "I'm sorry, Chaplain. Messer lost everything below the waist. But he is WIA, not KIA." As I stood in place, trying to maintain my composure, someone else walked up and said, "Hey Chaplain, I really don't want to be the one to have to tell you this. SGT Messer just died. I'm sorry."

I was crushed. I punched the door as I stormed outside and walked away in hopes of finding a private place where I could release my emotions. My entire psyche felt as though it collapsed not once, but twice. My hands did not stop shaking for three days.

Even though I spent those days dealing with the horrible event both spiritually and psychologically, I somehow managed to minister to the remaining embattled soldiers of Delta Company throughout the next week. Ultimately, I conducted a memorial ceremony for them to honor Messer and Given.

I will never forget any of the unit's warriors, but Chris Messer was a personal friend, a devout Christian, and the bravest man I ever knew. I learned from his life and death that fear does not determine whether or not a person is a coward; what matters is how they deal with those apprehensions. In SGT Messer's case, he heroically faced his nightmares—all the while believing he would die—and lived doing what he loved: being a soldier.

Despite the difficult losses of men like Messer, Given, and Scarface, I always looked forward to further visits to the troops at the remote battlefield positions. This meant circulating through a collection of locations scattered in the Triangle of Death: FOB Mahmudiyah, Patrol Base Yusufiyah, JSS (Joint service Station: a police station we created for Iraqi police), JS Bridge,

BP's #126, 132, 133, 142, the Water Treatment Facility (also known as 142 Alternate), 146, 147, 148, 149 (also called Hargawi), 150, 151, 152, 153 (also recognized as Inchon), Outpost Corregidor, 155 and 156.

As we increased the number of outposts, the enemy multiplied his attacks. This left us with no other option than to call for the cavalry and heavy armor.

A precursor of things to come: A Christmas photo of me holding a Bible, surrounded by my GI Joe toys, early 1980s

Basic training graduation at Fort Benning with my mom, 1991

Basic training graduation at Fort Benning, 1991

Dino Glasman, a man who changed my life.

Tanisha and me, wedding photo, 2004

Inner city ministry, Los Angeles, 2001.

Tent City: Camp Beuhring, Kuwait, 2006

Middle of the night flight into Mahmadiyah

View from my humvee while passing a damaged cargo vehicle on the Mullah Fayad Highway

Chaplain Assistant SGT Steve Tennant and me after returning from a dismounted raid of Qarghuli Village

The ominous Route Malibu

Hunting enemy forces with the Armored Warriors in an M1 Abrams tank

Fox Company mechanics and I (center) after pulling a transmission out of the vehicle behind us

Two black spots where the ambushed DUSTWUN vehicles burned (lower right foreground and by the last palm tree in the distance)

The Russian Power Plant, also known as "The Dragon"
(Department of Defense photo)

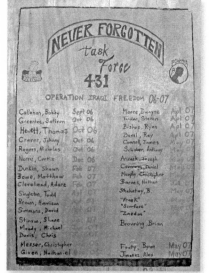

Memorial sign I made
to honor the brave
men who gave all

Setting foot on American soil after 15 long months of combat operations
(Wheeler-Sack Army Airfield, November, 2007)

# 10

# UPARMORING
# MY FAITH:
# MINISTERING TO THE
# MEN OF STEEL

N ow that we had secured a foothold inside Qarghuli Village, two things
became increasingly evident. First, the area for armed insurgent forces
(AIF) to operate in was lessened. Second, the AIF were reinforcing their
ranks with the most lethal guerilla operatives in Iraq. They brought in foreign
fighters from other provinces and we responded by bringing in an armada of
heavily armed M1A2 Abrams Main Battle Tanks and M2A3 Bradley Fighting Vehicles from the Army's armored and cavalry divisions.

Three "heavy" units were attached to the Polar Bears throughout the
deployment. They were the 1st Battalion, 22nd Infantry of the Fourth Infantry Division (Fort Hood, Texas/Fort Carson, Colorado); the 2nd Battalion,
5th Cavalry Regiment from the First Cavalry Division (Fort Hood, Texas);
and the 2nd Battalion, 69th Armor from the Third Infantry Division (Fort
Benning/Fort Stewart, Georgia). These units consisted of light infantrymen,
mechanized infantrymen, and tankers. They were battle-hardened organiza-
tions and eager for further action.

I rode with the team of four, 2-5 Cavalry tanks as they headed for the dangerous outskirts of Qarghuli Village, maneuvering and rumbling along dirt roads throughout the rural countryside. After the ferocity of the village, the high pitched whine of each tank's 1500— horsepower, jet turbine engine sounded beautiful. The treads clicked and clacked under their burden, leaving a smokescreen of dirt in their wake. Desert colored cannons, which reminded me of telephone poles, protruded over the bow of each machine, fluidly swinging to one side and back in search of enemy forces.

## INTRODUCING THE ARMORED CONGREGATIONS

### 29 March, 2007

The 1st Battalion, 22nd Infantry Regiment mechanized warriors were the first armored team I served. Originally assigned to assist the 101st Airborne, the tankers were now working alongside the 10th Mountain Division. In contrast to the Polar Bears, the tanks had been positioned mainly at the eastern quadrant of the Triangle, in alignment with the Screaming Eagles. When we moved our forces west, the mechanized troops of the "Ivy" Division rolled alongside us; they were instrumental in our battles at Al Taraq, Rushdi Mullah, and the Mullah Fayad Highway.

Shortly before the battle for the Mullah Fayad Highway, one of their most respected men, 2LT Johnny Craver, was killed while commanding his platoon of armored fighting vehicles along an intersecting network of roads near the Mullah Fayad Highway. The explosion was believed to have been directed at the vehicle in front of his, but flying shrapnel bypassed it and struck him.

When I conducted his memorial ceremony, Chaplain (CPT) John Hill visited in order to co-host it. Although Craver was with a small group of his men in our area, his assigned unit was located near Baghdad. The day after the service, Chaplain Hill received a request that he call his unit regarding an emergency. We went together to my command building and he responded by radio.

As he spoke with a soldier from his unit, his eyes watered up.

"John," I asked, "Is everything alright?"

The phone slipped from his grasp and dropped to his side.

"A catastrophic IED just hit one of my unit's vehicles," he said. "Everyone in it died. They're dead, every one of them. How could this happen only a day after we finished Craver's ceremony?"

I asked him, "Do you mind if we step to the side of the room here, brother? I would like to pray for you and your men. You're like brothers to us, you know?"

After finding a quiet corner, I prayed a heartfelt prayer of concern, "Almighty God, I ask for your help right now for John's unit. Give them courage to face this terrible loss. Please help his men make it through and sense your peace. Amen."

Within the hour, he left for his unit in Baghdad on a convoy my commanders had organized for him.

The 2-5 Cavalry Regiment replaced the 1-22 Infantry. The main difference between the two units was the amount of territory they would cover inside the Triangle of Death. The later in the deployment each unit served, the farther and more extensive their operational environment became.

One time, while I was visiting at one of the 2-5 Cavalry's battlefield positions, their company commander, Captain Rich Ince, approached me.

"I'm sorry, Chaplain, but your battalion took a casualty a little bit ago. I wasn't able to get his name, but I did get the name of the company: Bravo."

I said, "Thanks for letting me know. SGT Tennant and I need a ride to Rushdi Mullah so we can be with them. Can you get us there?"

He replied, "Absolutely! I'll have a convoy ready for you within an hour."

Steve and I stood outside the building with our gear, eager to get to the Bravo Company troops, when four Bradley Fighting Vehicles pulled up in front of us. We thought we would be fortunate to get anyone in the sector to reroute humvees for us, but armored vehicles were over the top. They took us to Rushdi Mullah, with a few stops in between to pin the 25mm Bush Master Chain Gun on some suspicious individuals. Fortunately for the suspicious figures, their courage faltered. Any plans they might have had for evil were shelved in exchange for self-preservation. After being targeted by our big guns, the men quickly left their questionable tasks.

Waiting a few minutes, we then proceeded on our trip. When Steve and

I arrived, we walked out the back ramp of the vehicle, looked at each other, smiled, and laughed at each other.

Steve said, "Wow, Sir! That was the coolest escort I have ever had!"

"Me too," I replied. "I wonder who's in the other Bradleys?"

The Bravo troops greeted us and said, "We thought that a general or somebody like that was coming down the road when we saw the armored vehicles."

Steve and I laughed but quickly the tenor of the conversation changed. "Who was it that was killed? What platoon was he in? Do you know where they are right now?"

Grateful for the presence of the chaplain team, one soldier, moved by emotion, said, "That's the awesome thing about you, Sir, you always come when we need you."

The last of the mechanized teams to roll into the Triangle of Death was the 2nd Battalion of the 69th Armor Regiment. They were a legendary team from the "Dog-Faced Soldiers" of the 3rd Infantry Division. Their unit arrived on 29 March, 2007. A week later, on 8 April, in what would be one of the most bizarre tragedies of the deployment, a Bradley Fighting Vehicle was destroyed while parked on Route Sportster. It was a day on which the 2-5 and 2-69 exchanged control of the southern boundary of Qarghuli Village. Quietly, in the middle of the day, two Bradleys sat stationary and monitored the area. It was the 2-5 Cavalry's last patrol before heading back to Baghdad and the first patrol for the 2-69 Panthers in the Triangle of Death.

I was traveling back to Yusufiyah from Delta Company's strongpoint position inside Qarghuli village when I noticed the two Bradleys moving into an over-watch position at the intersection of Route Sportster, Malibu, and the Qarghuli cemetery.

According to a video released by Al-Qaeda later, two men dressed in white man-dresses approached the vehicles unnoticed. They rolled some old truck tires filled with IEDs up to the vehicles and planted them underneath while the turrets passed slowly overhead. The soldiers inside the parked Bradleys were completely unaware of the enemy's presence.

About twenty minutes later, the convoy of trucks I was riding in pulled into Patrol Base Yusufiyah. Stepping out, we heard an enormous boom from the Qarghuli Village area. Nearly 600 rounds of exploding anti-armor ammunition sent up a brilliant flash of fiery light and catapulted pieces of one of the armored vehicles throughout the neighborhood.

The quick reaction force from both the 2-5 Cavalry and the 2-69 Armor rushed to the scene, but were unable to get close enough to provide aid because of the exploding 25mm and 7.62mm rounds emitting from the vehicles. When they were finally able to reach the site, the teams found that SSG Harrison "Ducky" Brown, PFC David Simmons, and SGT Todd Singleton had died. The only survivor, SPC Nick White, had crawled out of the burning hulk and worked fervently—while on fire himself—to extinguish the flames.

I immediately prepared my gear to go back out and help the units. That day, the injustice of war soured my gut as I considered the terrible price America had just paid for freedom. I stayed with the 2-69 Panthers as they continued patrols in their area and waited for the return of SPC Nick White from the Baghdad CSH where he had been evacuated after the explosion. For nearly a week I conducted religious services and stayed up late each night for crisis counseling.

I returned to Yusufiyah to prepare for the memorial ceremony I would later conduct for the three fallen heroes. It was there that SPC White, the lone Bradley survivor, found me in the chapel. He had just been released from the Baghdad CSH and returned via the brigade commander's convoy. My heart broke as I looked at his burned skin, lack of hair, and watery eyes.

He sat on a seat next to me. Describing the activities which had taken place during his brief stay at the CSH and subsequent return, Nick said, "Sir, I don't want special treatment. I don't want to sit down with VIPs and commanders; I just want to go back out and do my job."

It was clear to me that Nick was a hero in the truest sense of the word, with an unswerving determination to return to duty for the sake of others.

"Nick, you're an incredible man," I said. "Absolutely incredible!"

## PAYING A PRICE FOR VICTORY

*1-28 April, 2007*

I began venturing out with the Panthers and the Dealers on route-clearance patrols as Task Force Polar Bear sought to purge any remaining enemies from the overall battlefield. As we did, insurgent frustration mounted in direct proportion to their inability to defeat us. In desperation, they intensified the severity and frequency of their attacks. During the month of April, the Polar Bears faced one of the toughest periods of their deployment. By midsummer 2007, the war in Iraq reached an all-time high in political violence, a pinnacle that would never be surpassed. On 1 April, 2007, the 10th Mountain Division faced serious blows among its ranks. The 2-14 Infantry (the Golden Dragons) suffered the deaths of two soldiers from an IED. That same day, four soldiers from the 210th Brigade Support Battalion (BSB) were seriously wounded in a catastrophic IED incident while traveling on a major roadway known as a Main Service Route (MSR).

## CHRISTENING THE CHAPEL OF STEEL

"The Men of Steel," as one of our battalion sergeant majors, SGM McCormack, affectionately called the armored troops, continued with route clearance patrols throughout the sector as the enemy's activity escalated. The commanders of one 2-69 tank platoon, 1LT Jonathan Edds and SSG Michael Skarhus, asked Steve and me to join them on daring hunter-killer missions. Polar Bear 6 had once taught me an important lesson about being invited on such operations. He said, "Chaplain, when people fight to have a leader around, that person is probably doing something right. And that's a good thing. If they are fighting to get rid of a leader, that's a bad thing."

SSG Skarhus, also known as the "Hus" by his men because of his husky size, confirmed this point. "Sir, when you come out to visit, we aren't ever able to attend your services because of our missions. Either the missions pick up or we have to conduct required maintenance on our tanks. It just never works out for us. So we want you to know that when you guys go on patrols with us, that's our fellowship and service."

A little while later, while blessing a tank with anointing oil, I prayed, "God, please bless my men here today and watch over us. If the enemy challenges us, may You overcome them with the weapons You have provided us. I ask this in Your name, Lord. Amen"

The Hus then said, "Sir, that was awesome! I know we're in good hands now."

While fellowshipping with the tankers during the patrol, I thought, "I have the single coolest chapel in the world." It weighed nearly sixty-five tons and came with its own small congregation. As far as I was concerned, it was the sweetest deal that a pastor could ever ask for. The tankers gave me a nice, desert-colored tanker helmet to wear and taught me about emergency actions for crewmembers.

## PATROLLING IN THE CHAPEL OF STEEL

Although Steve and I patrolled with the Hus and his Dealers many times, the mission one particular evening centered on clearing IEDs in an ongoing effort to make the "impassible" Mulla Fayad Highway passable. As we drove along the dangerous road that skirted Baghdad's southern belt, I occasionally—and cautiously—lifted my head out of the turret to catch the breeze. The air felt good as it flowed over my face and around my tanker helmet.

Although the wind felt like a refreshing break from the heat inside the tank, the danger outside the vehicle was great. I always returned to the safety of the turret within seconds of cooling off because we could always be passing through the kill-zone of an ambush. That evening as I prepared to sit back down inside the tank, the Hus spotted the silhouette of a man walking through a field. I peeked back out, saw him, and spoke into the mouthpiece of my tanker helmet, "What is this guy doing out so late at night? What's he up to?"

SSG Skarhus responded though the headset, "He can't be up to any good this time of the night. I don't see any weapons on him, but I bet anything that he is planting IEDs."

We slowed down to a crawl.

Even with our night-vision devices we could barely make out the man's figure because of the thick vegetation and a distance of nearly two hundred meters. Even while we focused on him, we continued to scan around our tanks in a 360-degree radius, knowing that situational awareness in combat was critical. Distraction was one of the best weapons used by the enemy, and given enough time and space to apply it, they would do so masterfully.

Case in point: Months earlier, an Army unit that had been encamped in a remote battlefield south of the Triangle of Death received gunfire from the edge of a field. Their guards shifted attention toward the shots, leaving their rear and flanks unsecured. Out of nowhere, a truck carrying nearly 5,000 pounds of explosives raced down a road toward them. Before the soldiers comprehended what was happening, the vehicle rammed a perimeter wall, blowing it down along with the towers and buildings behind it, killing many.

With this incident fresh on our minds, 1LT Edds' spun the lead tank's turret and cannon around. The sights on the enormous 120mm gun squared the man up, influencing him to abort any plans of harming us. After standing perfectly still for a few moments, he slowly walked away. I thought, "That's the luckiest guy in the world." His life was spared only because he got rid of any weapons before we saw him.

Later that night, after we had travelled farther north on the Mullah Fayad Highway, we saw a beautiful but deadly array of neon-colored tracer bullets flying through the sky.

The drivers of both tanks slammed their throttles forward into high gear and raced toward the boundary of the sector. Understanding that a breach into another unit's area of operations would be an issue without a command authorization, 1LT Edds called the Polar Bear TOC and requested permission to cross the border and engage the enemy.

"Polar Bear Mike. Polar Bear Mike. This is Dealer 6. I am requesting authorization to cross the north sector boundary to engage AIF [Armed Insurgent Forces], over."

While we waited, the tracers from both Americans and enemy forces blazed paths across the sky. The phosphorus tips of the bullets, intended to illuminate enemy positions, streaked gracefully through the darkness like shooting stars. We sat anxiously, waiting for a radio response. Each second seemed like an hour when I thought about the effect we could have. I glanced around at the fields and hoped the only action we encountered would be as the reinforcement of the Americans engaged in the firefight. Finally, we received a response from the radio, but it was not one we wanted to hear.

"Dealer 6. Dealer 6. This is Polar Bear Mike, over."

"Go ahead, Polar Bear Mike."

"Apparently, the 2-14 Infantry is dealing with some AIF at this time. They are not requesting backup so we will not provide it. At this time, you are not authorized to enter their zone. Do you copy, over?"

We sat on the dark road in disbelief. 1LT Edds replied, "Roger, Polar Bear Mike. Dealer 6, out."

I was frustrated that we were going to have to sit to the side of the fight, in multimillion dollar tanks, when fellow Americans could use our help. But since we were not allowed to do anything more, 1LT Edds and the Hus discussed what to do next over their headsets.

The Hus then told the crews, "Go ahead and turn 'em around. We'll do a few more patrols through the sector in some other areas before we call it a night."

The turbines began their high pitched wind-up as we prepared to turn around. The platforms of steel jarred and shook us as their treads grabbed the ground. Then without warning, our driver abruptly slammed the tank forward and around at the same time, causing my face—mainly my teeth—to directly hit the turret's steel rim.

I tried to shrug off the pain and sit back down into the loader's seat. I swallowed the stream of blood flowing down my throat.

SSG Skarhus asked me, "Hey, Sir, you okay?" He then tried to make me laugh by saying, "You just got bit by the tank! It's what we call a 'tank bite' in the armor community."

As I continued to swallow, I laughed and said, "I'll be okay." I could feel the blood pouring down my throat but knew getting upset was not an option for a soldier sitting on a dark road in the most dangerous place on earth.

Seconds later, we were completely turned around. We raced back down the highway and after a few more patrols, eventually returned to the 2-69's base of operations.

The lives of our American service members weren't the only ones the tankers helped protect. The wellbeing of the interpreters who were assigned to the 4-31 Infantry was also at stake.

Zaedon was a bright, skinny young Iraqi who had joined the Coalition's cause in hopes that he would one day see a free Iraq. One afternoon, while on a dismounted patrol, his team was caught off guard by the enemy. Zaedon was killed by an IED explosion.

Frank, another interpreter, was an older gentleman who signed up to work with the Army to earn an honest living. Frank and I frequently drank chai tea together at BP #152 in his living space under a set of stairs. We spoke often about life, faith, and our friendship. That came to an end one day as he was ascending the interior stairway of position #153, a large house situated deep within an uncontrolled neighborhood.

A local, sympathetic to the enemy's cause, placed a rusty sewer pipe in a tree, tied it in place with an elastic inner tube, and managed to build a spotting device with a piece of cardboard. After punching an eye hole in the center of the cardboard, the insurgent taped it to the pipe and proceeded to load a 57mm Chinese rocket into it.

Boom! The homemade pipe launcher shot the missile through the air, over several neighborhoods, and directly into a small, yet barred, window in Delta's three-story mansion. The missile blasted into a wall next to Frank, causing him to fall to the cement floor several floors below.

One soldier told me, "As I ate my breakfast, a blast shook the house and filled it with dirt and smoke. Suddenly Frank's body comes out of nowhere. He tried to talk but he could only choke and gasp as his brains poured out on the floor around him. It was horrible!"

The carnage continued.

On 14 April, SPC Ryan Bishop, a Charlie Company soldier whose company had moved into a deadly area of the Triangle of Death known as Zone 310., walked with his patrol on a mission to kill Al-Qaeda fighters who were detonating accelerant-laced, firebomb IEDs against other American units in the area. After passing a small bridge in a field, his team was struck by a violent blast. SPC Bishop was killed by the devastating attack. The next morning, Bishop's platoon patrolled back to the same spot to complete the mission; this time I was with them. I conducted a memorial ceremony for him just days later.

At the memorial event, LTC Infanti said, "Charlie Company, Bishop's team while with this battalion, recently uncovered a weapons cache while conducting operations aimed at clearing the area of insurgents. In the cache was a cell phone with a text message. The message noted that 'The area cell has been disbanded, the Americans are everywhere!' This illustrates how the efforts of men like Bishop were not in vain."

Only days later, on 19 April, as Chief Warrant Officer (CWO) Dwayne Moore of the 2-15 Field Artillery Regiment was walking out of a building at Forward Operations Base Mahmudiyah, he was killed by an incoming rocket attack. His chaplain, Captain Richard West, was on leave at the time, so his commanders called for me. Almost immediately upon arriving at the FOB for pre-ceremony preparations, I sensed a sickening feeling in my gut that more soldiers would die over the next few days, a rather easy prediction considering the casualty patterns for the month. I was right: within hours, I received word that the Polar Bears had taken another casualty.

On the 21st, Charlie Company suffered another heartbreaking loss. SPC Ray Bevel was killed by an IED while taking part in a dismounted patrol in search of enemy caches. I left Mahmudiyah, intent on returning to conduct CWO Moore's memorial, and traveled to Patrol Base Corregidor.

While there, I sat next to an old building with PFC Phillips, a member of Bevel's squad, and said, "I'm sorry, man. I wish I could press a button and make our heroes like Bevel come back. But I can't. What I can do is stay out here as much as possible and keep walking missions with you like I did when Bishop was killed."

I would not have the chance to walk the patrol because only an hour and a half after I talked with Phillips, I learned that a soldier from Fox Company, at Patrol Base, Yusufiyah, had been killed.

I told everyone in Charlie Company, "I need you guys to be patient with me because I was already working on Chief Dwayne Moore's memorial ceremony before Bevel was killed, I am planning Bevel's ceremony today, and have just found out someone else was killed back at Yusufiyah by a mortar attack."

Throughout the coming weeks, the casualties mounted and I faced some of the most mentally grinding days I'd experienced yet. SGT Tennant and I sometimes conducted critical incident stress debriefings between memorial ceremonies. Many of the casualties weren't KIAs, rather WIAs (wounded in action) and members of the survivor's platoons who were required to press on without their comrades.

At various times SGT Tennant and I had so many ceremonies to conduct, that as soon as we finished one, we would immediately travel in convoys to conduct another.

## CONDUCTING A FIELD MEMORIAL CEREMONY
## FOR THE DEALERS

One memorial ceremony was for the Dealer tank platoon. Three soldiers from their home battalion at FOB Rustamiyah in southeast Baghdad had been killed by an IED attack on their vehicles. I was at BP 151 when a soldier informed me, "Sir, the 2-69 is calling on the radio for you."

I walked into the tiny house, grabbed the hand mike from the radioman sitting at a table and said, "This is Polar Bear Chaplain. Go ahead, over."

It was the Hus.

"Sir, we have something really important to ask you. Can you come back out to the Water Treatment Facility and talk with us?"

I said, "I always look forward to seeing you guys, but I just was at your place for an entire week. I have a whole lot of other soldiers I need to visit."

The Hus replied, "We know you're busy, Sir, but it's real important."

"You know I can't turn you guys down. Come pick us up and we'll talk. Polar Bear Chaplain, out."

Steve and I stood near the front of Outpost #151 that morning, waiting for the tanks. It wasn't long before we heard the rumble of high-powered jet turbines coming up the road. We cautiously made our way out of the perimeter, because the tanks could not fit inside the tiny yard, trying to avoid attention so that we would not be targeted by snipers, and onto Route Malibu. We looked at each other and laughed; the deadliest killing machines on earth, costing millions of dollars, were arriving just for us.

We climbed in and rode back to the Water Treatment Facility.

Inside the tank turret, the Hus told me, "Sir, the reason we needed you to come back out was because we lost three men back in Rustamiyah. We can't send more than a couple guys back there because of our duties here. So the boys are hoping that you will conduct a memorial ceremony out here."

I sat back, humbled. What chaplain could turn down such a simple, heartfelt request?

I told him, "I will be glad to do it, but there is just one issue. Since the men were not in the Triangle of Death, I can't officially do the memorial ceremony with everything a battalion would use since it won't be conducted by the task force. The men killed were in Baghdad when it happened and that's where their official ceremony will be. If *we* do it, it will just be Steve, me, you, and your platoon. I can't get a rifle volley or a bugler to play taps. Those things would be impossible to get for a twenty-five man event at a small checkpoint in the middle of nowhere. Those are challenges, but I promise that I'll do it with all of my heart, if it happens. It's your choice."

The Hus responded, "Got it, Sir. Whatever you can do for the boys would be more than enough. I knew that you wouldn't let us down."

Immediately, I told Steve to prepare for the ceremony. We would need three rifles, three bayonets, and three sets of special tanker boots from the Dealers, all to represent the three fallen soldiers. Two soldiers with SSG Skarhus's platoon managed to find an American flag and hung it on the barbed wire surrounding the small checkpoint. In its red, white, and blue glory, the flag provided the backdrop for the piece of plywood that served as the ceremony's stage for the rifles and boots. In less than a day, the hard work of the soldiers and SGT Tennant paid off. They had managed to turn a remote outpost into a platform of honor.

The location was actually a satellite outpost near the Water Treatment Facility, nearly fifty meters from the abandoned location of the 101st Airborne kidnapping. I did everything I could to make the ceremony as fitting as possible for the Dealers, including the use of a laptop for the National

Anthem, as well as background music for the portion in which soldiers would pay their final respect to their fallen comrades. I provided a personal message of inspiration and ended the event with a recorded version of taps. The honor I felt that day as the Dealers surrounded me in a half circle, listening intently to my message of hope, was unimaginable.

As I stood in front of them, I spoke about life and our fallen heroes. "Standing back up and continuing to live amidst grief is the healing process in a nutshell. Today, with the loss of our warriors, SSG Michael D. Moody, Jr.; SGT Chris Davis; and PVT Shane M. Stinson we have taken a fall. Five years into Iraq, with violence around us everywhere, we have taken many falls. But with God's help, the encouragement of each other, and the American spirit, we are rising again. God can help us in this tough time! Our enemies will never defeat our spirit to fight. We go on, always remembering these heroes. Yes, we go on. And they will go on with us."

Following the service, I offered each soldier a chance to say goodbye in his own way to the fallen warriors. It was the way I had personalized all of my memorial ceremonies. Yet this simple service became one of the most profound moments for me in my entire deployment. The tankers half-circle gradually became a line to the platform. One by one we all knelt and offered our respects. I knew at that moment that God had brought me to the Dealers' remote outpost so that I could deal his love and hope to them.

In the final moments, 1LT Edds and SSG Skarhus thanked me by giving me something special. In his deep voice, the Hus stepped forward and said, "I've been with the Delta Dealer Company since Operations Desert Shield and Desert Storm. Since then I've been in Operation Iraqi Freedom three times, including the initial invasion into Baghdad. In all that time I have only ever received one appreciation coin. Today, to say thanks from all of us Dealers, I want to give it to you."

The entire tank team stood in appreciation of what Steve and I had done. In my best attempt to deflect the credit to the one who rightly deserved it, Steve, I recognized his hard work and publicly thanked him.

I also noted that I was just doing what I should do, but the platoon was still set on presenting me with the appreciation coin. With that I humbly said, "I don't deserve this, but if you are set on giving it me, I have to give you something special back." I then unpinned two of my blackened combat crosses from the band of my helmet and gave them to 1LT Edds and the Hus.

After accepting my gift, the Hus spoke again. "We wanted to give you the coin not just for the memorial but also for everything you've done for us. We just found out this week that we're going to have to leave here soon because our battalion back in Rustamiyah wants us reattached to them. So you will always be our chaplain and we will never forget you, ever." With that they all nodded in agreement and clapped.

Despite the calamitous month, being asked to conduct the secluded field ceremony inspired me. It provided me with an opportunity to think about how important the role of a chaplain was, which would deeply motivate me for ministry to my support soldiers later.

A few hours after the homage to the fallen tankers, the Dealer's chaplain back in Rustamiyah called to offer his appreciation for my work with his men. Unfortunately, I missed the call because we had already ventured back out onto the dangerous roads of the Triangle of Death with the Dealers and the chapel of steel.

# BULLETS, BEANS, AND BIBLES: MINISTERING TO THE SUPPORT SOLDIERS

**W**hile patrolling the unruly sector with the Death Dealers, they gradually packed their equipment to leave the Triangle of Death. Within a month they were mostly gone and my unit had turned the empty outposts over to the Iraqi Army. As I walked through the ghost towns where our mechanized troops had once lived, I thought of the many great times Steve and I had there. Not wanting to miss a beat of action, Steve and I began setting in plans to canvass the sector with our Fox Company combat convoy teams.

On some rare down time back at Yusufiyah, I laid down on an old Army cot and drifted away into the only refuge from Iraq I knew, sleep. A short while later, someone woke me up. My journal notes, "Someone came running into my chapel tent. After waking me up, he told me that I was needed back at the command office because of an emergency. I quickly leaped from the cot, threw on my uniform, and hustled out the door toward the command building."

Reflecting the moment of my arrival at the battalion control center, my journal continues: "Once there, people stood in shock and silence. I assumed that a soldier had been killed. Polar Bear 5 informed me that SPC Bobby Callahan had died tragically in an accidental vehicle rollover. Originally assigned to Alpha Company, SPC Callahan was later moved to the battalion's mortar section. While on a patrol one night, his humvee skirted a canal too closely and flipped, landing upside down. The crew was trapped inside until some soldiers in his convoy were able to pull the men from the wreckage."

Walking past me, Polar Bear 6 said, "Chaplain! Can you be ready to leave here in 15 minutes?"

I said, "Absolutely, Sir. I just need to run back to my tent and grab my gear and assistant."

"All right, because a flight is coming in to take us to the boys on Callahan's team."

At that time, Steve was required to be in another area on some business, so Dusty, my former chaplain assistant, was with me. The Battalion Commander, Dusty, CPT Dreyer (unit intelligence officer), and I flew away into the darkness of the night. When we arrived at Yusufiyah, visibility for all practical purposes was limited to a few feet. We ran single file away from the wailing aircraft, to the best-guess edge of the landing zone.

I realized Polar Bear 6 was no longer in our group so I halted the small team and waited for him. That was when it dawned on me that he must be back at the helicopter for some reason. My journal reads: "He had run back to the aircraft because SPC Callahan's body, which had been placed in a body bag, was being loaded into the aircraft we just stepped out of. I ran as fast as I could toward the dim light of the aircraft to join them. As Dusty and I reached the helicopter, LTC Infanti and some of the helicopter crew, stood reverently in front of the unzipped body bag. After the medics positively identified Callahan, they re-zipped the bag and we loaded him into the UH-60 Black Hawk for flight."

Immediately thereafter, one of the crew chiefs signaled that he was ready to depart. I was the last man to leave the aircraft and as I began to help the crew chief close the door, I paused, put my hand on Callahan's concealed body, and said a quick prayer. "God, please help our unit get through this. Give Callahan's family help in whatever way they're going to need. Amen."

With that, I took a deep breath, knowing that it would be the last time I'd ever see him. Hunching down in order to avoid the helicopter's low, circling rotor blades, I hustled away, briefly looking back and upwards toward the sky to see the aircraft. As I reached a safe spot, I knelt on one knee and glanced back up at the dark heavens to see Callahan's flight one last time. The aircraft's rotor wind enveloped me, making me feel as if I had been overtaken by a hurricane. As sand and wind pelted my face, I thought about how much I hated combat. However, I couldn't imagine doing anything else. I was born to help soldiers.

## THE COMBAT STRESS CONTROL TEAMS

I managed to minister to nearly thirty more men in Callahan's mortar platoon that evening, until about 3:00 a.m. It was evident that our unit, which had been pressing forward in combat without pause, could use help regarding the mental welfare of its warriors. This help came in the form of combat stress control teams from Baghdad. Their efforts went far beyond the incident with Callahan and covered the spectrum of casualty operations throughout the deployment. They helped me conduct critical incident stress debriefings (CISD) after deaths and frequently counseled many soldiers. They were an astute group of psychologists, psychiatrists, and mental health professionals who included LTC Jones, MAJ Fong, CPT Landeck, CPT Leonard, MAJ Reins, SPC Brown and several others.

Many times, I faced multiple casualties across the sector and had to break free from day-to-day counseling. This was one of the times that the stress teams were invaluable. They would help troops in the rear, leaving me free to deal with everything else out in the badlands.

One frequently asked question I encountered, usually by journalists visiting our area, was what I referred to as the Million Dollar Question: "Who does the chaplain talk to when he needs to confide in someone about the troubles of war?" The answer was the Combat Stress Control Team. When I was able to talk with them, it helped me sort through and rise above the

crushing burdens I carried daily. They not only became my consorts in combat counseling, but also my personal friends.

## THE EXPLOSIVES ORDNANCE DISPOSAL (EOD) TEAMS

After the long, fatiguing night counseling members of Callahan's team, several of whom had been in the overturned vehicle, I decided to take a day for
mental recovery. While walking around the patrol base the next afternoon,
I ran into SGT Ewing of the Explosives Ordnance Disposal Team (EOD).
He was a great leader not only because he had exceptional tactical skills, but
also because he had repeatedly volunteered to extend his Air Force ordnance
disposal mission in the Triangle of Death so that he could personally train
incoming technicians.

He served as the senior bomb technician for the teams which lived in an
isolated portion of Patrol Base, Mamhudiyah. When I visited his group in
their 20 x 20 foot, camouflaged, net-covered portico, I thought, "Wow, the
Air Force lives well!"

Within the confines of their retreat rested a getaway that would have
made the Swiss Family Robinson proud. Large, sagging military nets hung
from the walls and draped across the open porch. I walked back through
their hidden maze of concrete barriers and plywood walls, to find the airmen
lounging in some rickety, old lawn chairs.

One of them opened his eyes, peered beyond the brim of his desert-
colored boonie cap and said, "Hey, Sir, come on in and relax."

Massive bomb shell casings (defused, of course) sat on the ground.
Fragments of destroyed IEDs rested on plywood shelves as ornamental deco-
rations and a graffiti-canvassed memorial on an adjacent wall honored the
many fallen EOD soldiers, sailors, and airmen who had given their lives on
the Mesopotamian battleground.

The fascinating setup would not have been complete without an inge-
nious assortment of robot parts that decorated yet another wall. Wheels,
sprockets, treaded rubber tracks, bolts, metal plates, and pieces of shattered
camera lenses canvassed the section like art in a gallery. Each piece, hung by a

nail, was a tribute honoring the sacrifices of the tiny mechanized warriors that had once served as the eyes and ears of their EOD masters.

The dates of their "deaths," their individual roles in combat, and even names (which ranged from geek titles to those of women in explicit magazines), were inscribed on the makeshift shrine: Johnny 5, The FNG (expletive new guy), Elisha, Tila, and Jenna. I often thought, "I'm not sure whether to laugh or cry at this crazy wall. Even robots aren't safe in the Triangle of Death."

I interacted with members of the teams almost every day. One such squad consisted of Technical Sergeant Timothy Weiner, Senior Airman Daniel Miller, and Senior Airman Elizabeth Loncki. Loncki, a young, spirited female airman, was on her first deployment as an explosives technician and had great aspirations of one day leading a team of her own. She once told me, "My dad really didn't want me to do this, but it's what I wanted to do more than anything else. I want to stay in and lead an EOD team one day."

"Stick with SGT Ewing," I told her. "He's the best because he cares about his techs and won't lead you wrong. Plus, he's been here a long time, and in the Triangle of Death, experience is everything." She could not have had a better leader from whom to learn.

Sadly, only weeks after discussing her life, her team was struck by several catastrophic IEDs.

In my journal I wrote, "7 January: SGT Ewing and his team, including the young female, were unexpectedly caught in a catastrophic ambush. As the team approached some reported ordnance, a hidden set of IEDs being monitored by insurgents were detonated, killing everybody except SGT Ewing. He was evacuated to the CSH and never returned."

I will never forget the countless sacrifices of the brave EOD teams. The loss of almost the entire squad crushed my spirit for weeks. Their efforts quelled the sting of death on the battlefield for the infantry every day. The Babylonian region was saturated with deadly IEDs, and any hope of surviving often rested in the hands of the bomb disposal experts. Later, when another element replaced SGT Ewing's team, I told one of the airmen assigned to it, "If we didn't have you guys here, we would have three times as many casualties as we do now."

## THE COMBAT ENGINEERS AND A GLIMPSE
## INTO HELL

Besides the EOD personnel, combat engineers served as critical support components, especially when it came to building secluded outposts. I worked with a small element from the 20th Engineer Brigade out of Fort Hood, Texas, along with their traveling ministry team made up of Chaplain (CPT) Ricky Wambles and his assistant, PFC Owens. Their armored convoy of flatbed trailer trucks, combat bulldozers, and dump trucks, all reinforced with thousands of pounds of steel plates welded on for protection, fortified many isolated battlefield positions for us.

During a rare break one day, our ministry teams sat around discussing life in Iraq. Chaplain Wambles prayed for me, "God, please bless Chaplain Bryan and SGT Tennant and keep them safe out here."

I told him, "Thanks, man! That's the first time anyone's prayed for me in a long time."

He smiled and said in his friendly southern dialect, "You deserve it, brother. We've heard all the way up in Camp Liberty just how hard your battalion has been working down here, so the Army thought we should come down and lend y'all a hand. And that comes with prayer."

The work the 20th accomplished with their amazing machines at several of our outposts would have taken my unit months to complete with our hands and a few shovels. I had quite a bit of fun hanging out with the engineers as they bulldozed the ground around the checkpoints.

I told one, "You guys have really cool jobs and some pretty neat machines to do them with."

The engineer replied, "Yeah, Sir, we like what we do, especially when we get to drive the dozers and the plows."

The 27th of February, was not one of those enjoyable days, though. Instead, it would prove to be a faith-testing time in which I would, once again, be fighting for sanity.

According to my journal, "Steve and I had just finished conducting a three-week cycle of visiting almost every one of the twenty-three outposts. We had planned on a couple days of rest at Patrol Base, Yusufiyah. We thought

how nice it would be to relax in the recently erected Polar Bear Chapel
—a large, green, military canvas tent with plywood walls, doors with small
rooms for our sleeping areas. A beautiful, seven-foot-tall wooden cross made
by our beloved Alpha Company Immortals, graced the sanctuary. A Navy
electrician, Petty Officer Third Class Sissung, a civilian contractor named
Chris, and a small team of Polar Bear soldiers helped construct the chapel
after a six-month absence of any place to call one.

"I appreciate all of your help, you guys," I said. "Without your support
there would be no chapel."

Sissung, Chris, and the gang of troops responded, "That's why we're
here, Chappy. Anything for you!"

While Steve and I rested in our comfortable retreat, a soldier rushed in,
short of breath. "Sir, SGT Tennant, there's an emergency at the TOC. You
may want to check it out."

I shook the sleep from my head and told Steve, "Make sure you have
your assault pack ready in case we need to leave here for a few days."

My thoughts, centered on the likelihood of someone having been killed,
were beside the point. It was always my duty to respond. If someone had
not died, then he was a survivor of some combat-related incident, and that
meant he probably needed a chaplain that much more.

A vehicle carrying three engineers and an NCO from Alpha Company
named SSG Mike Schlitz (who survived) had been struck by an IED in
the area north of the Triangle of Death known as Zone 310. Steve and I
sprinted across the camp to the SGT Hunter Aid Station. The medics, physician's assistant, and physician all stood in a tense semi-circle, waiting for a
vehicle to arrive with the remains of the three Brigade Special Troops Battalion (BSTB) engineers who had perished: SGT Richard Soukenka; CPL
Lorne Henry, Jr.; and SPC Jonathan Cadavero. SGT Schlitz survived and
was medically evacuated.

From my journal: "The three combat engineers, along with SGT Schlitz,
had been sent to an area some distance away, considered disastrous because
of horrible, fire-producing IEDs. While there, their vehicle was hit by the
blast of a hellish incendiary bomb and was subsequently crushed like an
aluminum can. SSG Schlitz managed to open one of the vehicle doors and

escape, but the horrific fire left him with third-degree burns on nearly ninety percent of his body."

We did not have long to wait before the recovery team arrived. I helped the medics carry the body bags—still radiating heat from the burned corpses inside—on stretchers into the miniature emergency room. We carefully laid them on waist-high platforms so that the medical team could positively identify them.

That day, I wrote in my journal: "It was the single most horrible thing that I had ever witnessed in my life. While carrying the bodies, the smell radiated everywhere without mercy and I wondered whether or not I was going to throw up. The overwhelming odor of burned human flesh overtook the entire aid station."

Standing next to the bodies of the men, I realized just how sacred being a military chaplain was. Not only was I one of a few allowed by the medics to remain with the casualties, but I had the privilege of praying over them. With LTC Infanti, the medics, and the handful of soldiers there, it was an incredibly somber moment in my life.

When Polar Bear 6 requested I pray, I reverently implored God to "please grant the families of these brave men solace. Help us honor these guys. Help us find the men who took their lives and help us make it through this tragedy. I ask these things in the name of the Father, the Son, and the Holy Spirit. Amen."

With that, LTC Infanti walked away from the aid station, saying, "I'm going to go find the men that did this and kill them."

Steve and I left the aid station in order to get some fresh air. As we did, we walked by a shed and found the recovered remains of the vehicle the engineers had been killed in. It had been purposely hidden behind the building and surrounded by a barricade of green, wet weather ponchos so that it would not draw attention from soldiers.

As we walked up to it, a soldier standing guard said, "Sir, I'm sorry. I am not supposed to let anyone see the humvee."

"It's okay," I replied. "It's SGT Tennant and me, the Chaplain."

We walked by him and then, struck by remorse, I turned around, and said, "I'm sorry, man! You're here for a reason and I shouldn't have done that. It was wrong of me."

He replied, "No problem, Sir. But I am feeling angry at some other guys who came by a little while ago. They were joking about it and taking pictures." Steve and I left and tried to forget that we ever saw the metal wreckage. I had seen many destroyed vehicles, but this one haunted me.

Throughout that week, I smelled the stench of burned flesh and relived the image of the men's charred bodies. Visions lingered in my head of them with their arms frozen in postures of failed escape, skulls broken open from the explosion, and charred tactical gear seared into flesh. The odor from the bodies saturated my uniform and was nearly impossible to wash out, even after several weeks. Every time I thought about the incident I relived every micro-detail. At times, I was so overwhelmed by the smell and accompanying images, I could not eat. The horrific mental images haunted me for weeks.

A horrible, tragic wound, it was by no means the only one we suffered. I found out that one soldier, PFC Isbell from Delta Company, had been shot through both legs by a sniper. His platoon had been embedding strands of sharp razor wire along Route Malibu when the crack of a rifle rang out. The shot, labeled a "through and through" because it entered and exited both legs, failed to stop him. Bleeding profusely, PFC Isbell limped to his beleaguered teammates at the side of the road in order to receive first aid. He was flown out fifteen minutes later by a medevac helicopter from Baghdad. After being released from the Baghdad CSH a week later, Isbell was returned to duty.

The bloody month wreaked havoc on our ranks. I watched the task force continue to pay in blood for the cost of freedom, but as horrible as that price was, the sense that I was providentially directed to the Babylonian theatre of war was electrifying. The frustration that came with hard-fought survival every day was balanced by an intense feeling of honor in being there. Each day was a struggle to make it to the next. This environment of desperate survival brought a deepening sense of appreciation for life and the diversity nurtured by it.

## THE DIVERSITY OF SUPPORT SOLDIERS

The combat engineers were not the only support entity belonging to the 10th Mountain's 2nd Brigade Combat Team (BCT). Besides the Special

Troops Battalion (BSTB), the regiment had the Brigade Support Battalion (BSB). The BSB was a group of soldiers oriented for more prolonged missions, such as maintenance teams for vehicle repair. In contrast, the BSTB provided a handful of teams, such as engineers and military police, to provide critical support to our temporary missions involving construction and interaction with locals. Together, they comprised a most diverse team: cooks, administration specialists, human resource specialists, truck drivers, both light wheel and tracked vehicle mechanics, water filtration experts, gunsmiths, veterinarians, machinists, electricians, computer repairmen, and sanitation specialists.

One evening, SGT Curtis L. Norris, a young, blonde-haired soldier from Fox Company, which was attached to us from the BSB in Baghdad, sat next to me in the small wooden, internet service building at Patrol Base, Yusufiyah. He joked with his team members sitting nearby. I loved being around men like SGT Norris because they laughed at life and brought life back to a war that seemed to lose it day-by-day. I couldn't count how many times that helped me make it to the next day in Iraq.

The next afternoon, SGT Norris was killed by an IED that exploded directly underneath his seat as he traveled on Route Malibu. He and his team were bringing supplies to the grunts at the farthest outposts.

Religious diversity saturated Fox Company: Wiccans, Jews, Mormons, atheists, Buddhists, and Christians of nearly every denomination. I often asked myself, "How do I best serve these troops without compromising my faith?" I realized that I didn't have to believe what they believed, just like they weren't required to believe what I believed. Theologically, we were worlds apart, but all were my soldiers and I was going to make sure their constitutional right to worship as Americans was supported.

Scripture teaches about loving our neighbors without condition. Nowhere does the Bible tell believers to love their neighbors only if they agree with us. Nor does it direct Christians to love their neighbors only if they spend personal time together. I had anticipated some passionate confrontation with a Wiccan soldier, SGT Taylor, but that never happened beyond theological disagreement. SPC Shamach, a Jewish soldier, and I frequently spent time together in a maintenance section of the motor pool while he worked on vehicles. One day I brought him a Jewish copy of the Torah and he, in turn, showed me Scriptures from the Psalms tattooed on his arms. Not long after, SPC Shamach was injured and had to be evacuated to the United States.

By an invitation from the mechanics, I often helped repair vehicles. While unbolting motors, transmissions, and rear ends, we discussed God. They frequently revealed, "Sir, you are some kind of different chaplain. Thanks for hanging out with us."

I usually responded, "No problem. I like hanging out with you guys. When are you coming to my chapel services? You know I don't work for free."

We would all break out in laughter. The truth was, with the horrible conditions of the roads and the constant plating and replating of armor on our vehicles, time for the mechanics and other support personnel to come to my services was scarce. Visiting these soldiers was my way of bringing God to them.

# SERVICE

As the support soldiers operated in their specialized areas of service for the sake of our mission, I was reminded of the role of servanthood in the Holy Bible. Jesus said that He came to serve, not to be served and this attitude was personified among this group of tireless warriors who worked hard, not expecting reward or recognition. The Fox soldiers simply did their jobs for the many warriors scattered throughout the Triangle of Death who depended on them. It was my privilege to serve them.

As I fought each day to retain some sense of personal humanity, the Fox soldiers always helped me to find it. Their love for one another was evident and once led me to think, "I hope I can somehow reflect their love for life and the kind of attitude in which things aren't taken too seriously." It was this perspective that God used to help get me through the worst of times.

Throughout my combat experience, I often found creative means of honoring fallen service and support soldiers. One way was attaching personal themes based on their occupations to the messages in their memorial ceremonies. The EOD teams were brave, and I remembered and recognized them for that bravery. The cooks were hard working servants, as seen by their efforts in the sweltering heat of our field-expedient chow halls, so I commended them for their brand of servanthood. The brave, self-sacrificing troops of Fox Company, the BSB, and the BSTB were among the most courageous, hard-working, and service-oriented warriors I had ever known.

It was, in fact, that appreciation I felt for my troops that always made it so difficult to see them suffer. But it was amidst their daily struggles in the Triangle of Death that each element of my battalion paid its own personal price for freedom. It was a cost that would become more expensive and more painful than we could have ever imagined. At that very moment, militant forces, mixed in with the local populace, gathered within Qarghuli Village. There, they planned something so great in magnitude that it could only be described as a nightmare; one that would change both me and the war in Iraq forever.

# 12

# DUSTWUN:
# A NIGHTMARE
# IN BABYLON

s long as I live, I will never forget the dreadful summer of 2007. It was
an intense time when my worst fears became haunting realities. It was
not enough that our task force had traveled across the world to defend the
Babylonian farmlands without support from the region's people. It was
not enough that the overall war in Iraq had sunk to record levels of political unpopularity. It was not even enough knowing that the number of
American casualties had reached an unprecedented high. Now, the fragile
Iraqi government decided to take a seasonal and highly controversial vaca-
tion, while America's president, George W. Bush, tried to sell a "New Way
Forward" to the people at home. The plan would surge forces by nearly
20,000 personnel and increase their tours from twelve to fifteen grueling
months. But compared to what would happen that summer, those things
were easy.

As the soldiers of Task Force Polar Bear continued hunting Al-Qaeda,
our men significantly reduced the enemy's areas of operations and avenues for
escape. The daily offensive operations pulverized the enemy's hope of an American demise or withdrawal. Al-Qaeda's failing supporters could only breathe

with gasps of desperation. Gradually their momentum of an unstoppable insurgency ran out of fuel. As a consequence, Al-Qaeda grew more desperate, recalibrating their terror with more advanced guerilla warfare tactics.

Meanwhile, back inside the menacing neighborhoods of Qarghuli Village, life consisted of a maddening game of psychological warfare between the locals and the Americans. For the residents, life seemed advantageous or fearful, depending on whose side they were on. If they sided with us, they prospered materially yet lived in fear of Al-Qaeda. If the locals sided with the enemy, they knew they were playing Russian roulette with us. But somehow they managed to carry on with their lives.

Throughout the bloody summer, I continued cycling through the sector with the tankers, visiting troops at all the battlefield positions. During these stays, I began sensing a palpable unease, even fear, among the men. Whispers of a looming enemy kidnapping began circulating through the ranks of the Delta Company soldiers who were based in Qarghuli Village.

Kidnapping has always been, and will remain, a potential threat in combat. This was especially true in our situation, with an enemy who was skilled in both torture and political statements. Further, with approximately 1,000 soldiers scattered throughout the Triangle of Death, usually occupying small, isolated outposts, we posed a potential target for a strong-enough enemy force.

So great was my concern, I brought it up to Polar Bear 6 during a battlefield update briefing.

"Sir, you know that I never bring things up as issues unless they are of the utmost urgency. When I say this, I hope that I don't come across as critical of Delta Company. I am deeply concerned about the possibility of a kidnapping on Route Malibu. I've spent a lot of time with the guys there, and almost every one of them feel that the daisy-chain IED incident that happened awhile back [one in which eight, 155mm IEDs; multiple rocket-propelled grenades; and machine guns were used against a four-vehicle convoy] was a failed attempt at getting some of our guys. Many of the men said that they had been entrapped with the disabled vehicles by an organized force and as they [Delta soldiers] tried to gain control of the situation, they were forced to move into a nearby house. Some felt as though five more minutes of the attack and the bad guys would have overrun them. The helicopter gunships that showed up that night saved the men from disaster."

The room became deathly silent.

His eyes widening, Polar Bear 6 asked, "What do you think, Chaplain? Do you really think this might happen?"

"Sir, again, I would never bring an issue up here unless I absolutely felt it was critical. No one can predict the future, but I would agree with the men. I think the daisy-chain attack was an attempted overrun, and I also believe they will try to hit us again, and maybe even kidnap someone. I think it's just a matter of time."

The intelligence officer cut in, addressing the colonel. "Sir, the report we received from Delta after that attack was that their vehicles had tires blown out and the situation was well under control."

I replied, "I got my information directly from the men in the attack."

Turning to the intelligence officer, Polar Bear 6 asked, "How do you explain it? What do you have to say?"

He responded, "Drama, Sir. Guys get excited and they get dramatic."

Not willing to let this pass, I pressed on. "Sir, SSG Tony Smith, an NCO from Delta Company's 4th Platoon, took charge and maneuvered the teams out of the kill zone [which subsequently earned him a Bronze Star with Valor] and into a house. Every last one of the men involved in the attack has told me that this saved them from being overrun. Would they have had to take a house if they were not in trouble?"

LTC Infanti placed his head in his hands, at odds with the conflicting information.

The meeting eventually ended, and as everyone sifted out of the old building, I ran into one of Delta's soldiers. He had been one of the men involved in the daisy-chain attack so I asked him to tell me again what had happened the night of the ambush.

"Okay, Sir. We were struck by seven or eight IEDs chained together along the road. As they went off, we began taking machine gun fire and rockets from every direction. There were lots of men on the rooftops of nearby houses, behind trees, and in the fields moving in on us. I just can't believe we lived through it."

As I walked away a few minutes later, I felt sure on two things. One, I was more convinced that an ambush would happen and second, I trusted that my commanders would do everything possible to prevent it.

In response to my voiced concern, the battalion commander ordered the elements in the area to prepare for such an attack. He had one specific platoon, near where the likely attack might happen, abandon their fortified position and move to a safe position a few hundred meters southward on the opposite side of the road.

Combat made me feel as though we were playing an ultra-high risk game of chess. It was one in which men were the pawns of fate and the battlefield was the playing board. I had complete confidence in my leaders—they were morally solid and tactically brilliant—yet I knew the enemy could be incredibly effective at their devilish game of guerilla-warfare tactics, especially when desperate.

Sometime later, on 11 May, 2007, our worst nightmare approached. Most of the Qarghuli community had strong sympathetic ties to Sunni insurgents in the area. While the village carried on with their normal lives, an extremely well-organized group of terrorists (some related to the villagers) finalized the plans for a complex attack to take place the next day. It would be one of the enemy's most lethal attempts at cutting the knees out from under the 10th Mountain in the division's history.

The morning of 12 May, 2007, arrived and with it a highly organized team of Sunni terrorists belonging to Al-Qaeda. A large portion of the covert group reportedly came from outside the Triangle of Death because the terrorists in it were unable to successfully pull off a kidnapping mission. Covertly moving through the predawn darkness, the terrorists forewarned their supporters in the village that the "big one" was in motion. Months of complex planning would soon reap great rewards for those waging jihad against the Americans. A vision of Al-Qaeda tyranny was about to manifest itself into a grisly wave of reality.

# THE NIGHTMARE

*12 May, 2007*

I was visiting the men of the 2-69 Armor at the Water Treatment Facility. It was there, on 12 May, 2007, that the war changed for me.

I had spent the week with the soldiers as they kept a close eye on Qarghuli Village. From the fortified windows of the abandoned buildings inside the compound, we watched the neighborhoods until late into the evening, finally switching guard shifts and going to sleep. At 5:30 a.m. I was in a deep slumber on a hand-built wooden bunk bed when noises, specifically yelling, startled me.

Some of the troops from the Bravo Company Panther element were shouting to one another.

"I don't care! Just grab your stuff and let's go, now!"

I pulled the makeshift blanket-my camouflaged poncho liner-over my head. I noticed a lack of movement from the many men resting nearby as well, and concluded, "It's probably just an NCO yelling at a soldier for doing something stupid." The slack trooper probably forgot his gear for some task, or maybe showed up late for sentry duty.

But something began to weigh on my mind. I sat up wondering whether or not the issue downstairs was an emergency. On the other hand, nobody had come for me and the men near me had no reaction.

Unable to sleep, I climbed off of the plywood board that I had slept on, donned my uniform, and then walked down the massive corridor of concrete stairs and outside to the "pee pipes" (waist-high, PVC pipes anchored deep into the ground and used for urinals).

Then, I conducted my daily ritual of shaving in front of a broken automobile mirror, which usually rested on a stick, and eventually brushed my teeth. It was a ritual performed by American soldiers throughout Iraq each day, a rite of passage for those who awoke on the front lines of combat.

When I finished getting cleaned up for the day, 1LT Joseph Tomasello, Delta Company's 4th platoon leader, approached me as I headed back to the Water Treatment Facility's main building. With a deadly serious look on his face, he asked, "Hey, Sir, are you aware of what's going on?"

"No. What's wrong?"

His reply shocked me. "One of our positions was overrun a little bit ago. Right now the battalion believes that five men at the site are dead and three are missing, possibly even captured. We're getting reports every few minutes and I'll let you know of any updates. As we speak, Commando 6 is on his way and he's bringing some investigators and military police dog teams with him."

"Do you know exactly which men were attacked?"

"Yeah, it was Delta's 1st Platoon."

Although it took a minute, I mentally ticked off the men: SFC James Connell; SGT Anthony Shober; PFC Joseph Anzack, Jr.; PFC Christopher Murphy; PFC Daniel Courneya; PV2 Byron Fouty; and SPC Alex Jimenez. I didn't know the eighth man at that point, an Iraqi *jundi* (the Iraqi name for a private) named Saaba Barak Shahatay, was with the team.

## ROUTE MALIBU

*4:30 a.m., 12 MAY, 2007*

All eight of the men had been awakened by the QRF leader during the late hours of the evening to conduct their mandatory pre-combat vehicle and weapons inspections before leaving BP 153 for the crater over-watch mission. It would require them to position the two vehicles facing away from each other on Route Malibu in order to protect the road from insurgents who might emplace IEDs.

During the night, the team loaded their two armored humvees with ammunition, water, and fuel. They ventured out the perimeter and down the road to the location where they would sit silently. Several hours into their watch, around 4:30 a.m., the team had reported seeing a suspicious silhouette near the road about 300 meters away. They saw it with their night vision devices, but determined that it was likely a wild dog. No one will ever know whether or not the suspicious images were feral animals or enemy operatives.

The only certainty was that armed insurgents, using four teams consisting of possibly three to four men each, positioned IEDs on the north and south approaches of Route Malibu. The explosives were placed several hundred meters away from each vehicle to detour American quick-reaction forces.

At some point, another enemy team parked a small, white truck, behind a house that lay nearly fifty meters away from the road. It would serve as the getaway vehicle for a capture team. Numerous other teams also waited in the dark for their chance to take part in the carefully planned mission, including a camera team, a security over-watch team, a torture team, and even an early warning team whose job was to notify the locals of the ambush.

Another element was the wire-breaching team: the insurgents successfully penetrated five strands of razor wire in order to gain access to the humvees occupied by the soldiers. This attack element was able to approach without being seen, cut the wires, and create a pathway for the other attack teams to get to the vehicles.

Once the razor wire was breached, the enemy set up a security over-watch position behind each vehicle. This would allow them, from the soldier's blind spots, to shoot anyone trying to escape.

Once all teams were in position, members of the attack elements began lobbing Russian military hand grenades into the gunner's turrets of both vehicles. The explosions ripped through the night and pierced the dark neighborhood.

The ambush was now in full motion. Insurgent gunmen kept close attention on the small doors of the smoking humvees with their flashlight-wrapped AK-47s, shooting the only soldier who made it out, PFC Murphy. He managed to squeeze his trigger and place several shots into one of the insurgents, seriously wounding him.

Despite his near-fatal wounds, Murphy mustered his energy and ran to get away, but was surrounded and forced to fight hand-to-hand. He swung his bloodied fists, striking his opponents until he was able to escape, but was caught moments later and killed. The insurgents placed his lifeless body near the road and booby-trapped it with explosives.

On the heels of the initial attack came an onslaught of satchel charges (homemade explosives stuffed into portable containers) that could best be described as overkill. Someone in the village—reportedly relatives of its sheik—had carefully fabricated the satchel bombs. The insurgents dropped them into the gunner's turrets, then jumped off and took cover as the explosives produced a huge fireball that melted the vehicles into metal skeletons. The severely wounded Americans, already injured from the grenades, were trapped inside, burning alive.

The next phase of the ambush involved the capture of PFC Anzack, Jr.; PV2 Fouty; and SPC Jimenez. Trails of blood bore witness to the three soldiers who had been taken from the vehicles and dragged along the road to a pre-positioned truck.

Except for the flickering pillars of fire and toxic smoke, debris on the road, and sporadic bursts of exploding ammunition leftover in the burning humvees, the road was now lifeless. Radio calls to the patrol went unanswered, "Delta One-Seven! Delta One-Seven! This is Delta Mike, over! We are requesting a SITREP [situation report] from you. We have elements throughout the area reporting gunshots and explosions near your location. What is your status, over?"

As radio traffic throughout the area overflowed with requests for reports, concern began to grow.

CPT John Gilbreth (Delta 6), Delta Company's commander, demanded immediate action. Members of his quick reaction force (QRF) piled into their vehicles, rolled out from BP Inchon, and drove south about 700 meters to the proximity of the ambush site. They were forced to stop short because of enemy-emplaced IEDs, visible in the middle of the road.

They called back, "Delta Mike, this is Delta QRF. We have two IEDs on the road and we can see two vehicles on fire at this time, over."

The QRF refused to wait. They dismounted and walked around the IEDs to the ambush site. The BP Inchon TOC (Tactical Operations Center) called, "Delta QRF, this is Delta Mike, over. We received your message that two vehicles are on fire at this time. Continue on with mission, we are contacting Polar Bear Mike [the battalion command center], over."

The QRF dismounted their vehicles and walked to the destroyed vehicles. There, they found the fragmented remains of the soldiers, footprints, expended bullet casings, and blood trails.

I recount the following, taken from a member of the QRF, "I found a helmet placed strangely in the middle of the road. It had a necklace and a St. Christopher's medallion tucked neatly inside of it." The enemy hadn't booby-trapped the helmet, but instead put a religious pendant from one of our soldiers in it."

The patrol began calling in. "Delta Mike, this is Delta QRF. The patrol conducting over-watch has been overrun and we may have some men missing, over." Without hesitation, Delta 6 called the 2-69's Panther element (the

Bradley Fighting Vehicles) for immediate security at the ambush site. It was their scrambling that awoke me that fateful morning.

By the time the two Panther vehicles from the Water Treatment Center arrived, the battalion had launched its EOD and crash-recovery teams into action for the clearance of the bloodied scene. I knew that I had two missions that needed to be conducted in the midst of the chaos. First, I decided to call battalion headquarters and let them know of my whereabouts so that they would know I wasn't in any of the ambushed humvees. Second, I needed to get to Delta Company's main battlefield position where most of its remaining soldiers would be. The ministry of suffering is important in that it bonds people during crisis. When people bond; they communicate more effectively. I believe this type of ministry helped the Polar Bear soldiers hang on to their faith and professional focus. In this case, both the ministry of presence and suffering would help my men through the most catastrophic event imaginable.

I walked into the command and control room at the Water Treatment Facility and saw the senior leaders of the Panthers and the Dealers: CPT Crary, 1SG Moslett, a couple of lieutenants, and SSG Skarhus discussing their response to the devastating ambush. Thinking about all the men who had been killed or captured brought deep, painful emotions to the surface, but I fought to hold them in. My grief was intense, but I held it in so that I could be strong for the others.

I stood silently in front of a motley collection of military radios with my helmet, body armor, and black glasses on. Everyone's attention seemed to be on me. I took a deep breath and collected my thoughts before calling my commanders back at the Yusufiyah TOC. I took the radio handset and called, "Polar Bear Mike, this is Polar Bear Chaplain, over."

The Polar Bear command center answered, "Go ahead Polar Bear Chaplain; this is Polar Bear Mike, over."

"I'm checking in and am going to move up to Delta Mike's position, maybe to the attack site, if it works with you, over."

"Polar Bear Chaplain, this is Polar Bear Mike. You have the go ahead but be careful, over."

I replied, "Roger. I appreciate it and will be available if you need me. Polar Bear Chaplain, out."

CPT Crary immediately stepped forward and offered his assistance. "I can get you on a ride up there. But to be honest with you, the brigade commander's convoy should be here shortly and it might be quicker to just jump in it. If that doesn't work, I'll make sure you get there."

Inside my soul I continued the fight between reason and anger. My mind bounced back and forth between wondering who had been captured and how we could make every villager pay for this heinous crime. My mind filled with thoughts of retribution, including an all-out siege against the town. I believed that most of the residents knew of the ambush and failed to do anything about it. With these thoughts tumbling through my mind for nearly twenty minutes, I heard the rumble of vehicles outside; it was Commando 6's convoy pulling into the rural outpost.

By the grace of God, Commando 6's convoy had a couple extra seats and I was able to take one. I pulled a small bottle of anointing oil out of a flap on my body armor, dabbed some on my finger tip, and made a small cross on the seat in front of me.

"God, please grant me strength and wisdom as how to best help our troops," I prayed. "Please help them and also give the commanders wisdom in this mess. Lastly, Lord, please help us find our missing men. Amen!"

We carefully moved along the dangerous road, dodging IED craters, each one a miniature nightmare from the past. I gripped the front Velcro flaps on my body armor firmly and closed my eyes tight. Questions continued flashing though my head. "Was the ambush really over? Did the enemy have another trick up its collective sleeve? Would there be a secondary attack?"

Only a few things were certain at that point. The American commanders at every level in Iraq were sure to do everything possible to deal with the matter. But that effort was going to be more difficult than we could imagine because the incident had happened nearly an hour earlier and our investigative teams were just arriving from their near hour long trip from Baghdad. The perpetrators likely understood that Americans were going to be everywhere within hours, and therefore, began fleeing the area.

Finally, after about ten minutes of traveling, we approached the neighborhood where the ambush had occurred. Because of the IEDs that had been placed on the road during the attack, and the critical need for investigators to examine the scene for leads in finding our missing men, no vehicles other than those of the 2-69 and the EOD were allowed near the carnage.

Until investigators could arrive and scour the scene for vital clues that might lead to the whereabouts of our missing men, only authorized personnel were allowed. The two Bradley teams that were providing security, scanned the dangerous neighborhood with their absurdly powerful 25mm guns, protecting the now-sacred ground where the brave men had met their fates. Their secondary function of the Bradleys was to block any traffic on the one-lane deathtrap known as Malibu. It was clear that it was going to be a while before that section of the village was open to traffic, so I asked the driver in the brigade commander's convoy to drop me off at BP 152.

"That's too easy, Sir. We need somewhere to park anyway."

They halted the armored motorcade at BP 152, an outpost just south of the ambush site, maybe a little less than a quarter of a mile away. As the brigade team walked the rest of the way up the road to the site, I stayed with Delta's 2nd Platoon to begin helping them spiritually process the ordeal. By spending time with the soldiers, I hoped my presence would show them not only that the unit's leaders had not forgotten them, but that God hadn't either.

These were the comrades of the ambushed men, waiting to relieve them when their shift ended. As a small group of us stood around in a semi-circle, I prayed, "God, I ask for your healing in this tough time. Please help us find our men as soon as possible and also the wicked men that did this. Keep the rest of us safe and give us wisdom in making it through it all. Amen."

They said, "Thanks, Sir. We needed that."

Smiling through the grief, 1LT John Dudish, the platoon leader, yelled down to me from the position's rickety tower, "Hey, Chaplain! You need to come up and see this!"

I thought, "Oh great! What else could go wrong today?" Out loud, I said, "Hey man, I don't need any more surprises!"

When no response came forth, I sighed and hunched my way into the battered tower and climbed the frail ladder. When I reached the top, the lieutenant pointed out the small window toward the road.

The sight of the nearly half-mile-long, Iraqi army motorcade traveling toward us nearly knocked me off my feet. A small MITT team (Military Transition Team) walked in front of the armada of vehicles, guiding them through the neighborhoods. It was one of the most awesome sights I had ever seen in combat; knowing that the people who had tormented our battalion for many months were now in for their own difficulties.

The MITT convoy came to a stop almost in front of our encampment and the Shiite troops inside dismounted and began searching houses near the road. The mostly Sunni village, who had allowed killing and kidnapping to flourish, now looked fearful. Justice felt sweet as we watched the Iraqi soldiers search the village. Information regarding the missing Americans was critical and no stone would be left untouched in the search.

The Iraqi soldiers rounded up hundreds of villagers and assembled them near the congested road. Blindfolded and kept under close guard, the villagers trembled as they came to grips with the fact that their community's decision to attack and kidnap our men was nothing less than disastrous.

Considering that not even one individual in the community had opposed the attack, I thought, "Who's bad now? Who's scared now, Ali-Baba? Come fight us now. You're not so bad now, are you?"

The Iraqi soldiers had their own emotional frustrations to deal with. They were fully aware that one of their own had been mercilessly slaughtered and desecrated during the attack. The tide of the conflict had suddenly reversed, leaving those who had often maliciously grinned at us through the pungent smoke of IEDs, humbled and subdued.

I climbed back down from the tower to hear radios screeching information traffic to all elements in the area. "All listening stations, all listening stations. Fox recovery teams will be passing through the area shortly to pick up Delta's destroyed vehicles, over. Keep all traffic on nearby roads limited for them, over."

After Fox Company received orders from the battalion commander to recover the humvees involved in the attack, they sent a fleet of vehicles to the site: including two M984 HEMMTs (Heavy Expanded Mobility Tactical Truck which serve as wreckers and recovery vehicles). As their security convoy provided protection, the HEMMTs harnessed the burned hulks upright and onto their long-bed trailers. From there, they began their slow journey back to Yusufiyah, passing my location at BP 152. We could hear the rumbling of the 450-horsepower engines as they rolled along the road toward us. I rushed out and one soldier followed me to the edge of the road.

As they passed, I could see SGT Campbell, a mechanic from Fox Company, driving the lead truck. Wanting to revere the sacredness of the vehicles, which were essentially coffins, I promptly saluted, making eye contact with SGT Taylor and the other drivers as they passed by.

The soldier next to me rendered a salute with me.

Finally, after the last one was gone, I lowered my hand. I hoped that the crews of the trucks knew I was not only honoring the vehicles where the soldiers had drawn their last breaths, but the Fox teams also because of their effort at recovering the remains of the soldiers. Finally, after the last vehicle passed, we returned to the outpost's radio room to coordinate a ride to the incident site.

Within thirty minutes, a Delta Company patrol pulled up to BP 152 to get me. I cautiously walked out and stepped into a waiting truck. It only took about three minutes to reach the ambush site. As we stopped, the first thing I noticed were two large, black, burn spots on the ground, where the destroyed vehicles had once rested. I picked up an expended AK-47 shell casing—probably one used to shoot Murphy—from the ground. I wanted to remember the mind-boggling sacrifice the men had made. My stomach felt nauseous as I considered how the scattered debris and blood trails that littered the ground were the sole reminders of the soldiers I had once known.

I told the Delta convoy, "Alright, I've seen enough. Let's get to 153 so I can see the rest of our men."

# INCHON

We got back into our humvees which had been parked to the side of the road, and drove away. As I watched the ambush site fade away through the cracked window, I said a heartfelt prayer, "Lord, please help. This situation is definitely one of the worst I've ever faced, and the guys up at Delta Company's strongpoint are going to need lots of help. Grant our unit power from the Holy Spirit so that we can make it through this. Give our missing men help to survive until we find them, and please give me strength because I'm exhausted. Amen."

Concerned about the surviving platoon members, I asked a soldier in our humvee, "Do you know which 1st Platoon guys were supposed to be at the crater over-watch site but might have been left back with Delta's main element? Somebody probably had to have been bumped from the seating list because ten guys at the most would fill two vehicles. If they had nearly fifteen men in their platoon, and eight were involved, who were the ones left behind?"

He said, "Sir, I think SPC York and 1LT Spring-Glace didn't go. I'll have to get back with you on the others."

Although I spun through a list of possibilities in my head, it didn't matter because the Polar Bears were going to search for any team member the same. No effort would be spared in finding any member of the battalion or the criminals responsible for capturing or killing them.

We soon reached the perimeter of Inchon (BP 153). What had always been a relatively low-key place was now a swarming colony of life because of the immense search for the captured soldiers.

Incoming troops and their equipment increasingly filled the parking area. As I stepped out of the vehicle, I sighed and began walking to the place where I knew most of Delta's soldiers hung out, behind the large building.

I passed a couple of miniature palm trees and some wooden, soldier-crafted toilets which were located next to the fortress. As I rounded a corner of the house, I saw the handful of surviving 1st Platoon soldiers. As they spotted me they stopped their conversation and walked toward me. The one remaining Delta Soldier not there was conducting guard duty on the roof of the house.

One said, "We knew you would come for us, Sir. Is SGT Tennant with you?"

"I came here for you guys. SGT Tennant's on leave right now, but I know that if he wasn't, he wouldn't want to be anywhere else but with you. As for me, I plan on staying for as long as you need me too."

They soldiers led me to a place that was more private where we could talk. I listened as they spelled out their frustrations, feelings, and fears. It humbled me knowing that they had anticipated my arrival.

Eventually, the group dispersed. When they did, I'm proud to say that they had a bit more life back in them.

I dropped my assault pack off in the room where Captain Gilbreth (Delta 6) and 1SG Galeana (Delta 7) usually slept. Throughout the coming days and weeks, I took part in many dismounted patrols and vehicle convoy missions to show the troops that the leaders weren't going to shirk from their duties or break down in fear, avoiding the front lines. The only standard that was acceptable in my unit was for leaders to lead by example, and this applied spiritually to me since I was the point man of faith.

Knowing that it was necessary to demonstrate courage during this rocky period, I recognized that continuing to conduct raids, reconnaissance, and cache searches with Delta Company was the best way to do this. Stopping missions because of chaos and death was not an option. If anything, I perceived leadership as increasing one's presence on dangerous missions so that subordinates and peers could be encouraged.

I also accompanied miscellaneous teams of Polar Bears on missions such as "Operation Polar Charade." It was a prisoner-of-war, search-and-recovery mission. It was composed of exhausting foot patrols through dangerous fields, daring raids into staunch anti-American villages, and tiring efforts involving the clearing of filthy canals. The Scripture I often thought about at this time was Psalm 23, "Even though I walk through the darkest valley, I will fear no evil, for You are with me; Your rod and Your staff, they comfort me."

Between missions, I frequently wondered, "What is the enemy planning right now? Are there more attacks coming soon? Do I know all of the things necessary in case I find myself in one? What do I do if I'm with a team whose position faces an overrun? And finally, "How can I better manage myself, mentally, physically, and spiritually after traumatic ministry?" The effort to encourage the troops also involved an exhaustive re-examination of my own tactics for circulating the battlefield and security of my ministry team. It was clear to me that the battalion could simply not afford another nightmare, especially one involving their chaplain.

Despite the horror-filled month, God showed his faithfulness. Not only did He protect me in the midst of numerous firefights and IED attacks, but He also illuminated the hearts of my men with His awesome mercy and love for them. One great testimony involved a three-day stint at a tiny house designated as Battlefield Position 152. In my journal I wrote, "I had been visiting the various sub-outposts belonging to Delta Company for nearly a week when I was awakened at BP 152 by a soldier at 4:45 a.m. His quiet voice abruptly separated me from my dream and I sat up, stumbled off of my cot, and walked into another room with him so that we would not wake the other two men who were asleep in the room. We talked about his increasing fear of dying for almost forty-five minutes. Eventually, we both prayed a prayer of Christian confession and salvation for him. We continued talking about life, God, and fear until he was ready to go back to sleep.

Many soldiers besides him discussed with me their fears and frustrations concerning the DUSTWUN incident. I always reminded them, "It's okay to be scared and angry over tragic things; it's what you do with those things that really matters. You can dishonor our unit and our fallen heroes by giving up your hope or you can honor them by channeling your emotions into productive efforts." I also told them, "Fear doesn't mean that you're not a warrior; all warriors have some kinds of fears, but they are people who know how to bring those emotions under control."

Playing to worldwide media attention stoked by the ambush, terrorists released an Internet video stating, "What you are doing in searching for your soldiers will lead to nothing but exhaustion and headaches. Your soldiers are in our hands. If you want their safety, do not look for them."

That same morning, LTC Infanti arrived at BP 153 and stood outside the building. He talked to a journalist about the video demanding an end to the search and his commitment to finding the POWs and the terrorists behind their abductions. He said, "I will never stop searching for my men, ever! I will use every asset that I have and anything I can get my hands on to find them. They won't be able to stop me unless they kill me or the Army chooses to send me home."

The next day, he spoke to a mass of blindfolded detainees who sat on the ground at Inchon. "Your only option now is to fight the bad guys. Join us and fight for Iraq! I can't ever let this place be the way it was before the vicious attack on my men. Your leaders must make that decision, and they must make it this week. If you're with us, we will help you. If you're against us, we will bring everything we have to fight you for our missing men and a free Iraq."

From the day of the ambush, the Triangle of Death swelled with reinforcements. By the end of the week, over 4,000 personnel from around the country and the world arrived for the search. Despite a traumatizing mixture of round-the-clock operations and false leads which wore us down to exhaustion, the soldiers refused to stop searching until their missing brothers were found.

The coming weeks brought many pivotal events. On 23 May, PFC Anzack was found floating in the Euphrates River nearly fifteen miles south of the Triangle of Death. His lifeless body, riddled with bullets, was wrapped in plastic sheets. While heartbreaking to learn that he was dead, there was reassurance knowing he was no longer in the enemy's hands.

Less than a month later a second video declared, "Your soldiers are now dead because you would not stop looking for them."

I remained at BP 153 for nearly three weeks before my commanders requested my presence back at the battalion's main camp. Once there, I organized and conducted the memorial ceremony for all of the men who died in the catastrophe, except for the two still missing. The memorial ceremonies were typically required to fall within a week, but this one was an exception supported by general officers in Baghdad because of the DUST-WUN search efforts. The brigade chaplain called me and asked, "Do you want me to send an assistant since SGT Tennant is on leave?"

I said, "Sure, Sir, I'd like to have Boyd because we've worked well in the past, but the magnitude of this one probably demands an NCO."

He said, "Okay. I'll send SGT F. down to you as soon as possible. "

SGT F. arrived and I discussed with him the possibility that we might have to venture back out to the Qarghuli area to see the troops near where the ambush happened. I stressed the fact that it was probably safer than it had ever been, because of all the forces responding to the crisis.

He replied, "Sir, I would rather stay here and work on things for the ceremony."

"You know, I have already gathered the boots, the helmets, and even an AK-47 to honor the fallen Iraqi Jundi." I told SGT F., "All you need to do is gather some M-4 rifles and, if needed, go with me back out to Qarghuli Village and serve as my bodyguard."

Upon hearing this, he frowned and looked at the ground.

Coincidently, about twenty minutes later, a soldier came into the chapel tent, "Sir, the battalion commander wants you to go back out to Inchon. He has a convoy waiting outside that will roll out in about ten minutes."

I replied, "Okay, I need to grab my gear. Tell the colonel that I'm on my way."

I've never been one to appreciate leaders who throw their power around carelessly. I felt that I shouldn't have to, especially with a chaplain assistant. Back at the beginning of the deployment, I had told both Dusty and Steve that, rather than ordering them to accompany me, "I will simply leave you back at the main camp and go visit soldiers myself." Both had proven themselves loyal and professional many times over and I assumed that SGT F. would be the same.

We walked out of the chapel tent and headed towards the waiting convoy. But as I veered right toward the vehicles, SGT F. angled off to the left toward the battalion command center. My heart sunk because I shook my head in disbelief as I contemplated how I had failed to influence him in facing his fears. I had tried to lead from the front, by example, but was deeply disappointed over the fact that SGT F. was going to save himself and allow me to go alone. I thought, "I could have ordered him to go, but I don't want a bodyguard with me who has to do his job under threat."

He stopped, turned around, and said, "I'm scared to go, Sir. I have kids. I want to see them again one day. I'm going to go call my unit to come get me." I had stopped to hear him, but immediately continued my walk to the humvees, shaking my head in disappointment.

Rarely had I ever been as angry at a soldier as I was that day. However, I knew that with a thousand troops to care for, I didn't have any energy to spare for SGT F. I climbed into a humvee, prayed, and did what I looked forward to doing each day, visiting the brave warriors on the front lines.

Later that week when I returned to Yusufiyah, the brigade chaplain phoned. "Jeff, I think there's been a misunderstanding between you and SGT F."

I told him, "Sir, I mean this with no disrespect to you, but there's no mistake. SGT F. is a stinking coward and if he ever comes down here again, he and I will have some serious problems. Can you please send me Dusty?"

PFC (Dusty) Boyd showed up a couple of days later, with PFC Mobley from the 10th Mountain's BSB. Each one was so motivated about experiencing front-line ministry that I had to stop them from arguing about who was going to venture to the outposts with me.

I said, "Listen! I need one of you to stay here and gather some rifles while the other rides back out to Qarghuli Village with me. We'll flip a coin to see who will go." Mobley won. In the end, both men journeyed back and forth several times to minister to the soldiers and prepare for the memorial event.

As with my other memorial ceremonies, I was determined to provide the best possible service to honor our heroes. I was adamant with myself about the attention to detail. However, others outside our battalion failed in this regard. Those who have died should be given honest recognition; however, people in both the military and the civilian media often over-generalized the fallen soldiers' accounts into meaningless headlines.

Usually a soldier's official death was generically packaged on the nightly news as "another soldier dies while on patrol in Baghdad." This typical misleading code was found on the military's official obituary for Bravo Company's PFC Brian Browning. He had died from a sniper's bullet while manning a rooftop at an outpost. One of our medics, PFC "Doc" Rogers, a medic, also died on a rooftop while selflessly defending his comrades with a machine gun from a violent, attempted overrun on their outpost. Both men were noted by the Army as "being on patrol in Baghdad." I didn't generalize or neuter any of my comments in the ceremony. America's heroes deserved better than that.

Coincidentally, Steve returned from the United States the day of the ceremony. He quickly stepped in to help Boyd and Mobley prepare for the day's mission by repainting our memorial ceremony equipment, including a podium and several platforms used for staging boots, rifles, and helmets which represented the fallen. Seeing Steve boosted my morale and, with the three best chaplain assistants in the world, I conducted the momentous event. It was difficult to comprehend however, that my battalion was conducting a service for six men; and possibly several others who were still missing. It was overwhelming when we had just two or three casualties at one time.

At the conclusion of the ceremony, I stood quietly to the side. As the chaplain, my job was to narrate the service and that job was over. With too much experience under my belt from memorializing over twenty fallen warriors since the start of the deployment, I remained at the position of attention as soldiers filed by to pay their silent, final respects to their fallen comrades.

As soon as the ceremony was over, Boyd and Mobley were called back to Baghdad. Steve and I picked up where we had left off: almost immediately, I coordinated a convoy and we traveled to some outposts to talk with soldiers about coping with the 12 May tragedy. On Steve's part, he had heard of the ambush while on leave and couldn't get back quick enough to minister to his comrades.

The 250 lb. biker from Ohio endlessly encouraged the warriors of the Polar Bear battalion, especially through his presence, words, and actions. There was nowhere that he would not go for our soldiers and no effort he wouldn't expend for them.

The weeks following the memorial ceremony consisted of hundreds of convoy patrols, raids, searches, and dismounted operations. Steve and I took part in many of them and witnessed the incredible array of assets, support, and detainees swelling the interior of each of our battlefield positions. BP 153 had bloated from about 30 men to over 400 in one week. Both American and Iraqi troops slept wherever they could find space. The ground; boxes of supplies; on top of, around, and under vehicles became temporary living quarters for the men. Other resources, including bathrooms, water, and food were stretched thin. The Iraqis preferred defecating on the ground rather than in our hand-crafted toilets and it caused much dissension. However this seemed minor in comparison to what our captured men might be enduring. We resolved ourselves to act with professionalism. Thus far, we had survived the most devastating punches the enemy could possibly throw at us.

But some of my fears shifted directions.

Nearly a month and a half passed after the deadly ambush. The crowd at Inchon, which had swelled to several hundred (4,000 across the entire Triangle of Death), began to shrink. This was much appreciated by Delta Company at Inchon. At one point, 1SG Galeana, the senior NCO of Delta, told me, "We just want our house back, Sir. Before all these people came, it was just us, and after the attack, they are everywhere. We appreciate their help but we liked it the way it was before."

As he said it, I thought, "If all of our help leaves town, the locals are going to hold a pretty big grudge against us for locking the city down. There will probably be retaliation like we've never seen before."

Little by little, the excess numbers of troops dwindled each day until only three or four outsiders were left at the Inchon outpost. Again, I wondered whether or not life would go back to the way it was: Everybody was pretty much gone; would the remaining guys be in danger?

I wasn't alone in my musings; many of the men scattered throughout Qarghuli Village felt the same.

If the villagers had not liked us before, they had reason to be twice as angry now. We had taken over their town and detained nearly every adult male in the city, in the hope of finding our captured soldiers.

After nearly two months, Steve and I were the only two outsiders left at Delta Company's main position. Among the departed elements were the mechanized armor teams. They had not just been moved away from the Qarghuli area, but from the overall sector. Their main unit near Baghdad wanted them back, and as the surge in forces brought calm to the sector, it was deemed by the military that their services were no longer necessary.

The sector was now considered safe enough that it could be turned over to Iraqi forces as part of the post-DUSTWUN restructuring plan and the services of the mechanized men were reportedly needed elsewhere.

As I looked around at the seemingly dead outpost, one which had flourished with life just weeks before, a tear rolled down my face. I was flooded with the magnitude of what that had taken place over the past month and the fact that the men at the center of it were nowhere to be found. Steve stood silently by as I knelt down and gently sifted a handful of dirt through my fingers. I reflected back on all the people that had passed over it and the many lessons I had learned.

I lived and continue to live with the indescribable pain and frustration of that nightmare. Although our men were still unaccounted for, I learned how faith and spiritual empowerment could bring someone through the worst trials. I thought of Daniel in the Bible, who was ironically imprisoned in this same Babylonian land and thrown into a lion's den. I recalled his courage as he trusted God while facing his nightmare. Both of us were normal men facing challenges that bore razor-sharp teeth. Like Daniel, I also sensed God's protection upon me as I struggled for survival.

Another important lesson I learned from the experience involved military tactics. Historically, militaries have succeeded or failed based on their flexibility. An army's ability to adjust to challenges in the face of battle often determines the outcome more than their weapons. I had seen the battle-hardened troops of the 10th Mountain Division successfully do this in the heat of the 2007 DUSTWUN. Now, Task Force Polar Bear was left with two major missions: finding our men and seizing control of the most important structure in the southern belt of Baghdad, the Yusufiyah Russian Thermal Power Plant, also known as "The Dragon."

For now, I had to come to grips with the fact that the ambush, the monstrous buildup of troops, and the disheartening stand-down of forces were things of the past. Although it would not be my last visit to BP 153, leaving was terribly difficult because I knew that this departure would signify an emotional end to an event that would change the war in Iraq. My experiences involved two months of intense, exhausting ministry, almost all of which took place at Inchon and its Delta satellite positions. However, I could no longer afford to stay; by doing so I would fail to serve the rest of my soldiers who were scattered throughout the Triangle of Death.

Safety for our remaining soldiers was a deep concern of mine. A departure would mean that they might face the indignation of the locals alone. My prayer was, "Lord, please protect these guys while I cycle the sector again. The rest of the soldiers need us, so please protect these guys until Steve and I return. Amen"

Dust clouds blew slowly across the silent, abandoned yard that had once served as a large, fortified parking lot. I stood next to my conveyance and rested my hand on the weighty door of the humvee. I glanced around one last time before stepping up. Our vehicles left an immense wake of dust behind as we maneuvered past a rusty barrier composed of metal poles, old barbed wire, and ragged sandbags. After we made our way out of the courtyard, we drove onto the treacherous Route Malibu, quickly and cautiously rolling southward through the village. On the way, we passed two large, blackened spots on the surface of the road; appalling reminders of fear, death, destruction, and the horrifying reality of war.

# 13

# TAMING THE DRAGON: THE 10TH MOUNTAIN DIVISION'S MARCH TO THE POWER PLANT

Following the horrific attack against the eight Americans in May, the Polar Bear soldiers stayed on course with their number one priority: finding the missing men and those responsible for the attack. However, any realistic hope of locating them rested on whether or not the task force would be able to increase stability throughout the problematic region. Prolonged search and rescue missions require substantial security. If the enemy was allowed even an inch of space in which to find refuge, it would exploit that advantage and jeopardize any mission to find our men. The 10th Mountain Division knew that to achieve stability and find our missing soldiers, it would need to seize the Yusufiyah power plant, or "The Dragon."

The power plant was a political landmark reportedly worth three hundred million dollars. Symbolizing a bygone era, one dominated by Saddam Hussein, it was also the one obstacle standing in the way of finding our men, stabilizing the area, and going home.

## EXAMINING THE OBJECTIVE

The decision to take the large Yusufiyah power plant was made by commanders at many levels between the Triangle of Death and Washington. While staging for the mission, the 10th Mountain commanders briefed their units on the operation. In those meetings, they discussed many issues, such as the risk of insurgents determined to defend the massive fortification and the likelihood of hidden IEDs throughout its enormous perimeter.

In one meeting, the digital projector's dim light painted eerie images of the nearly mile-long concrete walls that surrounded the Dragon, and the numerous dark corridors within it. The images on the wall reflected what seemed to be a total absence of humanity, except for a small element of 10th Mountain Division soldiers who served as an advance element. I tried to grasp the fact that we would soon attempt to seize and secure the entire complex.

I had seen the several-hundred-foot-tall smokestack from outpost rooftops throughout the sector. In the past, various units had conducted raids on the massive facility. Unfortunately, all had suffered heavy casualties to the point of overfilling helicopters. Nevertheless, their efforts were not in vain. Despite the toll, the units had successfully routed the enemy, thereby effectively destroying one of the largest VBIED (Vehicle-Bourne Improvised Explosive Device) factories in the country. A handful of men from the 10th Mountain Division's 2-14 Infantry had successfully moved into one section of the plant's main building in October of 2006, but miles of construction yards within the interior remained untouched. The 2-14 soldiers served as an advance set of eyes and ears for Task Force Polar Bear. If any enemy remained, we would clear them out and transform the power plant into our most important base of operations inside the war-torn province.

Polar Bear 6 made it clear after the DUSTWUN, that other than finding the missing soldiers, "The Dragon" was the most critical objective; both in taking this land back from insurgents and one day giving it back to the Iraqi people who rightfully deserve it. The risk involved with the mission was on everyone's mind, but by the end of the briefing, our unit was ready to move out and take the Dragon. Nearly 800 soldiers of the 1200-man task force waited for the radio call to begin.

Along the roads that surrounded Patrol Base, Yusufiyah and the parking areas within it, a long armada of semi-tractor trucks, humvees, and tanks idled bumper-to-bumper, waiting for go-ahead. Each vehicle was loaded to capacity with equipment, supplies, and personnel.

Polar Bear 6 directed Steve and me to depart at the onset of the mission. We would travel to an outpost located in the mid-area of the sector, in case an emergency. If one did arise, the ministry team would be located halfway to it from any direction. Steve and I found a humvee with two seats available and waited with the crew. We sat with heavy boxes of ammunition and food on our laps while we listened to the vehicle's radio. With one word, we would race across the Triangle of Death, seize the massive Russian power plant, establish a new base from which to control the recovery operations aimed at finding our missing men, and control the area once and for all. Anyone foolish enough to stand in our way was sure to die.

Finally, the call came from the task force's radios. "All listening elements, all listening elements. This is Polar Bear Mike (the task force command center), over. We are a go at this time! I repeat, we are a go at this time. Confirmation is needed from each commander immediately! Polar Bear Mike, out!"

The time to send a crushing blow to the enemy was at hand and the once unimaginable idea of putting men in the final stronghold of the Triangle of Death was now a reality. Aircraft filled with soldiers lifted into the sky as vehicles began pouring out of the rural base.

The convoy Steve and I rode in rushed through the dangerous farmland, bouncing with every pot hole and IED crater in the road. I was jarred so intensely that the top of my helmet slammed into the ceiling. I peered through the bulletproof window, being careful not to place my head too close to it. I knew that an IED explosion could instantly cause my head to become one with the reinforced glass. Because we were never allowed to lower the ridiculously heavy windows, the heat swelled inside, turning the vehicle's interior into a sauna. I knew it was for our own safety so I quickly turned my attention to the road, scanning for threats.

After nearly twenty minutes of the fast-paced, jarring ride, we slowed to a crawl and eventually stopped on the one lane road. Refocusing my attention on the road ahead, I wondered what the trouble was. What I saw next shocked me. Passing within only inches of my window was the largest convoy of American support vehicles I had ever seen. Our halt had been for the sake of the traffic coming from the other direction. The convoy had driven into our area from Baghdad and stretched at least two miles. Like an army of ants, they systematically poured into our sector to support the missions of finding our missing men and establishing operations at the Dragon. The roar of their engines reminded me of a thunderstorm as I watched them pass by on the shoulder.

Not only were such convoys on back roads rare, but the outrageous amount of supplies that they carried overhanging the tops of the vehicles, was amazing. Small wooden buildings, sky-high pallets of water, combat bulldozers, generators, wood for construction, fuel, food, piles of razor wire, tires and everything else imaginable passed by my window for close-up viewing.

"This is the most fascinating parade I have ever seen," I thought. "I wish all of our men who had died could see this." I felt a surge of appreciation as I considered this show of support for our battalion's mission, a tasking for which so many had given their lives. I felt a new sense of gratitude for other soldiers in the brigade, many of whom I thought did not care about the deadly battles we were waging in areas they would never see. Instead of outsiders, they now were comrades.

With the surge of troops, I sensed that the enemy's remaining hope for victory in the Triangle of Death was waning. Defeat, in the form of reinforcements and American determination, was sweeping over their land like an unstoppable storm. Although we were still on insurgent turf and the 4,000 troops for the DUSTWUN had left, we were not alone. The convoys traveling in from Baghdad were signs that the other elements of the 10th Mountain's 2nd Brigade were coming to reinforce our efforts.

However, my optimistic contemplation began to be tempered with concern.

I turned to Steve and yelled, "It would be far too easy for the bad guys to ambush us here, right now. There's no room for our trucks to turn around. It's the perfect time and place for them to hit us."

On the other hand, the enemy would be risking everything if they attacked us. There were simply so many American forces at that location, at that time, that any attempt to hurt or hinder us would bring the wrath of a brigade-strong force. I glanced back through the dirty little window and prayed, "Lord, you've gotten me through too much to let me die here. Please protect all of us on the roads today. Amen." Using the sleeve of my dusty uniform, I wiped the sweat from my face and sank silently back into the seat.

The original plan was to reach a small outpost within an hour, but the busy traffic transformed the ride into an all-day event. Unable to do anything other than sit on the road and wait, we baked inside the vehicle, our energy dwindling in the soporific heat. I watched through the window as the unforgiving sun punished the tropical farmlands and baked the countless piles of trash laying everywhere. Finally, after several more hours, my prayer was answered when our driver revved up the engine and carefully edged the vehicle back onto the center of the road. The convoy dropped Steve and me off at BP 147, near the village of Al Taraq, before continuing their way to the Dragon.

While visiting with the soldiers, I told them about the incredible caravan of support vehicles pouring into our area. As I told them, the men were encouraged by the news of the other 10th Mountain battalions coming to us from Baghdad. The enormous show of force aimed at seizing the power plant was reassuring because it demonstrated that the enemy's days of tyranny were nearing an end. After spending a few hours with the men at the BP, I used a radio to request a ride back to Yusufiyah. Once there, we boarded a UH-60 Black Hawk helicopter and flew into the heart of the Babylonian darkness: the Dragon.

## LANDING INSIDE

Charlie Company was the first element to officially set foot inside the power plant that evening. Armed with .50 caliber machine guns and fully automatic 40mm grenade launchers, they methodically swarmed in to secure the gargantuan perimeter and create a landing zone for the helicopters to bring in the remaining task force.

The Charlie soldiers cleared the area by searching throughout the night for enemy personnel who might have remained. They linked up with the Golden Dragon troops of the 2-14 Infantry and eventually confirmed that no insurgents were present. Within an hour of this confirmation, aircraft began swarming into the huge facility.

Late that night, a UH-60 Black Hawk flew to where I was located in the sector and flew me and Steve to the power plant. As we slammed into the ground, an immense cloud of dirt enveloped the large, roaring machine. It kicked up more dust as we quickly offloaded. As the aircraft ascended back into the dark heavens, it left me feeling as though I had just landed on the moon.

The lonely trek from the landing zone to the Dragon's main building was nearly half a mile. I told one of the six soldiers walking near me, "I can't believe the size of this place. If I didn't know the aircraft had dropped us off inside the place, I wouldn't actually believe I was in it."

We made our way into an abandoned building which had become pre-occupied by the initial force. There, after the massive fortress was officially safe, men found space to sleep. Steve and I spent the next few days sleeping on cold, concrete floors throughout the complex. Throughout the week, riflemen and supply soldiers continued moving vehicles and supplies in and out in a fashion that reminded me of a racetrack.

## SEARCHING

I spent the next few weeks with Charlie Company as they prepared the power plant for the arrival of the remaining task force. Steve and I walked through miles of barren construction yards, dozens of empty buildings, and countless lots filled with old vehicles. Amid the graveyard of equipment lay corpses of dump trucks and tractor trailers. Cranes stood silently as their sagging booms slowly lost their battle with gravity.

As we surveyed the huge construction yard, the wind blew thick clouds of dust over us. To pass the time, we peered through windows of abandoned trucks, scoured thousands of documents left scattered around, and investigated interesting pieces of construction machinery. Like detectives, we left no stone unturned and picked up a few souvenirs such as discarded spoons, tea cups, old ceramic plates, a stapler from a Russian office trailer, and several handkerchiefs. The relics would commemorate our time at the Dragon.

The more we searched the massive structure, the spookier it became. With almost every footstep, I wondered about the rumors I began hearing from soldiers about Iraqi people who had reportedly been brought to the power plant and eventually disappeared. Was it because they had opposed Saddam Hussein or Al-Qaeda? I also thought about the three 101st Airborne DUSTWUN soldiers who had been captured and brought to it in 2006.

On another day, while Steve and I searched the construction yards within the facility, I discovered a burned Camelback (a backpack-style of canteen often used by American forces) half-buried in the sand. I picked it up and guessed that it was old, particularly since it was tan, an obsolete color rarely issued to American forces anymore. I turned it in to someone in my unit who worked with evidence in the search for our men. He wrapped it in an evidence baggie and sent it to Baghdad for DNA analysis. I never found out whether or not the canteen belonged to the Screaming Eagles who had been captured before our deployment, but it had belonged to some American who was no longer around. That was enough evidence for me to believe that it was worth checking out.

By the end of the month, most of the task force who were going to move in had done so. With the transition came a significant increase of patrols and raids that caused the sector to come under a respectable state of calm. When we weren't with the troops on missions, Steve and I continued exploring the monstrous Dragon. Besides the eerie buildings and vehicles scattered throughout the vast construction yard, the absence of people gave me the creeps.

On one exploratory hike, we saw two massive steel beams protruding from the ground, reminding me of the twisted debris at New York City's Ground Zero. I began feeling as though death were following me throughout the large compound. When I passed by a large pile of dirt, I would wonder if it was a grave. The bag we discovered that contained someone's glasses, clothes, and shoes-did it belong to an Al Qaeda victim?

I also pondered the outcome of the people who had once occupied the colossal structure of steel. Asking around, I received varied answers regarding the fate of the Russian workers.

Some said, "They came to hate Saddam at some point and simply returned to Russia."

Others told me, "Saddam had them all killed."

Still others reported, "Saddam stopped paying the Russian government in 1991 during Operation Desert Storm and they left."

"The terrorists overran the Russians working on the construction during the 2003 invasion and forced the workers to leave."

Whatever happened to them, the architectural riddle they left behind became an insurgent stronghold, a fortress in which the fires of civil war were started. The only certainty surrounding the Russians was that they had lived in a sectioned area of the compound known as the "Russian Worker Village," near the main gate at the front entrance.

The Russians and the insurgents left most of the Dragon either thoroughly destroyed or utterly untouched. There was little that was in-between. Steve and I walked through one group of small buildings and noticed tables still covered with Russian paperwork, coffee cups, worker's hats, pencils, and pens. The rooms looked as if someone had stepped out only for a brief moment. Everything was perfectly in place.

However, a second group of buildings told a completely different story. Blood-spattered walls and ceilings had been peppered by machine gun bullets. We stepped over piles of clutter and broken furniture. In one place we saw a pair of shoes resting next to a pool of dried blood.

Some of the more disturbing portions of the camp looked as if a militant force had ransacked them with explosions. One day, Steve and I crawled over some mangled barbed wire that surrounded a collection of small, mysterious buildings. Once inside the encampment, we walked by an abandoned guard tower overlooking a knee-high yard of ashes.

I told Steve, "I have a grisly feeling about this place. What's all of this burned stuff? Maybe they held prisoners of some kind in this place. Maybe they burned them."

"Maybe so, Sir," he replied. "I bet the insurgents used it to house real important ones, too."

The area was filled with charred sidewalks, burned buildings, chairs, bunk beds, singed file cabinets, homemade tripods for machine-guns, and expended machine-gun shell casings. Sunlight poured through collapsed rooftops that had been crushed inward, possibly from aircraft ordnance.

After we left the mysterious yard that resembled a prisoner holding area, we made our way back out and into the larger construction yards. We came across another strange item, a large bamboo cage, about 6 feet by 8 feet in size. It was hidden between two trailers and concealed with large pieces of scrap metal and tin roofing material. The miniature holding cell was covered with piles of palm tree branches, possibly as camouflage so as to appear like a pile of branches. The cage was tied together with steel wires, which crisscrossed bamboo shoots, possibly to hold something with considerable power in it. Inside was a dirt floor, covered with human feces, and the remnants of an American MRE (an American military food ration). I always wondered whether or not the small cage had once held American prisoners. After reporting the haunting findings, we left the Dragon to visit our outposts.

## CONTINUING TO SUFFER

On 17 July, 2007, Steve and I returned from a three-day sojourn to the outposts to find that one of our men had been killed. In my journal I wrote, "SGT Nathan Barnes from Charlie Company was killed today by enemy gunfire as his UH-60 Black Hawk helicopter tried to land for a raid. The team he was with was seeking high-priority enemy leaders. SPC Smith, who was with Barnes's team in the aircraft, was also wounded by gunfire. Now, I am working on preparations for Nathan's memorial ceremony at our new home, Patrol Base, Dragon."

I thought about the lesson Polar Bear 6 had taught us earlier in the deployment. "In combat, it ain't over until it's over! Until you get on the aircraft for the flight home, you're still in the combat zone." This simple yet brutal truth had been a staple in my mind, reminding me that the nature of war was terrible, and the only escape from it was a post-victory flight home. It was a good thing that I had remembered it because 18 August brought another deeply painful tragedy that God would have to help me through.

While walking around Patrol Base, Dragon, I strolled into the battalion

TOC. A lieutenant asked, "Hey, Chaplain, can you answer an e-mail that was addressed to you but sent to me?

I replied in the affirmative and asked to use his computer since it had Internet capability.

Sitting down, I logged into my Army e-mail account and quickly ascertained the message that needed to be retrieved. Opening the e-mail, my heart sank.

"Sir, it's the 2-69 Armor here. As you remember, we were moved out of your area and back to Rustamiyah. We are requesting your presence for a memorial ceremony for 1LT Jonathan Edds. He was recently killed when his vehicle was ambushed. Although we understand that you are not our unit's official chaplain, coordination has been conducted with him and our commanders so that you may do the event. All the men in the platoon are asking for you to conduct the memorial ceremony. Again, they are asking for you. Please respond as soon as possible."

Our XO, was already aware of the e-mail regarding Jonathan's death, because the person who had talked with me had also spoken with him at some point. When I went to the major's office, it was clear he already knew what I would ask. It was also clear that his answer would be no.

Although hard to hear, I understood the XO's decision. He did not want our unit to appear intrusive toward another unit and its business.

The Dealer's chaplain was capable of conducting the service and he was with them. If I conducted the service, it would make him look bad. Distance was another factor. Major Manns (PB5) believed that if I were to travel several hours away and our unit faced an emergency, it would take too long to get me back.

Although not what I wanted to hear, it was his decision and I would respect it. I e-mailed the soldier who had sent the e-mail from the 2-69 Armor and told him I couldn't come. Within fifteen minutes he requested me once more. My heart bottomed out as I had to write yet again and tell him, "I'm sorry! My commanders won't allow me to visit you for the ceremony. I would do it for you in a heartbeat if possible. Tell all of the Dealers I send my heartfelt condolences."

It was a great honor to be asked by the Men of Steel to conduct the solemn service. They always told me how much I had blessed them, but they were wrong. I was the one blessed to be called their chaplain.

Trying to hold my emotions in, I made my way out of the office and searched for Steve. I eventually found him and said, "Hey man, we need to go somewhere private to talk about something real important."

Steve said, "Is everything all right, Sir?"

I responded, "I'll tell you in a second. Just give me a moment."

He could see the pain in my eyes; it was clear to him that something was bitterly wrong. We eventually found a private place near the top floor of the power plant.

I began, "Remember 1LT Edds?

"Sure, Sir."

"He was killed in an ambush yesterday."

As I said it we both broke down and I covered my face with my hands. We had all bonded on the tank patrols and had come to recognize 1LT Edds as one of the most outstanding gentlemen we knew, a Christian man with strong moral and spiritual convictions. After a few hours of talking about the times we had together, we discussed what had and would continue to bring us the most comfort: God's faithfulness, our families, and our close confidence in each other.

## THE FINAL ROUND

After processing the grief and continuing on with our daily duties as a chaplain team, Steve and I increasingly realized over the course of the next few months that the exhilarating experience of on-the-edge combat ministry seemed a thing of the past. More control over the sector meant less enemy presence in the area. Those who remained rarely attacked us as we forcefully continued our search for the missing Polar Bears, PV2 Fouty and SPC Jimenez.

Our battalion did, however, succeed at establishing a battlefield position on the opposite side of the Euphrates River during the final two months of our deployment. With the sector nearly at peace, most missions to the outposts, including the newly-established Euphrates position, were quiet visits rather than daring adventures. The soldiers wanted to fight the enemy but were left with observation duties most of the time. I walked the farmlands with the troops as they continued to conduct search and rescue operations, but information concerning the whereabouts of SPC Jimenez and PV2 Fouty was difficult to gain from Iraqis. Most of the information obtained from locals proved either erroneous or intentionally misleading.

The final few months of the deployment crept by, bringing us closer to returning home. It was during this time that I began to realize just how much of a challenge that departure would be. Leaving the war zone would bring an end to the fifteen months of traumatizing, full-throttle combat, but it would also begin a new battle. I had spent more than a year expending my physical, mental, and spiritual capacities so that I could fulfill my duties in a place considered nightmarish by the troops sent before us. Many of the soldiers I had cared for so deeply had bled and died here. As far as I was concerned, leaving would be tantamount to abandoning them. In leaving the real battlefield, I would have to step onto another one: my mind.

I had struggled for my emotional, spiritual, and psychological survival and now it looked as though I would continue to do so beyond the battlefield. Even though I looked forward to returning home, having fulfilled my mission, I was indifferent about going on with the rest of my life. Everything I had worked so diligently to learn about survival in combat would soon amount to nothing. All the risks taken, the countless relationships developed, and the unbearable pain I faced would soon be left behind. The fragility of life, the volatility of combat, and the excitement of fulfilled purpose were uniquely tied to the battlefield.

What good would any of these be in a life without war?

# 14

# RECALL: PREPARING TO LEAVE THE TRIANGLE OF DEATH

As I prepared myself to bridge the unforgiving relationship between war and peace, I felt lifeless inside. I had considered myself a reasonably easygoing guy, but the steady grind of violence in combat had altered me into a hardened man. Each morning, I would wake up and wonder why I had so many questions about myself. I wondered how I would go about readjusting to the United States when, for the last fifteen months, I had risked my life to acclimate to Iraq.

I wondered if a connection could still be made between people back home and me. They would not understand the pain of my experiences. With the exception of my wife, the warriors serving around me were the only community with whom I felt comfortable. The numbness that had overtaken my soul was something of a sacred badge bestowed upon me while desperately risking my life for the Polar Bear soldiers on the bloodied fields of battle.

What I would have once considered impossible, I had survived. Now my reward was to spend the rest of my life fighting the memories in the dark, lonely trenches of my mind. My conformity to the chaos could be reflected in the words of the famous Russian novelist, Fyodor Mikhailovich Dostoevski. "Is there suffering on this new earth? On our earth we can truly love only with suffering and through suffering! We know not how to love otherwise. We know no other love. I want suffering in order to love."[1]

I had managed to adapt to the most horrible environment in the world: war. After learning to live daily with bombings, gunfights, stillness, missing comrades, now a new battle waged in my heart. I needed to regain my humanity and find my normal self. It was unsettling to recognize this blunting of my senses. I remember telling Steve, "I hope we survive this hellhole because I want you to know that, if God ever gives me back my humanity, you'll see I'm a normal guy who loves God and cares about people."

For now, smiling and laughing were only relics from the past, replaced by thoughts of dying insurgents and personal survival. I knew that spilling the enemy's blood was appalling, but from my vantage point it meant overcoming evil and increasing the odds that my men and I would live another day. Such things haunted me because I knew God would never want me to be controlled by hate.

I asked the Lord, "What am I supposed to do with all of this war stuff in my head?" The fear, the excitement, the death, and the sacredness of being His agent sometimes caused my emotions to dramatically rise and fall. All that I had hoped for, I had seen come to pass. Now, all I wanted was to wake up from the nightmarish deployment and regain my sense of self. It was clear to me that if I had any chance, God was that hope.

## SITTING BY THE EUPHRATES

One day I sat next to a half-destroyed portion of the Dragon's concrete perimeter wall that contoured the marshy banks of the Euphrates River. The barrier was situated in a field of bright green vegetation near the edge of the rear perimeter, isolated from the activity at the large patrol base.

I rested against the wall and contemplated the words I had just read from my Bible. I scribbled it in my journal: "Psalm 137—By the rivers of Babylon we sat and wept. There on the poplars we hung our harps, for there our cap-

---

1   Fyodor Mikhailovich Dostoevski, *Dream of a Ridiculous Man* http://www.fyodordostoevsky.com/quotes/bookquotes.html.

tors asked us for songs…How can we sing the songs of the Lord while in a foreign land?"

The psalmist sat next to the same river, thousands of years earlier, and meditated on his own dilemma, involving life, death, separation, isolation, terror, peace, and injustice. Watching the quick, yet quiet current, I wondered about the patriarchs who had journeyed along the famous waterway. I began to feel less like I had been forgotten by God and more as though I had been specially called to go to a sacred land where America's heroes fought and would continue to fight. The undefeatable power of God's love pierced my anguish, my fear, and my trauma, helping me to want to make it another day.

I knew that war was not going to stop its merciless rampage on my senses. Although weary, I knew, deep in the cold depths of my soul, that God had helped me make it through everything thus far. His love was an anchor that had girded me during the stormy trials of war. I also knew that with His help, I could not only expect to make it through the rest of the deployment, but also beyond.

As I rested that afternoon near the Euphrates, I scribbled the words of Jesus in my journal: "I am the Good Shepherd. I lay my life down for my sheep." Although the turbulent experiences of pain and suffering had left me feeling forsaken by God, I knew that He had not. God had ordained me to minister to soldiers. He knew exactly where I was. And He knew precisely what I was going through. The fifteen months of front-line pastoral ministry was not punishment, instead, it was a divinely guided service to American troops, a ministry of presence that meant going wherever they went. With the difficult challenge of enduring, I realized that more than anything else, my personal faith in Jesus Christ, which had gotten me through war so far, would see me through the effects of post-combat life as well.

As I sat there, my thoughts turned to our POWs. "Where are our missing men? Why haven't we found them? Are we going to be forced to leave without them?" Although the troops showed no hint of easing their search for the missing soldiers, they were tired from the ongoing frustration. The war had dealt its damage and continued to demand every ounce of energy from a hard-pressed battalion fighting against the clock of redeployment back to the States.

Even though it was relatively quiet in the sector, the threat of attack was ever present. After the 12 May ambush, the enemy had either fled the area, been killed, or were laying low as evidenced by the decrease in attacks. However, assaults still occurred and as they did, they reinforced the wisdom of Polar Bear 6, "The combat zone is still the combat zone, regardless of how quiet it is." An incident involving the 2-14 Infantry underlined this.

SGT Travis Atkins had been with a small team over-watching a road when a group of Iraqi men approached them. Atkins walked to the men in order to check them out and quickly realized that they were wearing suicide bomb vests under their clothing. As one of the Iraqis reached to detonate his explosives, SGT Atkins tackled him. The ensuing explosion killed them both.

Chaplain (CPT) Kent Coffey, the 2-14 chaplain, called me from Baghdad. "Can you visit my guys? We had another casualty here at the same time SGT Atkins was killed. I could use some help with my guys down there. They need someone to help them cope after the incident."

The request from my friend would not require me to travel more than a couple of miles to be with his unit's men and was something I earnestly desired to do. "I'll be happy to do it. You guys are like brothers to us and helping you during this tragedy is the least I can do." I visited SGT Atkins's team over the next week, helping them get through the tragic loss of their brave hero.

## AWARDS

Upon my return from the four-day excursion to console the Golden Dragons, my unit conducted an awards ceremony at Patrol Base, Dragon. They held one nearly every week of the deployment, no matter where the battalion was located. Although I had been involved in at least twenty-something engagements with the enemy, my duties required me to circulate the tropical Euphrates River Valley and thus was unable to attend most events. I happened to be at Patrol Base, Dragon one day and observed the preparations for one award ceremony when someone said, "Chaplain, you need to be in the formation today; you're getting an award. I think it's from a firefight earlier in the deployment."

Surprised, I quietly walked to the rear of the formation. After presenting the ranks in front of me with their awards, Polar Bear 6 and Polar Bear 7 approached me. I saluted the battalion commander, and returning the gesture, he said, "I have a real combat chaplain." He followed the statement by adding something that meant more than any award. "You can never understand what your efforts mean to me." I was humbled because I knew that the soldiers in front of me honestly deserved all of the accolades. My reward was being their chaplain.

## EXTENSION

Sometime during our final two months in theatre, rumors began circulating among soldiers that the Army was going to extend the deployment of its forces out by another few months. The Army did, by three months. I told Steve, "It's been real tough, but our guys can handle an extra three months. If the Army is crazy enough to do it again, however, they can expect the morale of the troops to do a serious nose-dive." I also thought that if American troops were going to repeatedly be ordered to stay, with deployments becoming two years or more, mutiny would certainly brake out across Iraq.

Apparently, the fuss of a second extension circulated so quickly around the country, that the commanding general of the coalition forces in Iraq sent every unit in theatre a personally verified statement stating that a second extension was not going to happen.

In his letter, the general wrote, "To the troops throughout Iraq, who have been extended for the fifteen months, you will see no further extensions." I felt that since he had personally endorsed the statement, things were likely going to be okay.

## THE NPR INTERVIEW – 13 OCTOBER, 2007

Over the next couple of weeks, preparations to return to the United States picked up speed. Planning for everyone's flights and the logistics of packing consumed each day. One morning, Steve and I were awakened by a loud knock on door of the recently erected Polar Bear Chapel. Steve and I staggered sluggishly off of our cots to answer. Tom Bowman, a journalist from National Public Radio (NPR) had been interviewing members of Task Force Polar Bear about the DUSTWUN soldiers and their morale after the extension.

I never figured out whom, but someone advised Bowman that I would be a good person with whom to talk. Beginning the interview, Bowman asked, "Chaplain Bryan, how are the men doing after the ambush?"

I found that journalists usually came in two flavors: either they're out for a story to support the military or they want to undermine its efforts. In just a few minutes with him, Tom Bowman seemed to belong to the former group. I offered him a seat; he sat back and prepared his recording equipment on a small table. I politely responded to his lineup of pre-planned questions.

"What kind of relationship did you have with Jimenez and Fouty?"

I responded, "I knew every one of the eight guys in the ambush pretty well, with the exception of Barak Shahatay, the Iraqi soldier."

We went back and forth for nearly two hours, all the while my tattered nerves warring with my weary brain. Warning signals flashed inside me, but I ignored them. I felt strongly that the American public needed to hear exactly what soldiers on the front lines felt. The radio program *All Things Considered* sent Tom all the way to Iraq, and its audience—the American people—deserved the truth. Besides that, shouldn't a chaplain be honest? Nothing I was going to say involved classified information of any kind, so at worst, listeners might disagree with me.

Or so I thought.

I wanted to provide Americans back home an honest-to-goodness perspective on the war. Tom asked me my opinion of the Iraqi people.

I said that in my opinion, most of them are liars, cheats, or thieves. I have no doubts that an average Iraqi would take five dollars to kill me or any other American. The good-hearted people of Iraq, especially those in the Triangle of Death, still have not rallied behind us to find Fouty or Jimenez. We have sacrificed irreplaceable amounts of time, energy, and money in the search only to be given heaps of faulty information by local nationals. If there were good in them, they would fight their own fight and we wouldn't have to.

As we neared the end of the interview, he asked, "Is there anything else you would like to add?

I answered, "Yes, a couple of things. Someone, Abraham Lincoln I believe, once said that people who are not willing to fight for their freedom, or who deny it to others, don't deserve their own freedom. I think we should consider this wisdom when we examine the role of the Iraqi people in this war. Six months passed before I saw even one Iraqi soldier do something as simple as filling a sandbag. How many of them have died for our troops? The other thing I would like to say is that the American military will never quit looking for Fouty and Jimenez." Shortly thereafter, I thanked Tom for allowing me to share my thoughts with the American public.

He said, "Thank you, Chaplain Bryan."

Within a week of the interview, a handful of people from the battalion expressed unease about it, including my executive officer. "Jeff, Polar Bear 6 mentioned to me that he heard the NPR interview and was upset over some of the comments you made. He said that you must really hate the Iraqi people. Is that true? Do you hate Iraqis? I told him that you were just upset and didn't hate them. Do you, Jeff?"

I replied, "Sir, I don't want to hate anyone, but it's true. I have a lot of anger towards them because the deaths of our soldiers. It tears me up when I think of how the local nationals could have intervened so many times and didn't. Many of these folks have been players in the deaths of our guys, and that's a fact that I am going to have to work through for awhile. They haven't taken the lead in anything, including our search for Fouty and Jimenez. I just don't want anything to do with them, except for maybe the Iraqi Army, and trusting them is a risk that may yet end up getting us killed."

The commander walked away in silence and my stomach immediately began stirring with stress at the possibility of a fractured relationship with the battalion commanders, especially after we had worked so well together for so long. I felt a headache coming on as I asked myself, "How in the heck do I end up in some of the frustrating situations that I do?" I headed toward the main building that housed our command and control center. As I walked across the dark, dusty field, I hoped I might salvage the relationship between me and the commanders. Once I arrived, I found the executive officer and asked him if I could again speak to him. He accepted my apology over the controversy that had been caused with the interview.

He said, "You know, Jeff, there are some good Iraqis. We just never hear about them or the countless ones who die each day fighting alongside our forces around the country. I appreciate you coming back up to talk about it. Polar Bear 6 and I also appreciate your hard work."

With that, we smiled at each other and said goodnight.

By the end of the next week, many opinions about my interview drifted though the unit. Some felt I had disrespected the people of Iraq by stating that the overwhelming majority of them I had dealt with were untrustworthy. Others believed I had forfeited my military bearing by providing any personal opinion. Many agreed with my frustrations and told me what I had said was right. Right or wrong, I was honest.

## SAYING GOODBYE TO STEVE

*15-25 October, 2007*

During the closing month of the deployment, small teams of soldiers began making their way back to the United States. Because the chaplain team's ministry in Iraq was approaching an end, I asked the 31st Infantry commanders for permission to send Steve home with one of the initial manifests. He had exceeded any expectations I had of him for over a year and I wanted to show my appreciation by placing him on an end-of-deployment flight home as soon as possible.

Steve and I sat outside the chapel at Dragon underneath a large, overhanging, camouflaged canopy and held our last discussion in theatre. I said, "Hey man, let's go for a walk."

"Sure, Sir."

We walked away and stood near a dirt mound that separated the chapel from a giant smokestack I'd nicknamed the Tower of Babel. We spoke about his final few hours in the country. Because we had been together for so long, I had difficulty grasping that he would leave the next day. After what seemed like a lifetime of close and faithful comradeship, the time to part was at hand.

"This feels like a graduation, kind of bittersweet," I told Steve. "During graduation, everyone is always happy to see each other, but sad to face the departure because it signifies separation and a life without them."

It would be challenging for me because he was not only my bodyguard, but also my friend and confidant. We had only been separated on the battlefield a few times. I hated to be without my comrade for even a few minutes, but the good side was that it signified an end to our time in the Triangle of Death. Steve, like every other warrior in the battalion, had more than earned his trip home.

Before Steve's flight the next day, I was called away to visit outposts #162 and #165. I hurried back from the brief visit, still hoping to celebrate Steve's departure and tell him goodbye. We had saved two Sobe energy drinks that Tanisha had mailed in a care package months earlier for our final day in the war zone.

When I made it back to the chapel, I found an empty Sobe bottle on a table, marking Steve's lone celebration.

He was gone.

# INTRODUCING THE RAKKASANS

The fight was pretty much over for the task force except for the ongoing DUSTWUN search, which would continue until the very day that the last troops boarded the aircraft for home. While managing to balance the search for our missing soldiers and preparations to leave Iraq, CH-47 helicopters filled with men from the 3rd Battalion, 187th Infantry began arriving at the Dragon.

I watched each day as our replacements ferried into the large patrol base. It reminded me of the beginning of our deployment back at Patrol Base, Mahmudiyah. Uniforms adorned with patches of Screaming Eagles began appearing more each day as the 101st Airborne Division ranks increased and those of the 10th Mountain tapered off.

The grunts that I had served alongside were now leaving for home. I watched long lines of them, exhausted from war, somberly make their way toward the noisy aircraft.

I sighed inwardly. "God, I am so grateful that another group of these great soldiers get to go home. Thank You for that."

One evening, I waited patiently on the landing zone with a team of air control guides, watching the sky and monitoring radios for the helicopters carrying the 3-187 chaplain team. On the flight were Chaplain John "Clark" Sneed and his special duty assignment NCO (a soldier providing chaplain assistant support in the absence of a chaplain assistant). Together, our religious support teams would swap the spiritual baton of ministry.

When Task Force Polar Bear initially landed back in the fall of 2006, the outgoing 2nd Battalion, 502nd Infantry passed along vital information regarding life and operations in the sector. Although the reports were disconcerting to take in, hearing the unvarnished reality was important because it painted an honest image of what we would face. It was my hope that the 3-187 unit ministry team would also have an opportunity to learn, succeed, and survive through the hard-earned knowledge that I and the Polar Bears would pass on.

The new ministry team and I maneuvered our way around the dark, concrete hallways of the Dragon to the chapel, and reclined in some old, beat-up aluminum chairs. I wanted to immediately set them up for success by describing the style of ministry that worked well in this area of Iraq. It was a model that placed the chaplain and his assistant second to soldiers and demonstrated a steady faith in God.

I told them, "Faith in God always pays off on the battlefield," and "Never forget that ministry here is always about the soldiers."

Late into the night, we discussed life inside the Triangle of Death. I quickly realized that Clark was an incredibly smart guy and my respect for him grew as I learned of his love for his family and his unit. I had acquired quite a bit of practical knowledge about our portion of the combat zone after nearly fifteen months in it, and he allowed me to share as much of it as possible.

We talked about our personal lives, laughs, and loyalties late into the evening, highlighting ministry within the turbulent environment. Although I sensed that it was unnerving for him to hear about my experiences, I felt that anyone who was willing to take on this ministry deserved nothing less than the truth, regardless of how unsettling it might be. His safety was my first priority—because I would be crushed if anything happened to him. Some people hesitate to pass information along to others when that information risks their personal reputation. For me it was uncomplicated. I would rather have somebody perceive me as dogmatic or overly passionate when discussing threats than to have him or her die due to a lack of knowledge.

Clark and I quickly bonded because we sensed in each other a likeability, trust, sincerity, and respect. I also saw a growing sense of respect for our enemy. He concurred when I told him that the insurgents were intelligent, incredibly patient, endlessly adaptive, and thoroughly efficient in almost everything they did.

The next morning, I had an opportunity to show my support for Chaplain Sneed by briefing his unit's commanders on the importance of chaplain ministry in combat. I shared some heartfelt stories with them, including my relationship with SGT Chris Messer, the routine visits to the men who were later captured, and my constant presence with wounded Polar Bears. They deserved brutal honesty and it was what I was going to give them. Their lives could depend on it. At the end of the briefing, I said, "Gentlemen, this has been my case to you in hopes that you will support Chaplain Sneed and allow him to be on the front lines with your soldiers. Thank you for allowing me to brief you today, and may God bless you."

## CONDUCTING MY LAST MISSION IN THE TRIANGLE OF DEATH

The next day came, and with it the necessary mission of cycling the battlefield with the 101st chaplain team. It was an emotional experience for me as I would say goodbye to the locations I had known so well, where so much of my life had been invested, and where so many heroes had sacrificed their lives.

After hours of escorting Chaplain Sneed and his assistant around to the various battlefield positions, we returned to the Dragon. To decompress, we watched movies on a computer laptop until 2:30 a.m.

We were all ridiculously tired throughout the next day, but seeing that no other missions remained for me other than packing for the trip home and leaving, I spent the afternoon cleaning, organizing, and handing over the wide assortment of equipment I had collected throughout the fifteen month deployment. Lastly, I organized my personal gear for the last time, saying to the Lord as I did, "I can't believe I lived to see this day. There are so many men that deserve this more than me. Thank you for your mercies on me and never let those men be forgotten. Amen."

After weeks of tiring preparations for a handover of operations, everything was complete and I waited for my flight. I decided to walk through the offices at Dragon, now mostly filled with Screaming Eagles, one last time. Making my way through the small hallways of the soldier-crafted operations center, I saw my battalion executive officer. I had always wanted to tell him how much his support of my ministry meant to me, but chose not to because I didn't want to appear to be a brown-noser. However, as our efforts in the Triangle of Death were drawing to a close, I decided now was a good time to show my appreciation.

I said, "Hey, Sir, do you have a minute?"

"Sure, Chaplain. What's going on?"

"Well, Sir, I just wanted to let you know that I appreciate all of the support you've shown SGT Tennant and me throughout the deployment. Any credit to us as a successful chaplain team rightfully belongs to you."

He sat back in his chair and said, "I appreciate it. You guys deserve the credit because you both earned it."

I was finally able to express my profound thankfulness for his incredible leadership. He, along with Polar Bear 6, had allowed me to spend a great amount of time with the men at the battlefield positions. Had I walked away from combat without telling him, I would have committed a great disservice to him, and I would have regretted it for the rest of my life.

I walked back to the chapel that evening and sat on my cot. I was filled with gratitude for the fact that I was alive after combat. Now the most important person whom I needed to thank was Christ, for working all things out for my good.

Later, after making final preparations to leave, I replayed the last fifteen months in my mind. I pulled out my journal and wrote, "Today I called

Tanisha and said that my journey home would begin soon. Also, I was able to talk with Polar Bear 5 about my gratefulness for his leadership."

Clark came in at one point and sat down on Steve's old cot. He observed my journals and said, "That's really cool. How long have you been writing in them?"

"Practically as long as I can remember. I brought two blank journals with me to Iraq and have almost filled them both with notes." I eventually placed the leather books back in my bag and pulled out a photo of Tanisha to share. We looked at pictures of our families and said, "You're an answer to my prayers, Clark."

He smiled and asked, "How?"

"Every day throughout the fifteen months, I asked God to send an exceptional chaplain after me and he did."

He laughed. "Are you serious?"

"I am! I did not want a half-baked, half-hearted, half-stepping chaplain that doesn't care about anybody but himself. I'm blessed to know a guy like you, but I am doubly blessed knowing a guy like you is carrying on the mission after me. Your unit is *really* blessed to have you as their chaplain."

He shook his head in disbelief, proving my point about his humbleness. Shortly after he departed the chapel, I wrote in my journal: "This is my last night of Operation Iraqi Freedom, 2006-2007. I want You to know, Lord, that I love You and am grateful for Your goodness. You have been faithful to me in indescribable ways, not only by allowing me to live to see this day, but also in that You have given me the opportunity to write it all down so others might one day read about it. Please help me to never forget all that You have done for my men and me."

Following a few hours of sleep, I grabbed all of my gear, stepped out of the chapel, and looked back one last time. Storing the memory, I turned and made my way to the interior atrium of the Dragon for a flight manifest check. Once there, I dropped everything on the ground next to a small group of soldiers also waiting to leave. Sitting down next to my gear, my thoughts drifted to my beautiful wife back home. It was there Chaplain Sneed found me, to say a last farewell.

"I want you to know that I feel like I've known you for years, brother.

Thanks for your hard work here. I think you and your men really deserve this flight."

"You know, I feel the same. I hope we get to see each other back in the States someday."

In such a short time, we had become as close as brothers.

Once the night shrouded the land in darkness, we received the signal to prepare to leave. The group of waiting men and I walked to the aircraft landing zone. We sat quietly off to the side, shivering against the chilly night air. I considered the moments, knowing that they were my last ones in Iraq. One soldier, lying nearby, next to his bags, tried to read a small paperback book with a miniature flashlight. Everyone else sat silently.

## THE LAST POLAR BEARS TO LEAVE
## THE TRIANGLE OF DEATH

A soldier broke the silence. "Hey, I think I hear some aircraft in the distance."

We all sat still, listening. Then another person yelled, "Pick your gear up! The birds are inbound!"

Sure enough, the blacked out (meaning all lights are turned off) aircraft could be heard tearing through the black sky. They came whooshing in out of nowhere, churning up clouds of dust and debris as if a tornado had touched down within a few feet of us.

We all jumped up and made a single-file line. We began running toward the helicopters as their rotors screamed. Sporadic bursts of machine-gun fire echoed around the perimeter of the patrol base.

Even though it was chilly outside, sweat ran down my face as I hustled to the dim, green lighting of the CH-47 Chinook's ramp. My legs nearly buckled under the weight of my gear: two duffel bags, one rucksack, an assault pack, and my heavy ceramic body armor. I tried to move faster as the gear flopped around, but my body succumbed to the overwhelming weight, and my run quickly became a fast walk.

I prayed for the Screaming Eagles, "God, please keep them safe and strike fear into the enemy tonight. Amen!"

Almost at the helicopter, I glanced back at the dark landing zone one last time. In those final few seconds, I felt both sadness and pleasure. My heart was deeply relieved to be hustling in the direction of freedom, but it was also filled with anguish as I remembered the many men who deserved to go home, but would not do so alive.

Reaching the ramp of the aircraft, I stepped onto it, and turned around to regard the dim lights twinkling in the dark horizon. With a deep breath, I pivoted and shuffled into the interior. After helping others pile their gear in the center of the aircraft, I sat down in a hanging net seat, closed my eyes, and took another deep breath.

After the crew counted everyone, the massive machine shuddered and then gradually took off. I reopened my eyes and looked toward the semi-closed ramp as the faint lights of Patrol Base, Dragon grew steadily dimmer. It was only then, as the Triangle of Death disappeared into darkness, that I grasped that I was actually on my way home.

With a deep sigh, I re-wiped the sweat from my brow and sat back against the aircraft's interior wall. I remembered the many courageous men who had given their lives in this land. I choked up for a moment. I didn't know whether to celebrate or grieve. We had fought so hard, for so long, that to experience such a moment was overwhelming.

Perhaps this is what President Ronald Reagan felt during his final address to the American people on January 11, 1989. "We've done our part. And as I walk off into the city streets, a final word to the men and women of the Reagan revolution, the men and women across America who, for eight years, did the work that brought America back. My friends, we did it. We weren't just marking time. We made a difference. We made the city stronger. We made the city freer, and we left her in good hands. All in all, not bad. Not bad at all."[1]

And it was not a bad job! Our unit had fought with all its might, facing prolonged confrontations with chaos, day-to-day bouts with danger, and moment-by-moment misery. The task force had effectively organized "Concerned Local Citizens" (groups of Iraqi civilians trained by Americans to fight insurgents) and successfully equipped and trained an Iraqi military battalion of nearly 800 men. With the blessing of God, American soldiers

---

1  *Ronald Reagan: An American Hero*, (New York: DK Publishing, Inc., 2001), 249.

had reconfigured their lives toward the hope of one day transforming the "unchangeable" and "uncontrollable" Babylonian Triangle of Death into a place where freedom and peace would flourish.

Against what many Americans and Iraqis considered insurmountable odds, the 10th Mountain Division overcame the impossible.

# 15

# THE ROAD HOME

A s we ascended out of the Dragon and began racing through the dark sky to avoid being shot down by enemy gunfire, I prayed, "Lord, I can't believe I've lived to see this moment. I'm finally on my way home."

I glanced around the inside of the helicopter at my fellow soldiers resting in their seats and the vigilant crew chiefs keeping watch out of their small windows. About twenty minutes after the flight started, the CH-47 Chinook's tiny wheels slammed down firmly onto the cold, hard pavement of a desolate Baghdad airfield.

We piled out, re-oriented ourselves and our gear, and closely followed one another to a corner of an airfield. There we waited for nearly two hours for a vehicle to pick us up. The redundant pattern of "hurry up and wait" for our transportation reminded me of the uncomfortable trip to Iraq 15 months earlier. Finally, the buses arrived and drove us to Camp Striker, a small American base comprised of several tented neighborhoods, several miles away. While there, we were told, "These tents are your home for the next three days. Relax and enjoy yourselves."

After the first risk-free night of sleep in over a year, I awoke to a bright morning and enjoyed breakfast at Commando Café, the camp chow hall. The challenge now was to believe that leisure was a real thing. As I consumed my food, my mind drifted back to the men who had not lived to make the final flight out of Patrol Base, Dragon. They should have been here to enjoy the entertainment: gyms, movie theatres, pizza cafes, hamburger restaurants, even the comfortable bathrooms with ceramic toilet seats. Eating proved difficult as I contemplated the things my fallen brothers would never see or do again.

After breakfast, I wandered around the new base and found an MWR (Morale, Welfare, and Recreation) entertainment tent. Housed within were games, snacks, countless shelves of movies, and soldiers enjoying them all. I remembered having no electricity, lights, heat, air-conditioning, or even a chapel for many months. Memories of using baby wipes or bottled water to clean my body for almost the entire tour reminded me of how rough it could be. Now the toughest thing I had to do was decide which kiosk to shop at or what form of entertainment from which to partake.

Later, I took some men from my unit to the entertainment tent to watch some movies on a large screen television. I sat wondering whether or not the soldiers playing Ping-Pong nearby had ever ventured out of the large American base. Sitting back in a recliner, I spoke to God in my heart. "Lord, I can't believe that I'm alive and enjoying these things. It doesn't seem real." The combat I had left behind was something found in movies, video games, and now in my memories.

Before heading back to the tent where I would sleep, I returned to Commando Café for dinner. While there, I saw SFC Eric M. Talken, an NCO who had served as my squad leader in the 506th Infantry in Korea 14 years earlier. We recognized each other instantly.

"How the heck are you?" I asked.

He replied, "Good, Sir! How about you? Are you coming or going?"

"My unit just came out of the Triangle of Death. That's about twenty miles southwest of here. Now were heading home."

We made some small talk about old times and then eventually went our separate ways.

I thought, "Maybe life outside of hell really is possible."

By 2 November, 2007, we had been at Camp Striker for three days. The static visit reminded me of the film *Castaway*. In it, Tom Hanks played a successful businessman who survives a terrible airplane crash only to face a life-and-death struggle on a remote island. When he returns to civilization many years later, he feels completely out of place. Basic things, which he had fought so hard to find and keep on the island, were instantly available, with little or no appreciation for them by the people surrounding him. Life for the castaway suddenly seemed pointless.

Life at Camp Striker felt that way. For many of its inhabitants, life revolved around shopping, eating, and walking. I heard many permanently assigned soldiers complain each day about the limited selection of pizza restaurants, coffee shops, hamburger kiosks, and amusement trailers offered to them. In Commando Café, troops murmured about the terrible choices of ice cream available. I was not sure whether to laugh or cry at the ridiculousness of it. I was thankful for the camp's entertainment, but I missed the simple life that I had left behind in a small section of the world that felt a million miles away.

The Triangle of Death was a place where I had come to know the most dedicated and courageous people I had ever met. Regardless of whether they believed they were going to live or die, they lived life to the fullest and complained little. Although I treasured my newfound safety and freedom, I felt more out of place now than in the Triangle of Death. My time there was filled with purpose, focus, and appreciation for the few things we possessed. I had discovered a different lifestyle in the torment there, and now I missed it.

Despite countless opportunities for rest and recreation, I felt like an outsider at Camp Striker and was anticipating the flight home. The next day, we received the call from our commanders to prepare for that flight. As I sat with my men on an asphalt road near the airfield, a soldier from my unit approached me.

"Polar Bear 6 needs you, Sir. It's pretty important."

I hustled down the street where he was located and greeted him with a salute. "Sir, you called for me?"

"Hang on for a moment, Chaplain."

I had no idea what was happening, but my suspicions rested on the possibility that somebody had been killed.

"But who?" I wondered.

Hadn't all of the Polar Bears other than the few of us already left for the United States?

The person needing that care turned out to be a young lieutenant who was in our unit. She had flown into the large camp just days earlier. Strangely, one of her best friends was assigned to the Rakkasans and had been killed by an IED shortly after arriving in the Triangle of Death. Reportedly, the 101st had sent a team that included our lieutenants' friend, to reconnoiter an area. Her element was struck by an IED; the friend was killed and four others were wounded. It had been less than twenty-four hours since we left.

One of the wounded was Major Jones, the senior operation's officer of the unit. I had met him at chow during one of my last nights in the sector. In talking about the missing soldiers, Major Jones had this to say, "We will never stop looking for Fouty and Jimenez. They are American heroes and brothers to us. We promise that we'll never let the search end, Chaplain."

"Sir," I replied, "there's no guarantee they will ever be found, but knowing that you guys will keep looking means everything to us."

I was told by someone later that after the IED strike, he was evacuated by aircraft and lived.

Our lieutenant already knew about the incident, but Polar Bear 6 wanted her to have an opportunity to talk with me. As we stood together, I tried to comfort her. Although grief-stricken, she said, "Sir, I'd like to just spend some time with one of my team members standing over there. I'll be okay. Thanks for your help."

"Okay," I replied. "As long you're dealing with the grief in a positive way. I know you're going to be okay, but if you do need me, don't hesitate to ask. I'll be wherever this group is."

Inside I thought, "Here we've left the Triangle of Death, but it refuses to leave us."

Returning back to the asphalt and my gear, I thought about Chaplain Sneed, his commanders, and all of their soldiers. I wondered how they were coping after facing casualties so early in their deployment. Recollections of the brief time we spent together drifted through my mind. Deep down in my heart I felt the 3-187 Infantry would be fine.

I also realized just how capable the suffering of war was able to transcend the battlefield; it was already returning home within me.

## WAITING IN BAGHDAD FOR A FLIGHT

My group spent the remainder of the day waiting on the quiet road for a flight home. Sometime in the late afternoon, someone called out, "Hey, everybody up. We're going to walk to an airfield up the road, get on an aircraft, and head home."

Like the journey to Iraq, this one also seemed slow, but at least it was moving in the right direction.

Almost an hour later, we reached the final airfield. My heart pounded as I thought about the bittersweet moment: I felt a sense of joy for leaving, and unending pain for the absence of Jimenez and Fouty. I knew that when I took my final look at this airfield, it would be a closing glimpse of the toughest chapter of my life. For over a year I had known nothing but ministry in the perilous farmlands of Babylon.

Straining once again under the weight of my bags, I walked with the team towards the large C-17 aircraft. The twisting formation of troops making their way across the tarmac reminded me of a snake winding itself around its prey. We drew to a halt near a long concrete barrier that separated us from another portion of the airfield. I saw a large element of soldiers from the 101st Airborne Division departing the plane we would soon be boarding. "They're coming and we're going," I thought. "I wish all military operations were this simple."

As the 101st soldiers offloaded the aircraft, they gradually made their way past the small barrier near me. Fifteen months before, I'd made that same walk into the country. I choked up as I thought about these new soldiers walking by us and how some of them were certain to never leave the war zone alive. Glancing into their faces some appeared as scared as I had once been. I desperately longed to encourage them, but couldn't because my flight was boarding. I would have to leave it in God's hands and pray that their chaplains would take good care of them.

Our team began walking again as the passing troops cleared the runway. Standing just behind the aircraft, I felt its hot exhaust envelope me. Suddenly, I was situated at the massive, metal ramp that led into the dark, cave-like tunnel. It was a deeply somber moment for me as I realized that each step was bringing me closer to a world I had left so long ago.

With one step I prayed, "Lord, please never let me revisit this land." And with another I petitioned, "God, I also ask that you never let me forget the awesome ministry I took part in while here."

In that moment I thought about how much I loved being a chaplain, but at the same time considered how I had experienced enough trauma, fear, and death to last several lifetimes.

So goes combat's cycle of life. I was not the first to experience it, and I would not be the last. The soldiers who had just come off of the plane were not all going to die, but some likely would, and that is one of the terrible things about combat.

You never know who will.

I had faithfully served my time, fully knowing that I could be killed. Nevertheless, I answered the high-risk call because it was what I had been destined to do since birth. Now, preparing to board the massive C-17 Globemaster aircraft, I understood the meaning of Ecclesiastes 3:1: "Everything that happens in this world happens at the time God chooses."

I had come to bring God to soldiers and with the Lord's amazing grace, had finished and lived to tell about it.

However, I also understood that getting on a plane and flying out of the combat zone was not going to end the heartache from losing men I cared so much about. The answer was not an easy one, but perhaps it was an honest one: God. His peace had been with me as I maneuvered along the deadliest roads in Iraq. Now I would need it to navigate the upcoming highways of "normal" life.

With these thoughts swirling through my head, I stepped up onto the hefty metal ramp and looked back over the runway of the Baghdad International Airport one last time. I could see the last few soldiers closing in behind me as they walked toward the ramp. Polar Bears 6 and 7, as well as a handful of other soldiers, stared somberly at the ground as they did. Before I turned around and walked into the aircraft, I said a quick prayer for them: "God, please help us get through this difficult day. We shouldn't be leaving without our men. Thanks for giving us the opportunity to make it this far. Amen."

I describe the moment in my journal, "I glanced back just before I stepped into the massive tunnel and looked at the men forming up behind me. I figured that the day was difficult for them because Fouty and Jimenez were still missing. Then, with a deep breath, I said goodbye to Iraq, turned, and continued my walk out of hell and into the belly of the plane."

I found a seat and sat down, thinking how fortunate I was to be alive. A tear escaped and ran down my cheek. The last few troops boarded the aircraft and sat in seats lining the inner walls. The piercing whine of the engines grew louder as the machine prepared for its taxi and takeoff. Staring back at the ramp, I watched it slowly ascend until it locked with a resounding clank. In inverse proportion, the burning Babylonian sun dimmed until it was completely out of sight and darkness filled the titanium hull.

The loud hydraulics jolted me back to reality. The days of an explosive environment were finished. Bullets, rockets, and insurgents were now things of the past. In the deep covering of darkness inside the C-17's belly, I sat back against the wall as we taxied along the runway. With an ear-splitting whine, the aircraft lifted off. My journal notes this moment in time: "We flew out of Iraq and headed for Kuwait. Life began to seem reasonable again, and I had not felt that way in a really, really long time."

God had gotten me out of the Triangle of Death alive and now I would be able to go home, be with my wife, and live the rest of my life.

## KUWAIT

After quite some time in the air, we landed in Kuwait. Stepping off the plane, I immediately basked in the cool temperatures of the fall season. With the blistering heat behind us, a gauntlet of customs checkpoints lay ahead. After hours of inspections, the team was able to rest in a secluded tent city and wait for their turn to take the last step along their re-deployment home. I found some books to read and occasionally walked around the area to ward off boredom. Like many camps I had seen outside the battlefield, it hosted plenty of entertainment, restaurants, and sales kiosks.

One of the soldiers slept for nearly the entire three days we waited, refusing to come out of his sleeping bag as though he were a cocooned caterpillar.

A handful of other officers and I teased him and tried to get him to wake up, but we were unsuccessful. At one point they placed bets on who could irritate him the most before waking him up. Simple entertainment, but it kept us from dwelling on the fact that we were nomads in the middle of a desert, thousands of miles from home.

## FLYING HOME

*2 November, 2007*

Finally, everyone was cleared for the next stage of our journey. We climbed aboard white touring buses and ventured more deeply into Kuwait's barren wasteland to another remote airfield. Once there, we boarded a spacious civilian airliner. The flight attendants had taped small yellow ribbons to the interior walls of the aircraft, providing comforting reminders that fellow Americans had not forgotten us. The crew was nice, greeting each of us individually as we stowed our gear and found seats. Within twenty minutes, we were airborne.

The flight was peaceful. Most of the men either slept or were occupied by their thoughts. I reflected on how much I missed my wife and our home at Fort Drum, NY. Considering how to celebrate our reunion, I pictured taking her to a small Thai restaurant we had found just before the deployment. Thinking about her beautiful smile and dynamic companionship caused me to miss her that much more, and the lengthy flight that separated us seemed to drag.

It seemed as though we had flown for nearly a week by the time we landed at Fort Drum's Wheeler-Sack Army Airfield. We arrived at the start of a bitterly cold winter, but no one cared. We were simply happy to be alive, back in the United States, and near our families. Furthermore, the cold felt comforting compared to the draining heat of the Middle East.

After touching down, we spent the next few hours turning in our equipment, conducting accountability checks on personnel and, once again, participating in our favorite pastime: loading into buses. While most of the troops chose to be transported in this way, a few of us walked to the location of the homecoming celebration because we had our fill of riding buses. Besides, it was only down the street to the final destination: McGrath Gym.

McGrath Gym was the place where the war chapter of life would finally end and the rest of our lives could begin. Standing in formation and shivering outside the sports complex, the anticipation of seeing our families overcame us. Someone opened the door, probably to catch a brief glimpse of his loved ones. That was all it took. A tidal wave of family-starved soldiers poured into the building, reminding me of a crowd at a rock concert. The double aluminum doors nearly broke off of their hinges at the force brought on by the rushing soldiers. As the men stormed in, the crowd of families erupted with cheers of celebration.

The commanding general of Fort Drum spoke for a few minutes, extolling the virtues of the unit's performance in Iraq. "You soldiers did a great job over there. Thank you for your sacrifices. The families and community here at Fort Drum appreciate them." It was all the families could do to stay in the bleachers. As soon as the general concluded, they rushed down onto the floor and became one with the mass of troops.

Tanisha and I found each other within moments. She was even more beautiful than I recalled. Overcome with joy, we kissed, held hands, and just enjoyed each other's company as we walked to the car. When we arrived at home, I barely recognized the house I had seen for only three days before deploying in 2006. Back then it had only contained packing boxes from our recent move.

Tanisha and I spent much of the remaining evening catching up on our lives. I walked through the house before going to bed and prayed, "God, thank You again for letting me live to see today. Thank you for keeping Tanisha safe. I don't know how to express my appreciation. Amen."

The weeks ahead brought lots of snow to the area and many memories from Iraq. I was frustrated at how difficult the psychological readjustment was. Rewiring myself back to life in America was going to be easier said than done. Even something as simple as unpacking evoked strong memories and emotions. As I removed items from my military duffel bag, I would think, "Holy cow! I haven't seen that since I hung out at BP 133."

I wondered how many other soldiers were dealing with the same thing.

Over time I found out that most of them were struggling, too. Many soldiers told me about their battles with the memories. One said, "I was shopping at a store a few days ago and I saw a Middle Eastern man walk by. My heart started beating really hard and my hands began sweating. I told myself everything was okay, but my body felt like it needed to react."

My commanders frequently asked about the morale of the unit. "Chaplain, how are the men doing?"

I told them, "I think they definitely need some time with their families. A few are having serious issues. I can't tell you because of confidentiality, but those men are essentially dealing with leftover trauma from the war. As far as PTSD, it's hard to determine how many have it compared to normal combat stress, because PTSD is a disorder generally measured over a few months. If issues persist, that's probably what it is. I keep counseling our soldiers in order to help them work through post-combat related issues."

The commanders did everything possible to support the troops during their reintegration. One thing especially stood out as brilliant. The staff reasoned that if the unit could bring the families of its wounded and fallen soldiers to Fort Drum, psychological healing would be facilitated for everyone involved with the deployment. The troops and the families of the casualties could meet at a restaurant and discuss anything they desired. The families would have the opportunity to visit the unit's area where their loved ones had once spent time, and talk with the troops they had served alongside.

Mick Fouty, the father of our missing soldier Byron Fouty, was one of the visitors. When I discussed Byron with him at the restaurant, I remembered an important business card in my upper jacket pocket. It held sentimental value to me because it had photos of both Fouty and Jimenez on it with the inscription: "American Heroes, 12 MAY 2007. Byron Fouty and Alex Jimenez. MIA/POW. Never Forgotten."

I told him about how a 101st soldier gave it to me shortly before leaving the Triangle of Death.

"One of the Rakkasan commanders, Major Jones, handed it to me one evening while we ate dinner. He had just arrived in theatre only hours before and gave it to me as a promise that he and his team would never give up the search for the missing heroes."

As I handed Mick the card he grabbed it and said, "I want it. Can I have it?" As he continued to look at it, his eyes watered.

"Absolutely," I told him. "I think Major Jones and his team would want you to have it. "You know, Mick, I could never imagine how tough it must be for you to go through this. I obviously was not related to Byron, yet my heart has been broken."

"Thank you!" Mick replied.

"For what?"

"You're the only person I've talked to who's been honest enough to say that. Most people tell me that they understand exactly how I feel, when they can't; unless they have lost a son like Byron."

I sat back in the chair and continued talking with him for the remainder of the afternoon. As we walked out of the building to go our separate ways, I told him, "I promise you that our country will never stop looking for Byron and Alex."

He smiled, turned around, and walked away.

Over the course of the next few weeks, the Polar Bear battalion changed in many ways. The Army promoted LTC Infanti and assigned him elsewhere; LTC Richard Greene arrived from Alaska and became the new battalion commander. Similar changes occurred among most of the remaining staff.

The ranks of enlisted also changed over as the Army reassigned them elsewhere. Some soldiers were immediately sent back to Iraq. Worse yet, a few soldiers actually returned to the Triangle of Death. These men had left our battalion upon returning stateside and were reassigned to the 101st Airborne Division at Fort Campbell, KY. Once there, the division placed them in the 3-187 Infantry, the very unit that replaced us in Iraq. For these men, the 15-month nightmare of the Triangle of Death was relived for another year.

I do not doubt that the Polar Bear command would have done everything possible to stop the back-to-back deployments for the men had they known. By the time I found out, it was too late. Sometimes the Army shifts its troops without investigating important aspects of the warrior's life. To a chaplain, soldiers are people, but to an organization, they can easily become lifeless numbers.

A few soldiers retired from the military. Others, whose service obligations expired while in combat, left the Army shortly after returning home.

Those who stayed in were understandably fed up with the seemingly endless rotation of deployments. I empathized and was saddened as I watched many courageous troops grow weary as the Army prepared to send them back to Iraq with minimal recovery.

A few months later, Steve and his family moved to Italy. It was incredibly difficult for me to tell him goodbye. After all, I was not an experienced chaplain with years of combat under my belt when we served together. I was a new chaplain who was forced to learn in the heat of battle. Steve was an integral part of our ministry; he surpassed every expectation and went all-out for the troops. That is partly why I never heard a bad word said about him during our nearly two years together. He protected me during countless high-intensity attacks, serving as a trustworthy confidant when we both felt like giving up. He was the best chaplain assistant with whom I could ever have worked. I would never have made it without him.

As for Tanisha and me, we remained at Fort Drum for a few more months until the Army assigned us to Fort Jackson, SC. Before I left, it was my privilege to conduct several reintegration events for my unit: soldier retreats, marriage enhancement seminars for families, prayer breakfasts, chapel services, and frequent crisis counseling so that the troops themselves could readjust to life outside the combat zone.

## CONTINUING TO FIGHT

Since my return from Iraq, I have often been asked "How do you cope with the memories of war?" Attempting to explain how I dealt with the tour has been as challenging as describing my feelings surrounding it. I have frequently asked myself, 'What am I supposed to do with all this war junk inside my head? How am I supposed to readjust to a "normal" life after holding wounded soldiers in my arms, carrying burned skeletal remains, or the stirring images of our missing comrades in my heart? How am I ever supposed to overcome these painful memories?'

In the Bible, the third chapter of Ecclesiastes teaches, "There is a time for war, and there is a time for healing." The more I considered the age-old words, the more I recognized the need to endure after combat.

Tanisha not only helped me resolve my question of how to deal with the baggage of war, but also the value of a healthy relationship when it comes to successful reintegration from combat. Along with God, she was the consistent strength of my soul, not giving up when I felt helplessly enslaved by post-traumatic stress. Whether through her sacrifice during the war or selfless patience after it, my chance at successfully resetting myself to normal without a solid partner would have been minimal at best.

I have learned that combat veterans face their toughest battles when they return and have to confront their demons. As much as I hate to use that word as a chaplain, I consider it necessary because the demons that warriors deal with are not necessarily spirits, but rather haunting images of the past. Combat veterans return only to encounter conflicts within their minds. But there is a light at the end of this tortuous tunnel.

Many people have asked, "How were you able to cope with all of the suffering as a chaplain?"

I frequently tell them, "Faith has never led me to believe that I am immune from the troubles of life. In fact, I sometimes feel divinely placed in dilemmas to help others."

Someone once said, "Courage is the mastering of one's fears." I was probably the most terrified soldier on the battlefield, but I put my faith in the Lord, went out and conducted my duties, and He brought me through each day. Although staying afloat during tribulations is always easier said than done, and often feels as though its an unwinnable battle, it absolutely is winnable. Faith in God can overcome any pain.

Also, trust in one's family or friends can help alleviate the fear and loneliness. God designed us to stand alongside one another during tough times. When we transcend our trials, we are able to help others make it through their dark nights. Trustworthy relationships are important because they provide confidence and comfort. The Bible notes the importance of relationships in Proverbs 27:17; "As iron sharpens iron, so a man sharpens the countenance of his friend." Jesus Christ, of course, has always been recognized as the greatest friend; He is described in the book of Proverbs (18:24) as "a friend who sticks closer than a brother."

Faith has served as an anchor in my life through many desperate times.

It always connects me spiritually to the Designer of all purposes; the One who continues to transcend all suffering; and the One who masters mercy and forgiveness. God's mercy, grace, and love are always available through a relationship with Him. I hope that the examples found in this book illustrate not only how I fought, but also how I achieved victory in the toughest battles of my life. Regardless of the depth of your pain or the dynamics of your loss, help is always available and hope will always see you through if you allow it.

For me, telling my story has been a significant way to go on with life. Although remembering and writing the events necessary for recounting my personal narrative was emotionally difficult at times, I promised myself to one day provide people with the story of combat, including the legacy of those who were either wounded or killed, from a chaplain's perspective.

From 2003-2008, Iraq's treacherous Triangle of Death was America's nightmare. It was an uncontrollable area that voraciously claimed lives. In October of 2008, international media sources reported that combat operations in the Triangle of Death were over. The region had been brought under enough control by American forces that coalition authorities were able to officially hand the reins over to the Iraqi government. Parades took place along the once bloody, impassable streets. Children played freely; elderly residents shopped in markets that had, at one time, been forcefully closed by insurgents; and a destroyed economy was brought back to life.

The mission to save Iraq's most treacherous area from itself was accomplished. What the Iraqis do with that success can only be revealed over time. This victory certainly won't end all terror, for chaos shall have a home as long as man rules the earth. Hopefully, men and women of faith will step forward and continue to march to the beat of freedom and faith with those who fight against unholy terror.

As for me, I await my own future challenges—whatever, wherever, or whenever they may arise. Prior to leaving for Iraq in 2006, I wrote a question from Jesus (Matthew 16:15) inside one of my combat boots. The Scripture was intended to serve as a personal reminder to me of who God is during the testing of my faith. Jesus asked Peter, "Who do you say that I am?" This question, although directed at Peter, summons all people to an understanding of who Jesus Christ is. When we understand who He is, we can comprehend what He can do for us in trials. This knowledge is important because we cannot fully grasp who and what we are without an understanding of our divine purpose, which comes from the divine Creator. When life turns desperate, our greatest challenge will always be to remain steadfast in who we are and what we represent. I pray that you will acknowledge God, receive His amazing love, pray for His providential wisdom, and discover His divine plan for you on the battlefield of life.

# EPILOGUE: PRO PATRIA

The following are the brave men that were killed during Operation Iraqi Freedom 2006-2007 who had served with Chaplain Bryan, PV2 Boyd, and SGT Tennant.

CPL Joseph J. Anzack, Jr.
SGT Nathaniel S. Barnes
CPL Ray M. Bevel
SPC Ryan A. Bishop
PFC Matthew C. Bowe
SSG Harrison "Ducky" Brown
SPC Brian A. Browning
CPL Bobby T. Callahan
PFC Adare W. Cleveland
SFC James D. Connell, Jr.
CPL Daniel W. Courneya
2LT Johnny K. Craver
SGT Chris Davis
SGT Sean M. Dunkin
PFC Nathaniel A. Given
PFC Satieon V. Greenlee
PFC Thomas J. Hewett
SGT Christopher P. Messer
SSG Michael D. Moody, Jr.
CW2 Dwayne L. Moore
CPL Christopher E. Murphy

SGT Curtis L. Norris
SPC Nicholas K. Rogers
SGT Anthony J. Schober
PFC David N. Simmons
SGT Todd A. Singleton
PVT Shane M. Stinson
SSG Steven R. Tudor
Barak, Shahatay (Iraqi Soldier)
"Frank" (Interpreter)
"Scarface" (Interpreter)
"Zaedon" (Interpreter)

Declared Captured and Missing (Remains recovered in July, 2008):

SGT Alex Jimenez
SPC Byron W. Fouty

CPSIA information can be obtained at www.ICGtesting.com
Printed in the USA
BVOW022015081111

275632BV00001B/16/P